M & N Hanhart, Lithographe

CITY OF LAHORE.

Woven Masterpieces of Sikh Heritage

The Stylistic Development of the Kashmir Shawl
under Maharaja Ranjit Singh
(1780-1839)

Woven Masterpieces of Sikh Heritage

The Stylistic Development of the Kashmir Shawl under Maharaja Ranjit Singh (1780-1839)

Frank Ames

Antique Collectors' Club

ISBN 978-1-85149-598-6

British Library Cataloguing-in-Publication Data
A catalogue record for this book is available from the British Library

Frontispiece. Kashmir long shawl (detail). See WM20, page 121 COLLECTION INDU PUNJ. PHOTOGRAPH SUNIL JAIN

Title page: Maharaja Ranjit Singh. See Plate 55, page 87

Mixed Sources
Product group from well-managed forests, controlled sources and recycled wood or fiber
FSC www.fsc.org Cert no. SGS-COC-003548
© 1996 Forest Stewardship Council

Printed in China
for the Antique Collectors' Club Ltd., Woodbridge, Suffolk

The Antique Collectors' Club

Formed in 1966, the Antique Collectors' Club is now a world-renowned publisher of top quality books for the collector. It also publishes the only independently-run monthly antiques magazine, *Antique Collecting*, which rose quickly from humble beginnings to a network of worldwide subscribers.

The magazine, whose motto is *For Collectors-By Collectors-About Collecting*, is aimed at collectors interested in widening their knowledge of antiques both by increasing their awareness of quality and by discussion of the factors influencing prices.

Subscription to Antique Collecting is open to anyone interested in antiques and subscribers receive ten issues a year. Well-illustrated articles deal with practical aspects of collecting and provide numerous tips on prices, features of value, investment potential, fakes and forgeries. Offers of related books at special reduced prices are also available only to subscribers.

In response to the enormous demand for information on 'what to pay', ACC introduced in 1968 the famous price guide series. The first title, *The Price Guide to Antique Furniture* (since renamed *British Antique Furniture: Price Guide and Reasons for Values*), is still in constant demand. Since those pioneering days, ACC has gone from strength to strength, publishing many of today's standard works of reference on all things antique and collectable, from *Tiaras* to *20th Century Ceramic Designers in Britain*.

Not only has ACC continued to cater strongly for its original audience, it has also branched out to produce excellent titles on many subjects including art reference, architecture, garden design, gardens, and textiles. All ACC's publications are available through bookshops worldwide and a catalogue is available free of charge from the addresses below.

For further information please contact:

www.antiquecollectorsclub.com

Antique Collectors' Club
Sandy Lane, Old Martlesham
Woodbridge, Suffolk IP12 4SD, UK
Tel: 01394 389950 Fax: 01394 389999
Email: info@antique-acc.com

——— or ———

ACC Distribution
6 West 18th Street, 4th Floor
New York, NY 10011, USA
Tel: 212 645 1111
Email: sales@antiquecc.com

CONTENTS

To the unknown Kashmiri weaver of yore

Kashmiri weavers at work. Painting, possibly Lahore, c.1867. After Kyburg exhibition catalogue, 1988, London

A creative act enhances the beauty of the world; it gives something to the world, it never takes anything from it – Osho

Acknowledgements

Woven Masterpieces of Sikh Heritage, which began six years ago, was not intended to wind up as a treatise on Sikh period shawls. In fact, it began while taking notes in anticipation of a catalogue for a private collection, which never took hold. By then, however, my notes and ideas for a new book had swelled, and my immune system had succumbed to the research bug. A few years later a title emerged, which seemed to sum up the work and illustrations nicely, and added élan to the text. Had it not been for Janet Roberts, to whom I owe an enormous debt, the shaping of the material might have taken an entirely different turn. From the get go, Janet, editor-at-large, jumped on board and, whether lecturing in Kosovo, Shanghai, or on assignment for the UN, greatly inspired my efforts. Without her background in things Central Asian, her consummate editorial skills, and 'laser eye', pointing out inconsistencies, errors or ambiguities, this project might not have seen the light of day.

Of the many kind people who offered advice, information, suggestions, or hospitality, I would like in particular to thank: Jean-Marie Lafont, who shared unstintingly his encyclopaedic knowledge of France and the Punjab. Jovial and witty, Jean-Marie, went out of his way to provide some rare images, and welcomed me warmly as a kindred spirit into his New Delhi home, where I met his gracious wife, Rehana.

I'm indebted to my wonderful Kashmiri friend and colleague, Mujtaba Shah. Mujtaba's heartfelt passion for the old *kani* weavings is matched only by the beauty of the Sufi energy he brings to reviving the industry in Srinagar. When we first met years ago, I learned that, to shawl lovers and cognoscenti, Mujtaba had given away over a hundred copies of my first book on shawls! To his spirited encouragement and generosity I extend my sincere gratitude.

I could not be more grateful to Cornelia Punj, whose lavish hospitality made my stay in Delhi festive and exciting. The strength of our Indo-Tango connections and Cornelia's love of Indian art, dance and Kashmiri shawls overcame Delhi's bureaucracy to obtain images, as difficulties seemed to vanish under the spell of her alchemical charisma.

Also in New Delhi, Jyoti Bharany as usual has been wonderfully generous in opening up his Ali Baba backroom trove of 'woven jewels', giving me free reign and assistants to photograph on his roof top.

I particularly want to thank the affable Sam Josefowitz who invited me to study his growing collection at his home in Switzerland; to Vicky and Ermes Gnemmi, for their gracious welcome in Milan and enthusiastic support.

I am indebted to the effervescent Joan Hart, from the Hoosier heartlands of the US. Joan is still unconvinced I drove the seven hundred miles to her home in ten hours! Imagine finding a world-class shawl collection, tucked away in the Corn Belt! Great thanks go out to Joan and her husband, Jeff, for inviting me for a pleasant stay at their 'foxy' abode, allowing me to wreak havoc on their back porch with my photo equipment and to rummage through their garage for scaffolding.

To Andre Heget, warm thanks for inviting me and Vimala to Budapest and allowing us to photograph his collection. Andre, raconteur par excellence, awesome polyglot, not only led us on a tour of the land he loves, but also introduced us, very joyfully, to the epicurean and oenological heart of Hungary's ancient Roman provinces.

I would like to express my gratitude to Barbara Schmitz for sharing her knowledge on Kashmiri manuscripts; Jeevan Singh Deol, for his kind emails on Sikh manuscripts; Robert Skelton, for his perceptive thoughts on flowers in Mughal painting; Steven Cohen, as always, for his insightful and generous clarifications and enormous understanding of Indian carpets; Willem Floor, for his vast knowledge on Persian history and trade; the late Stuart Carey Welch for his copiously filled emails; Pratapaditya Pal, for support in seeking publication.

Gathering images for a book of this type is frequently an uphill battle, and moreover a fiscal challenge. Among the institutions and private collectors that proffered generously, I would like to thank:

The TAPI Collection of Shilpa and Praful Shah, Surat. My innumerable visits over the many years to the Shah's offices in Churchgate and home in Malabar Hill are filled with warm memories of lively conversations on Indian art and textiles over wine and savoury vegetarian dishes. Shilpa, Praful and their helpful staff extended every effort to see that I was able to obtain excellent images of shawls from their collection, one of the finest in the world. The 'sun and sands of Goa' is little match to the beckoning and exciting events that continually seem to unfold within the Shah's bright field of energy;

The Rhodes Island School of Design and their efficient staff: Joanne Dolan Ingersoll, Curator of Costumes and Textiles and Department Head; Kate Irvin and Laurie Anne Brewer, Curatorial Assistants, and Erik Gould, museum photographer;

The Indianapolis Museum of Art, Niloo Imami-Paydar, Curator of Textiles and Costumes.

In addition I am indebted to the Museum of Fine Art, Pamela Parmal, Curator of Textiles and Fashion, Boston; Antonio Ratti Foundation, Francina Chiara, Curator, Como; Israel Museum, Jerusalem; Textile Museum, Washington, D.C.; The Government Museum and Art Gallery, N.P.S. Randhawa, Director, Chandigarh; Jagdish and Kamla Mittal Collection, Hyderabad; National Museum, Delhi, Anamika Pathak; Musée Guimet, Amina Okada, Curator of Indian Art and Aurélie Samuel, Curator of Textiles; New York Public Library, 42nd St., its research staff, especially to those in the Asian and Middle Eastern Division: John Lundquist, Usha Bhasker and S. Soucek; New York Botanical Gardens Library, Bronx; Bharat Kala Bawan, Varanasi; Guimet Museum, Vincent Lefevre, Paris; *Hali* Magazine; Maharaja Sawai Man Singh II Museum, Jaipur; Thyssen-Bornemisza Museum of Art, Madrid; Al-Sabat Collection, Kuwait National Museum; Morgan Library, New York; Habibganj Library, Aligarth; Rao Madho Singh Trust Museum, Fort Kotah; Royal Museum of the Armed Forces and Military History, Brussels; Sheesh Mahal Medal Gallery, Patiala; Musée de l'Armée, Paris ; Musée Jean de la Fontaine, Château Thierry; Royal Library, Windsor Castle, Windsor; Sackler Museum, Harvard University, Boston; Khalili Collection, London; Staatsbibliothek, Berlin; Musée du Louvre, Paris; The Trustees of the Chester Beatty Library, Dublin; British Library, London; Victoria and Albert Museum, London; Beauvais Carpets, New York.

I have relied on the following colleagues, scholars, collectors, friends, dealers and Indophiles, all of whom have in one way or another shared their thoughts, ideas or suggestions:

Asaf Ali, Joyce Ames, George and Dan Anavian, Susan Bean, David Bernstein, Dilys Blum, Martha and Tom Boyd, Jim Burns, Christopher Buyers, Mark Cohen, Rosemary Crill, Virginie and Michel David, Jacqueline and Marc De Bolle, Rajat Deb, Layla Diba, Ben Evans, Marc Feldman, Esther Fitzgerald, Bertram Frauenknecht, Jim Ffrench, Ray Furse, Chet Gadsby, Elisa M. Galiardi, Francesca Galloway, Vasant Gideon, B.N. Goswamy, Joss Graham, Ingo and Mia Grill, Marie-Hélène Guelton, Navina Haidar, Harideva, Peter Harris, Ann and Fred Holmes, Jenny Housego, James Hurley, Guy and Marie Joubert, Karuno, Rakesh Kaul, Lawrence Kearney, Alan Kennedy, Ann Loseff, Vishnu Lall, Gale Martin, Tina and Nirmal Mattoo, Susan Meller, George Michell, Alim Mirza, Michael Phillips, Rashmi Poddar, Krishna Prem, Janet Rizvi, Keith Rocklin, Clive Rogers, Peter Saunders, Britta Sauter, Claude Seligman, Dan Shaffer, Mark Shilen, Jeff Spurr, Hamid Tavakoli, Jon Thompson, Allen Tobias, Andrew Topsfield,

Louis Van Leeuwen, Rolf von Beuren, Dan Walker, Julian West, Jim Williams, Wolfgang Wittrock, Marilyn and Marshal Wolf, Junnaa and Thomi Wroblewski, Dara Zagar, Anja and ZouZou, Magali Regis and Sylvan Leroux; and to Vimala Roberta Berton, for computer skills I couldn't do without. Her equanimity in face of panicky moments of image organization and her unerring support has been my good fortune.

Lastly, this list would be incomplete without mentioning the continued support over many years and renowned publishing reputation of Antique Collectors' Club: Diana Steel, publisher; Prim Elliott editor.

It may not have been possible to name everyone who, during the course of six years, had an input to this project. For those whom this list might have inadvertently overlooked, rest assured that to them I'm extremely grateful.

Dochalla (detail), Afghan Period, late 18th century. The blue has been retouched.
Private Collection

Detail of WM13 (see page 101). Sikh period, c.1835.
Tapi Collection of Praful and Shilpa Shah, Surat, acc #. 97.1419-S1-75

Introduction

Flowers exploding like rockets on the Fourth of July; sharp spears intersecting bizarre fan-like devices and eight-pointed star-shaped lotuses floating on a churning sea of semi-floral geometric motifs: do fantasies such as these sound like patterns we would normally associate with the Kashmir shawl? Maharaja Ranjit Singh's takeover of Kashmir in 1819 represented an important event in the Punjab's history. Few, however, realized it would have such an extraordinary impact on the legendary *kani* shawls of the Valley. Intriguing and mysterious, these enigmatic yet dynamic patterns appear to have surprisingly slipped through the cracks of historical examination by textile experts.

Since John Irwin's ground-breaking monograph, *Shawls*, appeared a half century ago, interest in this subject has spawned the publication of many books. However, none focuses on any one period of Indian history. In my first attempt years ago on the subject, I proposed four major historical periods in which better to examine the shawl's development. The Sikh period (1819-1839) was one of these periods. My conclusions in that chapter are worth citing:

> *The huge size of the sweeping botehs and the multitude of large architectural and curvilinear patterns began quickly to invade the whole surface area of the shawl. Hollow botehs detached themselves from the increasingly dominant ground designs to evaporate through scattered directions across a roaring sea of new images, exotic and enigmatic. The riotous agitation of the boteh's flora swept away practically all botanical reality in its path. It appears that, in one fell swoop, the Sikhs obliterated all graphic souvenirs which recalled the hard struggles against their Mughal and Afghan rivals, to vindicate their rights to Northern India. This close look into this boteh microcosm provides a clear distinction of the evolving key elements which eventually emerged, fused and detached anew to form the churning symbolism of the Sikh period.*

Indeed, this 'churning symbolism' is the subject of investigation in this book and, although it represents only one school of Kashmir design, its dramatic impact illuminates a key style in the decorative arts of a fascinating era in Punjab history. From collections around the world, an attempt is made to present to the public for the first time some of the best examples of shawls from this era.

Above and beyond the reigns of the Afghans (1753-1819) and Dogras (1846-1877), the Sikh period and the Mughal period are arguably the two most significant artistic periods. To be sure, Dogra rule was not without its exciting aesthetic moments, but by this time European influence was so enmeshed within the design repertoire that, to all intents and purposes, Oriental influence had faded dramatically. Certainly, there were exceptions to this rule, as can be seen in a few masterpieces of astonishing creativity (for example Plate 13 page 34). On the other hand, the Sikh period represents a truly indigenous and unique art form that appears to have direct roots in the soil of the Lahore-Kashmir-Khalsa link. The court of Maharaja Ranjit Singh and the Sikh culture of 'Brotherhood', in which Ranjit Singh ruled and flourished, produced a rare and exciting atmosphere in which shawl artists dramatically transcended the static forms of simple boteh repeats to evolve a unique repertoire of decorative graphic designs. Their exuberance in the playful geometry of arches, circles, and other unusual motifs, combined with the brilliant use of intense colour tones, suffuses these shawls with a kinetic energy that cannot help but elicit feelings of mysticism and awe. They are a visual record of a culture (for example WM26, page 134).

These artists appeared to be pursuing abstract and innovative strategies, using bizarre assemblages of patterns that responded to and emerged from the colourful frenzied environment that defined the Punjab. This avant-garde movement was not unlike that of the Dada artists, such as Duchamp, Man Ray, Picabia, etc., a century later, who, in their angst against established artistic norms, became captivated by evolving technologies and their existential side-effects. The Sikh artists, like their Dada counterparts, emerged in a period of rapid technological developments, spawned by the Industrial Revolution. The need to expand the artistic surface of the shawl may indeed have been due in a small way to the advent of the major European exhibitions of industrial products then beginning to take place in Paris.[1]

In this book, the viewer will see many bizarre patterns, patterns that could certainly titillate the Pythagorean senses of the architect, graphic artist, mathematician or engineer. Is there an inner meaning that lies embedded within their volumetric shapes? Are there rhythmical measures which the ancient Greeks called the 'Music of the Spheres'? Or, do they articulate movements responding to the musical modes *(ragas)* found in the *Adi Granth*? Perhaps these are mysteries destined to be forever sealed, only sensed rather than resolved. Speaking about Indian art, Stella Kramrisch once stated: 'There is something so strong, and at the same time so unique, in any Indian work of art that its "Indianness" is felt first of all, and what it is, is seen only on second thought.'[2] Whatever is the case, these patterns rendered something truly ethnic in nature, and represent, as suggested by the eminent Indophile, Jean-Marie Lafont, a new 'major artistic expression in the subcontinent'.[3]

The shawl is observed as an integral and important part of the world of decorative arts whose often symbolic, even heraldic, patterns reflect the fluctuating social conditions in which the shawl was woven. The intricacies of trade and commerce, the many sightings of the industry by foreign travellers, the conditions of the weavers and wool are really not the subject of this book, except where pertinent to our understanding of the decorative elements. These areas of research continue to be well covered by scholars in the field and for an overall view of the industry the reader is encouraged to consult the numerous works available. Except for the focus on General Allard and his expatriate cohorts, there is no general treatise on costume for this period.

What is presented is a sense of how these patterns evolved from the riot of ethnic and socio-political forces that impacted on textiles recorded in the Eurasian theatre of art history. Within this esoteric and multifaceted subject, the artistic influence of France somehow always finds a way to emerge from the depths of historical investigation. Be it from Pierre Vallet, royal gardener and embroiderer to the King of France, or the sixteenth century botanist, Carolus Clusius, whose narcissus flower, published in Antwerp, was copied by Mughal artists; or from the expatriate generals of Napoleon's militia; or from the great artists of the European shawl industry, such as Amédée Couder, Antony Berrus or Frédéric Herbert, whose popular designs drifted back to Kashmir, all these exotic influences found resonance in the Kashmir shawl.

Opposite:
WM1. Kashmir long shawl (detail)
In this fine transitional piece we see zoomorphic elements that may have found their way to Kashmir from the spectacularly creative period (late 1840s) of the French shawl designer, Antony Berrus. Notice the thick root stem at the base of the 'dragon' Paisley. This is surely drawn by an artist who was steeped in the late Afghan shawl tradition, when botanical elements such as this first evolved. Late Sikh period, c.1850 PRIVATE COLLECTION

A concerted effort is made to contextualize the stylistic development of a broader topographical sense of the artistic environment. On one hand, Indian painting is explored through the eyes of either known or unknown painters, observing artistic sensitivities as expressed through the rendering of their own inimitable rhythms, colour palettes, and affinities with costumes and textiles. On the other, it is explored through the complex of unique graphic forms and figures found in the *kani* weaves and embroideries themselves. While painting workshops existed in the Punjab, Kashmir and the Hill States, save for the obvious influence of the Mughal School, little about them is known; it is the same for the whims and fancies of the patrons. Thus, Imam Bakhsh Lahori, Nainsukh, and even the Hungarian Schoefft, for example, have left a corpus of works, the study of which needs to be balanced against the colourful atmosphere of the historical settings in which they painted. The extent that the artist enlivened his work with decorative textiles, rugs and dress accessories, or created chromatic moods, depended greatly upon his own unique surroundings. The most important of the known published works in this field affording a glimpse into this exotic world of painting have been consulted. In no way do these constitute a definitive examination of such a vast area in which much bound and private art material is still at large, often stored away in institutions around the world with little accessibility. Besides an attempt to contextualize Sikh designs, the overall intention is to explore and reveal areas of research which hitherto have gone unexplored.

In the case of Pahari and Punjabi painting, new information on the artists and patrons in the last few decades has only recently come to light and certainly more will become known over the years to come. Towards the end of the eighteenth century, due to a rapidly changing map of Northern India, artists began to migrate more and more. Outlying princely kingdoms scattered across India retained local artists, who seemingly may not have been connected with the region of Kashmir, except through the shawl patterns they personally created. Kotah is a case in point.

New information, as well, is becoming available, albeit slowly, on Persian painting. The recent spate of previously unknown eighteenth century Persian paintings coming on the auction block, dated and signed, is beginning to add important knowledge to the field. As a result, the curvilinear boteh can now be dated to almost a half century earlier than anybody would have previously guessed.[4] To this end, Shiraz's role, under the rule of Karim Khan Zand, is discussed through trade, costume and the painters, especially Muhammad Sadiq, one of Persia's pre-eminent artists of the eighteenth century. The unfortunate lacuna of any serious Perso-Kashmiri trade records prior to Moorcroft's visit to Kashmir in 1822, admittedly, presents serious challenges to the textile historian, and exposes frustrating complexities whose narrative seems to follow no particular straight path. The ebb and flow of market forces, consumer demand and political vicissitudes are such that the shawl's artistic development along with its inimitable patterns – especially as a reflection of shawls depicted in paintings – render the subject difficult to pen with precision. In a subject where the wool had taken on almost mythic proportions, where the pattern had become virtually a symbol of national identity, and where the shawl itself was a cause célèbre between nations fighting over tariffs, trade barriers, exhibiting national pride, jealousy and greed, we arrive at a subject whose material is as mercurial as its ability to quickly slip through a 'Manucci' thumb-ring.[5] This is perhaps one of the main reasons for the focus of this book: we have the unique opportunity to fall back on the extant shawls themselves.

Critical research in this field often depends on the ties between patrons and artists, of which evidence is sometimes found through manuscripts. To this end, the *Janam Sakhis* of the Sikh period are discussed, as well as other religious and secular manuscripts. Here again, many Sikh manuscripts remain elusive, tucked away in private collections, yet perhaps represent a critical future source of investigation. Highlighting a few of the known patrons and artist families active at the time of Sikh ascendancy not only sheds light on the creative environment of the region, but attempts a rapprochement between artists of all craft and artistic mediums. The painterly quality of some of the more elaborately embroidered, pictorial *rumals* (square shawls) is weighed against the prolific backdrop of Imam Bakhsh's brilliant world. Such assessments bring our awareness closer to the real life characters that brought so much woven beauty into the world.

With so many endlessly changing shawl patterns, one should always pose the question – bearing in mind the weaver's input of choice of colours, stitches, and pattern nuancing – 'what was the artist thinking, feeling, experiencing; what were the compelling forces that surrounded him; to whom was he reaching out?' At times patterns can be dense and filled in with so many tiny colourful flowers that the possibility of an artistic statement being obscured becomes real. Like Indian miniature paintings which captivate us again and again, because of subtleties we may fail to see at first glance, *kani* weaves equally necessitate a study which can oftentimes develop into an illuminating experience.

That textile scholars have paid little attention to Sikh period shawls is unfortunate, since many great pieces with often unbelievably rich, symbolist patterns have come and gone on the market, only to be swallowed up silently by anonymous private collectors. Important museums of the world, which usually rely on gifts and donations, rarely have made a sincere effort to build a comprehensive shawl collection. Thus, it is perfectly normal at this time to see large institutional collections without a single Mughal or high Sikh period shawl. Because there are no known collections per se of this genre, the greatest effort here has been to source these pieces from museum and private collections. While other schools of shawl art are also important, a complete study of the inventory of the symbolism, designs, and patterns of all the known Sikh period shawls in world collections is a project that needs to be addressed. The investigation should be done, if only for the simple reason that no other uniquely Indian period possesses as much literature and documentation. Time will show that these neglected weavings, which have yet to be fully discovered and appreciated, represent one of the most exciting Indian art forms and, furthermore, their dynamic design elements eventually dovetail with decorative European art.

Much of what has been set forth here represents the experiential views of the author, reflecting his personal observations, speculations, ideas, and musings through intimate contact with the subject over the past thirty years. While there are many good publications in this field which discuss basic concepts of the techniques of shawl weaving or the infrastructure of the industry itself, in this work the focus remains on the shawl's decorative elements. Nevertheless, if to any degree the public's imagination is stirred, the aficionado's interest is inspired or the art historian's critical eye is more widely opened, then my goal will have been accomplished. It is also hoped that the information presented here will raise awareness of the value of this remarkable Sikh legacy, which forms an integral part of the cultural patrimony of Kashmir, as well as of the Punjab.

Chapter 1

A Synoptic Overview

...I have neither seen nor heard of any country equal to Kashmir for charm of climate during all four seasons...the beauty of their [homes] exterior defies description, and all who behold them for the first time, bite the finger of astonishment with the teeth of admiration.

– Mirza Haidar Dughlat, Babur's cousin and ruler of Kashmir, writing in 1544-45[6]

In the flush of Mirza Haidar's indescribable astonishment, he needed more than to merely witness the amazing transcendent beauty he was experiencing; he needed to assure himself that he wasn't dreaming. In his incredulity he was not alone: other early and important travellers to this highly secluded, Shangri-la Himalayan valley had similarly been taken aback by the awesome beauty of Srinagar. The Mughal emperor, Jahangir, who may or may not have had a penchant for such gritty toothsomeness, none the less couldn't help but exclaim that the roofs were '...ablaze by the torches of banquet-adorning tulips'. Despite his poetic talents, he still found that in writing about Kashmir's flowers, fields and waterfalls, the beauty of the Valley was '...beyond all description'.[7] A hundred and sixty years later, the Comte de Modave was able to witness 'the whole town on fire, giving it the most ravishing look one can imagine'.[8] Legoux de Flaix who belatedly published his travels twenty-five years after leaving the Valley in 1782, immediately recalled his own astonishment at the flowerbeds that crowned all the rooftops, that left him with an unforgettably indelible image. It is no wonder that a city so immersed in the daily display of flowery pyrotechnics gave birth to such an exquisite art form as the Kashmir shawl.[9]

Ironically, Sultan Haidar's tactile eloquence and Jahangir's oft-quoted spiritual communion in Kashmir's 'Garden of Eternal Spring' must have obfuscated the legendary wonders of the *pashmina* shawls. Well-known medieval writers and Renaissance kings, conquerors and explorers have invariably spoken of the beauties of this valley with paradoxically little more than a mention of the fabulous shawls, whose very mystique surely contributed to making the Valley famous over time. Even today there exists among the oldest extant Kashmir shawls a mystifying elegance and charm that comes close to leaving the casual observer challenged in his powers of description; these jewel-like weavings represented an amazing synergism of rare natural dyes and high-altitude lustrous *pashmina* that dazzle the viewer with hypnotic brilliance.

Opposite:
WM2. Kashmir long shawl (detail)
Striking colours reflecting the talents of a master *tarah guru* (colour caller) and bold design, with ample free spacing, animates a brilliant pattern featuring small temples. Sikh period, c.1840.
COLLECTION ANDRÉ HEGET

Below:
Plate 1. Boteh jewellery decoration. This is one of the earliest appearances of the boteh. Gandhara statue, 2nd-3rd century.
ASIAN ART MUSEUM, BERLIN, INV. NO. I.76

Plate 2. Boteh motifs found on stucco wall frieze, Iran, 11th century.

There may have been other places in the world where one could find either craft being plied, but the miraculous, if not alchemical, fusion of these two, of dyeing and *kani* weaving, was unique to the Valley of Kashmir and rendered these unique loom products one of the true unsurpassed textile wonders of the world. These works of art, laboriously produced by the gifted, but yet anonymous Kashmiri weavers, recall the impassioned statement by Archer in his description of the Pahari painters: '...like a humble palace servant toiling like an interior decorator and in the process, producing as if by accident, works of consummate elegance and charm'.[10]

There is no doubt that the Kashmir shawl, at least in its undecorated form, with its smooth flowing and incredibly soft *pashmina* wool, has been around for millennia. What is less certain, however, is whether its fine surface was ever embellished during all or most of this period with any kind of *kani* pattern. From the various very brief mentions in the medieval and Renaissance literature of the Orient one can get an impression that, because it was so famous, nobody felt it necessary to write anything in depth about the shawl industry. Mirza Haidar Dughlat, cousin of the founding father of the Mughal Empire, Babur, took control of Kashmir in 1544. In his *Tarikh-i-Rashidi* one senses his powers of observation as he describes, for example, the 'dog tooth work' of one of the many temples in Kashmir, while further on he tells us of the crowded laughing and weeping figures within, such that the astounded beholder has not seen or heard of, in the rest of the world. The Mirza was also familiar with the arts and crafts that were practised in the Central Asian region for he goes on, at length, to point out the 'uncommon' trades that were practised in the Valley, the likes of which were not to be found in '...the whole of Mahvara-un-Nahr, except in Samarkand and Bukhara; these [crafts] are nowhere to be met with, while in Kashmir, they are abundant. This is all due to Zain-ul-Abidin'.[11] The Mirza cites stone-polishing, stone-cutting, bottle making, window cutting and gold beating, yet shawl weaving remains starkly absent. One can infer that the *kani* shawl, if it existed at all then, hadn't reached its full popularity and that, to him, shawl making was a common craft, unworthy of special mention.

Yet, one and a half centuries earlier, Srivara, the renowned chronicler of this era, in his *Rajatarangini* (1394), records one of the earliest references to weaving in Kashmir. It tells us that the people there learned to weave valuable cloths of silk and wool and that some of them were woven with patterns of creepers or variegated plants.[12] Were these 'cloths' shawls? Was the wool that Srivara mentions *pashmina?* It is not perfectly clear. Presumably, if Srivara talks about 'valuable cloths' in the Valley of Kashmir we can assume that he meant *pashmina*.[13] Srivara's use of the word 'woven' comes from a

Plate 3. Jhelum River, Kashmir.

historian uneducated in the techniques of weaving and must be taken with a bit of scepticism. Even François Bernier, the French doctor who accompanied Aurangzeb to Kashmir in 1665, describes shawl weaving as a 'sort of embroidery made on the loom'.[14] Although the term 'embroidery' is inaccurate, his observation of the pattern being made on the loom is correct, which implies, of course, the *kani* method. Yet, Bernier also fails to leave us with any description of design or motif patterns.

The mysterious aura of the Kashmir shawl was, by some, attributed to the washing of the freshly woven shawls in Srinagar's Jhelum River, the waters of which imparted a supposedly magical quality to the colours. Perhaps the lustre of the wool was due to the wild thyme and sweet marjoram on which the roaming goats gorged.[15] The Kashmiri dyers of the Mughal period had supposedly created over three hundred tints from the Valley's bountiful plants and minerals and thus it was not uncommon to encounter shawls with superb colours of golden saffron, luscious shades of peach, salmon pinks, and fuchsia; the intense saturated colours of the rubescent reds from lac or cochineal; gem-like hues of emerald green, indigo blues and deep crimson. The shawl was the quintessential synthesis of rare wool and exotic dyes. Few luxury articles of clothing except those woven, say, of gold and silver thread, could, by their chromatic effulgence, have created as mesmerizing a hold on the viewer.

Besides such a pyrotechnic display, the Kashmir shawl was – especially from the Mughal period onwards – more than the sum of its parts in so far as it articulated designs and patterns that reflected contemporaneous imperial Mughal culture. The shawl's end panels, known as *pallas*, form a kind of frame for the multitude of designs for which Kashmir is known. From the seventeenth to nineteenth centuries, the designs reflected contemporary floral and geometric art forms in vogue during the four periods in which Kashmir was ruled: Mughal, Afghan, Sikh and Dogra.

It appears that the first direct and imperial mention of the Kashmir shawl comes during the reign of Akbar (1556-1605). Akbar is credited as being the first ruler to pay intimate attention to the shawl industry. His court chronicler, Abul Fazl, recorded the qualities of the various wools and mentions the difficulties of dyeing *shah tus*. Probably the most important part of Fazl's notes is his description of how the shawls were donned:

> *In former times, shawls were often brought from Kashmir. People folded them up in four folds and wore them for a very long time. Now-a-days they are generally worn without folds and merely thrown over the shoulder. His majesty has commenced to wear them double, which looks very well.*[16]

Although this familiar quote is often cited, it must be understood that Fazl represents the first person responsible for not only unambiguously detailing some of the main characteristics of the Kashmir shawl but also for recognizing the scope of the industry. He is telling us that the shawl has been around for a long time. One gets a sense of the shawl having a history and of being carefully valued. We can also postulate that these shawls were more or less undecorated since folding them in fours would certainly not be the best way to display their finely woven and beautifully dyed flowers.

Plate 4. Sunset over Dal Lake.
PHOTOGRAPH BY THE AUTHOR (1982)

Because period shawls – woven in pairs, and actually stitched back to back – have only recently come to light, we are now able to confirm the meaning of Fazl's description. This discovery was the first proof that the Kashmir shawl was indeed woven in pairs *(dochallas),* at Akbar's instigation, and quite possibly confirms the notion that important embellishment first began with Akbar, with the innovation of a freely spaced shrub repeat on the then new idea of a *palla,* as a frame for floral display (Plate 5). In other words, the trend from this period on may have been to enclose, at each end of the shawl, a floral (boteh) repeat within a narrow rectangular 'box' *(palla)* delineated by *hashia* (border) meanders.

The very first shawl patterns were most likely small flowers which, over time and by dint of fashion, grew into a repeat of flowers or shrubs. Like many of the decorative arts and miniature painting of the Akbar era, floral styles were mainly Persian in origin or inspiration. Akbar's chronicler, Abul Fazl, informs us of his patron's intense interest in the shawl industry, but leaves us no inkling of fashionable motifs on shawls, if they existed at all. However, he was certainly struck by the contemporary fashion for exotic colours with which garments and textiles, including shawls, were dyed. For example, mauve, like the colour of some parrots, sandal wood, hay, pistachio, bluish-like China ware, mango, musk and 'fakhtah' pigeon are a few of the thirty-two colours he carefully recorded.

Akbar's Imperial wardrobe *(toshakhana)* was very precisely organized 'according to the days, months and years of their entries, and according to their colour, price and weight'.[17] Garments, textiles and shawls were weighed before being entered into the *toshakhana.* The text leaves the impression that shawls were not, in general, grouped together because it was more the 'character of the day' on which the garment was received that determined its place in the wardrobe. Thus certain garments, depending on the auspiciousness of their day of arrival, were more highly ranked than garments arriving on lesser days. Curiously, textiles of the same kind arriving on the first day (*Urmuzd*) of the month of *Farwardin* assumed a higher rank than those arriving on any other day of the month; should they have the same weight, then they were ranked according to colour.

It is interesting to observe how the Mughal ruler's penchant for astrology carried over into every facet of daily life, including the clothing worn. Indeed, Akbar had created a unique Imperial wardrobe providing him with a wide choice of costumes, the rankings of which, one might assume, would align, should the occasion arise, with his astrologers' predictions.

Finding no mention of flowers included in the organization of the Imperial wardrobe is surprising given the Mughals' sensitivity to the precise details of calendar, colour, weight, etc., especially since there was such prolific use of flowers on rugs, textiles and on almost every other form of decorative art. Certainly, flowers were admired and, certainly, they were imbued, as in other parts of the world, with ideas of power, authority, love, life, death and notions of redemption and resurrection. Akbar's close friendship with the Jesuits and his venerable respect for the Catholic Church may have exposed him to the symbolism of the latter two. Apart from Fazl's brief discussion of the various natural shades of *shah tus* and Akbar's unsuccessful attempts at dyeing *shah tus* red, nothing more, unfortunately, can be learned from Fazl.

The Englishman, William Foster, visited the Valley, but his eyes must have been more absorbed by the renowned beauty of the Kashmiri women, for the only thing he managed to put down on paper was: 'Here are made the rich pomberies (shawls: *pamri*) which serve all the Indians'.[18] The frustration of expanding our knowledge about the industry continues even under Jahangir's reign (1605-1627) who, in his memoirs, assumes that all has already been told of the industry by his father: 'The shawls of Kashmir, to which my father gave the name 'param-naram', are very famous, there is no need to praise them'.[19] Such a terse note evokes the notion that either he neglected to review his own father's memoirs or possibly a rare manuscript on the industry is still at large.[20] Nevertheless, Jahangir does state that he had presented a special shawl called 'phup' to Mirza Raja Bhao and thus we learn, for the first time, that flowers were indeed decorating the shawl's surface. At this point in time one might easily assume that such floral designs were *kani* woven. After Jahangir, a century and a half drifts by before scholars will learn anything further of the shawl industry.

The following discussion ponders and reflects upon the possibility that a special language is to be found among the flowers and patterns that adorn the shawl's surface. If, with that potential promise, new doors of understanding can be opened, then every effort should be made to find the keys. This is why I have, over many years of studying the Kashmir shawl, continually endeavoured to concentrate on the floral details that constitute

Plate 5. *Palla* detail of a multi-floral boteh, Mughal period, 17th century, Kashmir, fragment.
COLLECTION SAMUEL JOSEFOWITZ

the language of flowers and shrubs woven into the *pallas*. The emergence of this floral vocabulary – more meaningful if the styles found are identified and isolated from each other – can provide a clearer perception of the characteristics particular to the culture of Kashmir. The Napoleonic painter, Ingres, for example, a pivotal character in the study of not only floral language in period shawls but also in his total reverence for all things of antiquity, was a master at linking art and fashion. Whether the link was through an interpretation of orthodox neo-classicism, or the tactile and sculptured effects of the soft, voluptuous textiles he loved so much, Ingres succeeded in creating an imperial heraldic language through the iconography of pattern and design (for example, Plates 6 and 8).

When I began my research in the early 1980s, I had boldly set out to identify the various schools of art as applicable to the Kashmir shawl and associated with the history of Kashmir and India. To understand a clearer picture of the vast array of endless designs woven into the shawls, I felt that a kind of taxonomy could be established. On one occasion, while in Srinagar in 1982, I came across a pundit shawl dealer located near the Bund. Besides the few old *kani* shawls gathering dust in his store window, there were also a few old nostalgic sepia photographs of his shawl weaving family on display which grabbed my attention as I entered his shop. During those early years of my field research, I had the obsessive habit of always carrying 8x10 Ektachrome transparencies that showed dramatically exploded close-ups of interesting and early shawls. Holding up one of the photographs, I watched his face change as his eyes fell on an eighteenth century boteh. It was obvious he had never experienced seeing such wonderful 'high-tech' images. He looked at it in astonishment and pronounced the word 'Pathan'.[21] This moment will always be remembered as a turning point in the development of my classification, for the pundit's remark immediately validated the ideas I had begun to formulate about Kashmir's political phases impacting on design, and the 'Pathan' or Afghan period was one of them. Moreover, I immediately felt a real connection to the past through the presence of this person whose family had been so intimately attached to the industry. From this pundit's spontaneous remark, it was clear that there was much to learn about the early shawl styles.

Plate 6. *Palla* detail of finely woven, complete long shawl, Kashmir, second half 18th century, Afghan period. COLLECTION ERMES GNEMMI, MILAN

That connection and the warm contacts with the local tradesmen I had made that year in Srinagar brought home the feeling of being among a people saddened by the loss of a once great industry that will never again rise to the stellar heights it had once attained, and who were also saddened by not having anything to show for it, not even a statue erected to the unknown weavers who slaved away their precious youth. For hundreds of years Kashmir, with its unique crafts that achieved such a remarkably broad geographical diffusion, may be considered the shawl-weaving atelier to the Orient and the Western world. This tiny Himalayan country (about the size of the state of Delaware or the English county of Lincolnshire) had set an inimitable standard of weaving excellence that became the envy of so many countries. Yet, despite this, written history has left us little. With no artist's sketch albums, no sample books of early *kani* fragments, no early written references to shawl patterns, no important signed and dated shawls, and from what must have been, at one time, a huge number of shawl artists, no biographies containing writing about the Kashmir shawl, this is tantamount to a forensic case study of a deceased industry. Such regrettable lacunae of information, where so much was lost in the mists of antiquity, is not unlike Kashmiri painting, where from the eleventh to the seventeenth century identifiable works of art are virtually non-existent. If Kashmiris were tacking precious sixteenth century Mughal paintings to their windows to block the cold, we can only imagine, given the poverty they often suffered, what they actually did with the remains of their own shawl records....[22] Fortunately, over the past three centuries a large corpus of material has

survived in the form of very colourful weavings, providing – from various collections around the world – a rich source of research material.

Throughout these long centuries, however, and apart from the late arrival of the well-known investigator, William Moorcroft, with his dauntless scientific curiosity and tenacious writing, there had been no one to record the industry in detail.[23] Sixteenth century Kashmir desperately needed someone with the likes of Moorcroft's intense energy. For the textile historian, in the long history of shawl making, he was a 'Johnny-come-lately', arriving only in 1822.[24] Before this date we are left pitifully sparse phrases and tiny slivers of observations that tantalize us, yet often leave us, in their vagueness, with little to go on. Moorcroft's study of the industry, in a sense, confronts us with not only the blatant fact of just how rich and complex the industry was but also with the sadness of how much information is actually missing.

The study of the shawl, in my opinion, has yet to reach its full potential. The thousands of shawls spread out among the many private and institutional holdings still need a determined effort to collate the interminable and diverse branches of the flowing river of designs into their various categories of culturally expressive variants. Among the many designs found on the shawl – which are more closely examined in the following chapters – we have those which fall into the dense mosaic types and others with more open spacing in which the natural flowers breathe, while others appear drawn by artisans of the lacquer crafts. Then there are the comical and whimsical styles of the Mughal schools. In other words, the many designs found on the shawl begin to fall into distinct stylistic categories. Only when these categories are achieved are we better able to observe and formulate the terminology that the literature has hitherto denied us.

With the completion of such a study, museums, institutions and collectors might find it less perplexing when it comes to the questions: is it Islamic, Indian, Mughal or Himalayan? is it a costume accessory? secular or religious? if woven for the European market, Indo-European textiles? for the Indian market, simply Indian textiles; for the Persian market, Indo-Persian textiles? can we label them folk art? The fact of the matter is that these *kani* weaves, which came in all sizes and shapes, were made for an extremely wide variety of clients from all over the world. Unlike the Oriental carpet, which often carries, according to its design and weave structure, the tacit label of the tribe, village or city from which it came, the *kani* shawl's structure remained invariably unchanged and its provenance easily recognizable by the quality of its inimitable colours and soft wool. Those shawls falling outside this criterion were often judged to be of Punjabi or Persian origin.

Plate 7. *Palla* detail of a *dochalla* that was reconfigured most likely during the Napoleonic period. Afghan period, late 18th century. Size: 60cm x 280cm.
COLLECTION OF THE AUTHOR

Opposite:
Plate 8. *Dochalla* (detail). The thick branches and stylized blossoms show artistic impulses from the field of miniature painting. Identical to one at the Victoria and Albert Museum, although this one exhibits an all over *kani* boteh pattern in the *matan*.
COLLECTION SAM JOSEFOWTIZ

Chapter 2
General Classification

In the following discussion I begin by presenting a brief, if not broad, overview of the four principal political periods that impacted on the Kashmir shawl. Within this more detailed text, it is hoped that the reader will come to form his or her own understanding of the complexity of forces that bore influence on the shawl. The creation of this classification twenty years ago was not intended to set definitive time limits on a complex and evolving fashion, but was to establish a sense of order amongst a plethora of unending designs and hopefully to highlight key moments or possible stylistic schools of designs, to encourage a better understanding of a difficult subject. In this respect, one might argue, for example, that the Dogra, well before their rule of Kashmir, were already a formidable strength under Raja Gulab Singh. Nevertheless, this view must be weighed against the omnipotence of the Lahore Durbar, to which Gulab's power deferred.[25]

Finding a sense of order without any signposts amongst undated material is by no means an easy task and thus, perforce, the paradox of many speculations and assumptions cannot be avoided. Although these classifications were nothing more than initial assessments and groupings, hopefully, by their very nature, I may have succeeded in raising useful points of discussion, establishing a basis for continued study.[26] In addition, these diachronic periods coincide well with the available evidence of shawls; up to now, none of the shawls appears to be datable earlier than the reign of Shah Jahan (1628-1658). None the less, there are a few rare *kani* specimens containing patterns which may hark back to a much earlier period.This will be discussed in another section.

The apogee of the Mughal period came at a time when relative calm reigned throughout the Middle East and India. Both in Safavid Iran and Mughal India, trade and commerce flourished for many years during the sixteenth and seventeenth centuries, fuelled by a growing mercantile population spread across many borders and by Emperors, Sultans and Shahs who understood the value of such business activities and their importance to expanding the wealth of their dominions. The finely woven, freely spaced flowers of the Kashmir shawl during this time reflected not only this relative calm, but in a way represented a final frontier of an art form that had developed in Europe during the past one hundred and fifty years or so. The climate in Rome, for example, of extraordinary cultural aspiration and large opportunity, evoked by Pope Julius II, was not unlike that of the Imperial Islamic courts of Iran and India, where no expense was spared to obtain the best artists and craftsmen. Thus, the final frontier captures this 'minimalist' flower woven with grace and harmony on to the *kani* shawl (which also appears in miniature painting) and celebrates nature through a playful realism of botanical exactitude and organic unfolding. The Kashmiri artist/weaver, endowed with a rich imagination, would, at times, also capture with a lilting grace of efflorescence in the luminescent qualities of warp and weft a sense

---

Opposite:
Detail of WM26 (see page 134. Kashmir long shawl. Sikh period, c. 1835.
Courtesy, National Museum, New Delhi. Photograph by Sunil Jain

Plate 9. *Palla* detail of complete Mughal shawl, 17th century, Kashmir.
COLLECTION BHARAT KALA BHAWAN, BANARAS

of humour and an element of surprise (for example, Plates 9 and 14); one is always amazed at the limitless lyrical subtlety and whimsy one finds in the ornamentation, not to mention how the laws of perspective are, in the words of B.W. Robinson, 'humorously disregarded' by the artist's Oriental take on spatial organization. Finally, one senses that the artist has, in the quietude of his floral arrangement, expressed a particular experiential mood or feeling which strikes at the heart of those fortunate enough to be able to afford to bask in such luxuriousness. Such was the fecund ambiance, originality and inventiveness that reigned during the high Mughal period.

With the Afghan period beginning from the mid-eighteenth century, a new pattern began to take shape and its design impulse may have actually come contemporaneously from Iran. Known by various names such as the boteh, buta, cone, palm (in French) or Paisley, this curvilinear and bulbous, tear-drop pattern exercised a powerful and lasting effect on the development of future shawl designs (Plate 10). Somewhere, during this early eighteenth century time period, a vase was incorporated into the cone shape to better display a variety of floral arrangements. This fact undoubtedly acted as the catalyst in the development of curvilinearity. The variety of flowers multiplied and, oftentimes, the overly stuffed bulbous shape left little breathing space for flowers to take on a life of their own. The floral bouquet became more a schematic representation of chromatic silhouettes often centred around a radial flower device where the flowers and stems were arranged like the spokes of a wheel. Perhaps such a floral system was the foreshadowing of graphic devices to come. Reinforcing this bulbous shape of the boteh style was its adaptation as a powerful, almost heraldic symbol of fashion as epitomized by the Napoleonic painters, whose works, like the Italian Renaissance painters, were meticulously studied by art students from around the world, and from the Orient as well.

The French may have identified with the bulbous curvilinear boteh as a kind of exotic revolutionary symbol since it indicated a break from their Bourbon past. In fact, it is highly

Plate 10. *Palla* detail of very rare boteh fragment showing the early development of the curvilinear shape, c.1700, Mughal period. Identical fragments in Musée du Guimet, Paris, and Metropolitan Museum of Art, New York.
COLLECTION AUTHOR

likely that flowers, per se, such as the iris (fleur-de-lis) or the rose, perpetuated a stigma of *ancien régime* royalty, class separation and Christian rituals – all of which the 'sans culottes' and the Napoleonic era eschewed, if not completely repudiated. The natural and graceful beauty of the freely spaced flowers so associated with the Mughal period, and perhaps still popular in India, would not have attracted the interest of France's elite; and, surely, at that time they were available in the Orient. However, contemporary painters, seizing the moment, opted for a shawl pattern that spoke of sobriety and royal iconographic refinement. The embracing of the tall, bulbous, curvilinear boteh in painting and fashion reflected a culmination in the Empire's powerful intrusion into the Orient and thus became a perfect symbol to usher in the new era of Napoleon.

We can find a similar phenomenon in the Afghan domination of Kashmir, whereby the floral nature of the boteh appears to have become 'ensnared' within a sharp curvature (Plate 11), a kind of symbolic morphing of the boteh as a reflection of a changing political scene. Perhaps it was more a rejection of those floral styles popular under the Mughals than a conscientious shift in fashion. One has only to observe the flood of new patterns that ensued, following Napoleon's rise to power, along with the eponymous designs that later appeared with his imperial return from Egypt. In fact, Jean-François Bony, an important silk designer during the Empire period, was responsible for engendering the proliferation of many textile patterns like the laurel leaf, palms, olive branch, Greek vase, lyre, Napoleonic bees and the Imperial Ns, as well as the colour combinations of deep blue and golden yellow.[27]

The symbol of the laurel crown motif, often in the form of a leaf or group of leaves, as well as other Napoleonic design devices, could have made their way into the lexicon of shawl pattern repertoire via the French military community that already was well established on the subcontinent. The community was not remiss in the latest technology in warfare that had been, or was in the process of, developing in France.[28] Although the community was perhaps much more distant from Kashmir itself, the social dictates of fashion were never very far off in a country where commerce and merchants always found ways to overcome obstacles of war, and where clients had money to spend.

Plate 11. Kashmir shawl (detail), mid-18th century.
Collection Guy Joubert, Paris

The turn of the nineteenth century saw the dawning of a new strategic importance for Kashmir. With the British Empire steadily gaining control over the whole of the subcontinent and its slow but steady defensive push northwards to fend off an expansionist Tsarist Russia in Asia to the north-west and an aggressive China to the north-east, Kashmir suddenly saw itself as the contentious centre of foreign intrigue. Yet its reputation as a pre-eminent centre of internationally known crafts remained untarnished, and its cherished and highly lucrative shawl industry quickly adopted exciting new designs that reflected these churning developments.

The era of Sikh domination (1819-1846) might best be described as a new era of graphic art. The domineering influence of the boteh now took a back seat to other creative ideas emerging from the Kashmiri artist. An arrangement of volumes and spheres, of geometric forms and Art Deco textures began to invade the shawl's expanding size *(pallas)* to create a new genre of architectonic patterns (for example, Plate 12 and WM26, page 134, and WM4, page 37) that seemed to sweep away centuries of classicism. There was, in brief, an explosion of dynamic elements, of tensions and forces established by the juxtaposition of isometric compositions, that revealed perhaps a universal mystical order. Concerning a similar phenomenon, in the Art Nouveau period, for example, Gabriele Fahr-Becker observes 'Artists began to abandon the overworked recycling of historical styles of the past in favour of a self-conscious, artificial style of art'.[29] However, as much as the artists of that period were establishing a dynamic floral language that achieved a unique sensation of synesthesia, Sikh artists, through their own newly discovered language of graphic shapes, found a unique way to voice their moods and inclinations. As much as the Sikh religion drew from eclectic spiritual sources, it is also clear that the new Sikh designs drew sharply away from tradition to create patterns distinctly antithetical to Mughal heritage. Indeed, many of the new designs were virtually explosive in character and could easily be compared to a fabulous display of fireworks while others were equally celebratory in their profuse and even chaotic arrays of exotic foliage. Were these festive memorial shawls to pay homage to Ranjit Singh's many military conquests or were they an unconscious outpouring of renewed

Plate 12. *Palla* detail of complete Kashmir shawl showing 'Samadhi boat', c.1840, Sikh period. Detail of WM18, page 119.
COLLECTION NIRMAL MATTOO

WM3. Kashmir long shawl (detail)
A series of mihrabs (as in a prayer *saph*), lobed medallions locked in by embedded bent-tip botehs, and circles, form a wonderful architectural pattern that may reflect the sudden rush of building and construction the Punjab experienced during this period. Sikh period, c.1840.
COLLECTION JOAN HART

vigour symbolizing a shedding of years of Afghan tyranny? Perhaps there was even a parallel element of synchronicity that, in these early years of the nineteenth century, mirrored France's Revolution, whereby all from the *ancien régime* was abolished. At the same time, one should not overlook the importance of the holiday, Diwali, otherwise known as the Festival of Lights, often lasting several days, and celebrated by Hindus, Jains and Sikhs (for example, WM3 and WM23, page 129)

In assessing these new revolutionary patterns it should also be mentioned that, while Maharaja Ranjit Singh was known for his religious toleration, his officers and troops did not share his acceptance of the Muslims.[30] Perhaps, this intolerance among the people was one of the catalysts that helped spawn a new era of bodacious patterns, swept clean of an out-of-date Islamic jurisdiction. Yet the enigma prevails in observing patterns such as the harmonious mélange of Indo-Muslim shapes as in WM3. While many of these fantastic shawl patterns continue to baffle us today, it is clear that no other area of contemporary Indian art had ever witnessed on the subcontinent such a rapid shift in fashion and extraordinary artistic activity.

Despite the strong European influence, and contrary to popular belief, the Dogra period (1846-1877) was no less a fertile period of artistic development than its predecessor. This was due to the powerful competition of artistic energies that circulated in Srinagar, driven by a

Plate 13. Detail of Dogra period Kashmir shawl, c.1865.
PRIVATE COLLECTION

multinational force of foreign purchasing agents under heavy pressure to meet the demands of a luxury-hungry Europe, flush with bourgeois money. True, because of the dramatic increase in demand, great quantities of shawls had to be produced and quality suffered. French influence was pre-eminent in Kashmir, but, this fact in no way impeded the creative juices of the autochthonous artists, for some of the best masterpieces of *kani* weaving started to appear (Plate 13). Such pieces more than likely foreshadowed the coming of the Art Nouveau period.[31] In the Dogra period, designs in general, of course, often mimicked or copied those created by the French artists for the Jacquard loom. But, it is obvious, given the beauty and originality of extant evidence, that they also acted as a powerful catalyst for the Kashmiri artists.[32]

Over the years, tracing the origin and development of the Mughal flowering plant has been a challenging endeavour. In 1955 John Irwin, in a sense, laid down the gauntlet when he declared that the earliest surviving shawl in a public collection was a flowering plant fragment (Plate 14) preserved in the Calico Museum of Textiles, Ahmedabad.[33] He dated it to c.1680, based on similarities to a *patka* flower in a miniature painting from Golconda.[34] Since then, an identical fragment from the same shawl is now part of the Victoria and Albert Museum's collection. The *pallas* are patterned with rose plants, freely spaced and charmingly delicate, in the typical Shah Jahan style. Observing the plant's prickly leaves, one could almost perceive a slight easterly wind sweeping through these roses – their frail stems rising up to support a clutch of blossoms and buds that form the boteh's triple-flex pose. This classic pose (*tribhanga*) is the *ne plus ultra* of Central Asian forms and, in this case, its ultimate expression would seem to unite the regenerative forces of botanical nature with the resplendent might of the Mughal court. After many editions and over thirty years later, the shawl's graceful and poetic efflorescence continues to adorn the cover of John Irwin's ground-breaking monograph. That this rare

Plate 14. Colour tracing of *palla* fragment, Kashmir, 17th century. Identical fragments in Victoria and Albert Museum, London, and Calico Museum, Ahmedabad.

fragment, featured in so many publications, has to this day continued to pique our interest strongly supports the idea that court artists were intimately involved in world craft trade endeavours.

However, as much as Irwin's pioneering shawl research impacted on textile history, paradoxically his monograph had a tendency to remain fairly limited in its global purview. Irwin may have overlooked some of the shawls and shawl fragments in his study as being of a much earlier date. As laid out in the eight shawl tracings of his monograph, which he dates from 1680 to 1870, his arguments clearly show that his dating was based on a linear time progression of shawl patterns, beginning with freely-spaced flower bouquets that developed into botehs/cones exhibiting curvilinearity.[35] The strong impact of these simple sketches is such that it camouflages the parallel production of many other patterns that competed with the cone for shawl decoration, which, admittedly, is not an easy issue to tackle. Irwin, in establishing this linear progression, may have fallen into his own trap, as we shall see further on from a correspondence I had with him in 1980. This precarious step of establishing such a time progression leads us to believe that the earliest patterns began only as freely-spaced flowers with a mature degree of botanical accuracy when, in fact, there must have been concurrent or transitional shrub designs dating from the Akbar period or even earlier, given the long history of shawl making. The grace, poetry and botanical refinement of the beautiful floral weavings so associated with the courts of Jahangir and Shah Jahan indubitably created an immediate appeal to the aesthetic senses. It is all too easy to get swept away by this phenomenon but, in fact, the Kashmir shawl has a long history.[36] So little is known of those 'imperial' designs which did not represent the so-called flowering plants, designs that reflected other types of exotic flowers and shrubs – and there must have been many – which bore no resemblance to the seventeenth century Mughal archetype.

Twenty-five years ago, in Paris, when I first began my research, I had written to John Irwin (d.1997) asking him some specific questions about the Kashmir shawl. One of these was whether there was a correlation between the shawl's *palla* height and its age. Before the week was over, a typewritten reply on his letterhead stationery arrived from Hampshire:

> *Commodity textiles – that is, textiles made for the anonymous market as distinct from those specially commissioned for a purpose or associated with a particular personality – are notoriously hazardous to date. The truth is that side by side with the production of new designs, weavers commonly went on producing the old designs to meet the market of conservative taste. This more than ever applies to the history of Kashmir shawls of the 19th c. when production had to meet simultaneously the demands of a very wide variety of markets, some placing great importance upon novelty and fashion, others being ultra-conservative in taste. So I would never like to be dogmatic about the date of any Kashmir shawl unless there is independent evidence of a documentary nature. Perhaps one should not expect to do more than to place designs within the framework of the period they are first known to have appeared.*[37]

Having just made my first steps into researching the subject, Irwin's letter came as quite a surprise to me and I was extremely flattered by his taking the time to reply and impressed by his clear thinking about the complexities of a defunct fashion industry. His thoughts also helped clarify my own ideas of being, perhaps, a little too bent on tracing a pattern which may not have followed a precise linear chronology.

However, to equate such rich, opulent and labour-intensive weavings to a market without a name appeared to me, at the time, a difficult supposition to digest. Calling them 'commodity textiles' smacked of a certain aridity and debasement that left me wondering if, indeed, my interest should be focused more on the history of say, blue jeans, than the Kashmir shawl. By the time I read 'notoriously hazardous to date' I was almost convinced I had embarked on the wrong endeavour. It had never occurred to me that a market, especially a fashionable one, could be called anonymous, yet to read the words 'anonymous market' seemed at the time a marvellous absurdity.

Although the nineteenth century saw an explosion of trade to the West, Kashmir's

WM4. Kashmir long shawl (detail pages 38-39)
The complex display of broad serrated-edge arches, lobed medallions and bell shapes is like viewing a mechanical drawing of the insides of a clock. Indeed, Lehna Singh Majithia, Ranjit Singh's Hill States minister, was known for inventing horological devices. The artist has reduced the use of botehs to what are faint silhouettes, pairing them off with large spear separations. The majestic flaming arches that overlap the opposing botehs recalls the halos associated with Himalayan Buddhists sculpture. Under the arches, if one looks closely, it is possible to see tiny *gurdwaras* on each side, with a cypress tree on top. The metaphor of the tree is a divine symbol frequently cited in the scriptures of the Sri Adi Granth. Sikh period, c.1835.
COLLECTION AUTHOR. PHOTOGRAPH BY ADAM REICH

markets had already been firmly established and perhaps not so unspecified as one might think. Besides the whims and fancies of Mughal fashion, the kingdoms of the Deccan, such as Ahmadnagar, Golconda and Bijapur, had a long regional tradition for intense, romantic colour hues, and designs which may not have mimicked those of their rivals in the North. Speaking of certain floral patterns, the elder shawl wallahs of Kashmir still use phrases such as 'Hyderabadi' and 'Jaipuri'. Specialized shawl goods with geometric designs or abstract patterns, or prayer mats often in darker colours and deep reds, were a predilection of the hill

tribes of Afghanistan and points further north, towards Central Asia.[38] In any case, the closest Irwin and I came to resolving the issue of *palla* height and age of a shawl was the understanding that the earliest do indeed seem to be quite diminutive, at least on the *dochallas*. The *patka* (waistband), on the other hand, seems over the centuries to have maintained fairly constant its end panel's *(palla)* height.

Irwin's comments on market anonymity are not without a touch of irony. His monograph lists in the appendix ten pages by Moorcroft, written in 1823, carefully describing the various shawl products and their countries of destination, such as Persia, Hindustan, Afghanistan, Russia, Turkey, Deccan, Baghdad, Yarkand, Bokhara, Arabia, Turkistan, and Kandahar.[39] It is true that, even if they were woven with *pashmina* wool, the bulk of shawl goods were often of very common patterns and materials. In this case, lack of designation would be quite applicable. But at the other end of the spectrum were goods of top quality, woven with the finest grades of *pashmina* or more rarely *shah tus,* pieced together by the best *rafugars* (shawl tailors or seamsters), and most likely woven under the aegis of elite patronage. In many cases – as attested by extant shawls in collections – the shawl was woven, seamlessly, in one piece on the loom. It is usually these types of shawls that, found in important collections, dazzle us by their brilliance of colour and fineness of weave.

In fact, Irwin didn't seem very dogmatic about always dating designs 'within the framework of the period they are first known to appear'. This is understandable when considering once again the above-mentioned well-known Calico/Victoria and Albert Museum fragment. It fits quite neatly within the framework of floral styles seen in the *Padshahnama* c.1630, or about half a century earlier than Irwin's dating.

When I began in the early 1980s sorting out shawl patterns into four classifications, it was probably the voice of Irwin's letter about commodity textiles which most often resonated in my ears. For there is no doubt that Irwin was a clever and meticulous researcher and his insights often went right to the core of a problem, as one reads in the clear bell-tone quality of his prose. His groundbreaking study on the Kashmir shawl, despite its limitations, none the less established early on a high standard of research excellence, engendering a new aesthetic appreciation for the shawl. It marked a shift in attitude and taste for Indian craft which rendered the subject worthy of scholarly study.

In my first publication on the shawl (1986) I had explained that our search for earlier patterns appeared to be thwarted due to a lack of commingling of styles. Patterns and designs from the pre-Mughal period, or Sultanate period, were for the most part classic Islamic motifs, similar to those found in the Middle East. For *kani* weaves earlier than the late eighteenth century these graphic elements do not appear, either on their own or blended with traditional Mughal art. This, in itself, speaks volumes about the early beginnings of the Kashmir shawl. Extant evidence shows the earliest pieces decorated only with small freely spaced shrubs or flowers.

However, in my rather broad overview of the subject now almost twenty-five years ago, several fascinating if not enigmatic and unique *kani* designs (as mentioned above) were published which now appear to merit closer scrutiny than the passing attention they had originally received. They should be scrutinized with the understanding that certainly the earliest ornamentation of shawls did not begin with a delicate *tribhanga* flower (Plates 14 and 15),

Plate 15. Detail of silk and metallic thread palace carpet, Mughal, 17th century.
COLLECTION VISHNU M. LALL, AGRA

but conversely, and most undoubtedly, began with a much simpler floral type decoration. Among the purists of Mughal art, the flowering plant has become such an ensconced emblem that anything less notable in artistic merit has been systematically if not unceremoniously brushed aside. As much as this graceful sinuous form might express the height of Mughal interest in the flowering plant, one should avoid being blindsided to its floral antecedents. It is interesting to note that since John Irwin's monograph on shawls, almost fifty years ago, no seventeenth or eighteenth century Kashmir shawl has appeared with any kind of date woven in, embroidered or otherwise stamped on it. A few pieces with *toshakhana* stamps (Plate 16) from the late eighteenth century and several known shawls of the nineteenth century with embroidered dates exist, but this is, unfortunately, of frustratingly little help in this research study.

John Irwin, writing a half century ago, was the first to state that the boteh evolved through Persian art and advanced a dual theory as to how it came about. In the first he submits that the nineteenth century Kashmir cone was clearly the product of an independent development, from sixteenth century Safavid patterns, at a time when Persia and Kashmir enjoyed particularly close links. Irwin theorizes that the cone is the product of two motifs stemming from sixteenth century brocades and carpets: the cypress and a flowering almond tree. During the seventeenth century the frequent placing of the almond tree in front of the cypress caused a gradual merging of the two motifs into a 'common outline'. In Irwin's second hypothesis, which appears more valid, are two popular seventeenth/eighteenth century Indo-Persian motifs, the floral shrub or vase-and-flower, fusing together some time during the eighteenth century to form the cone.[40]

As much as Irwin's above ideas may appear reasonable, they really do not hold up under the scrutiny of pictorial or material evidence extant. As it will be shown in Chapter 7, it is quite possible that the cone's appearance may indeed be due to the quirk of spontaneous

Plate 16. Rare example of a *toshakhana* stamp on a Kashmir shawl fragment. Translation: 'We wish you good welfare', dated 1797.
COLLECTION MAHARAJA SAWAI MAN SINGH II MUSEUM, JAIPUR

fashion. That cone development may have been greatly influenced by the integration of the vase within the floral framework of the flowering plant appears to be a more reasonable argument.

As for the cypress-and-almond tree idea, I would tend to reject it on several grounds. First, there is no Kashmir evidence to support it. True, both plants are often seen commingling on carpets and in paintings, but the cypress tree invariably appears to stand stoic against the caressing and sweeping arms of the almond tree's advances – the cypress standing tall, not always with a bend at the top, while the flowering tree's branches spread in rather scattered directions. Nothing here would suggest the development of the cone.[41]

Notwithstanding the improbability of this type of cone development, Irwin's cypress tree theory, drawn from Persian painting and early textiles, represented at the time a prescient vision and indeed pointed the way towards Persia as the progenitor of cone development. Persia's medieval architectural history is replete with boteh motifs, motifs which more than likely evolved from the rich, swirling patterns of Islamic calligraphy (see Plates 1 and 2).

Before entering our discussion of the main topic of this book, namely the Sikh period shawl, it behoves us briefly to review in the next chapter the stylistic development of the shawl under the great Mughal emperors. Understanding the creative impulses surrounding the imperial courts will be of help in following the train of events that lead up to the Sikh period.

Chapter 3

The Development of the Mughal Style

Sweet are the uses of adversity,
Which, like the toad, ugly and venomous,
Wears yet a precious jewel in his head;
And this our life exempt from public haunt
Finds tongues in trees, books in the running brooks,
Sermons in stones and good in every thing.

As You Like It, Duke Senior, Act II, Sc. i
William Shakespeare (1564-1616)

In the imperial gardens of Kashmir Shakespeare would have felt right at home in Jahangir's own inimitable haunt, where the fragrant beauty of nature spoke to him, as it did in lyrical metaphors to the great Elizabethan poet. India, unlike Persia at the time, was a land of intellectual and religious freedom, where Persian poetry especially blossomed, more so than in its native country. According to the words of Abul Fazl (Akbar's chronicler), 'thousands of poets were continually at the court of Akbar', many of whom produced *diwans*. In fact, the great Emperors, Babur, Humayun, Akbar, Jahangir and Shah Jahan were all accomplished poets in their own right, surrounding themselves with talented people of the lyrical word. Poets were given *mansabdars,* some *jagirs,* while others received cash grants for their odes.[42]

The passion for poetry was not confined to the Imperial court. The aristocracy and professional classes revelled in this art form, which continued its popularity well into the nineteenth century; cloth merchants, goldsmiths and bankers stroked their appreciative chins, especially of the lyrical and romantic *ghazals* George Forster, while in Kashmir in the late eighteenth century, remarked on the huge popularity of poetry there.[43] Many important Imperial works of art would not have been replete without a poetic inscription. Shah Jahan had the Peacock Throne inscribed with the verses of Qudsi, whose effusive metaphors, enamelled into the throne, sparkled adjacent to the fabulous gemstones that adorned it. Abu Talib Kalim from Hamadan (d.1650) became the poet laureate to the court of Shah Jahan. Kalim's style, inspired by the great master, Mirza Muhammad 'Ali Sa'ib (1607-1677), as well as by his own sojourns in Srinagar in company with the great Kashmiri poet, Gani Kasmiri, gave voice to the important historical events of the time, rendering his poetry invaluable to the cultural life of the period.

The style of court poetry was often effusive and, at times, pregnant with enigmatic qualities and panegyrics infused with lyrical subtleties and hidden meanings. It is not altogether surprising that within this artistically stimulating and intellectually charged atmosphere we find patterns and designs among the various craft products which similarly exuded an enigmatic, if not poetic, nature. Extant masterpieces of imperial weavings such as the Aynard prayer niche carpet, arguably one of the greatest *pashmina* knotted Indian carpets in the world, showcases an artist's dreamscape conception where hooked tendril-like sepals create an aquatic-like effect of 'octopi' blossoms languorously floating against an intense crimson sky dotted with menacing dragon-

Plate 17. Aynard prayer carpet, knotted, *pashmina* wool, Mughal, 17th century.
COLLECTION CARMEN THYSSEN-BORNEMISZA, MADRID

head *tchi* clouds (Plate 17). To observe this bizarre concoction of voluptuous efflorescence is to enter into the surreal world of an artist's brilliant imagination, whose psyche may have been long steeped in the words of the fifteenth century poet Navoi who wrote: 'But there is an image of the world in this flowerbed, and the whole world is hidden in every flower'.[44] Equally indecipherable are the Akbar period red-ground 'grotesque' carpets where animal heads are drawn swirling in vine-like fashion, while other animals are being disgorged from their mouths.

Another masterpiece of knotted weaving is the fine *pashmina* Altman carpet at the Metropolitan Museum of Art (Plate 18). Its spectacular main border was obviously drawn by the painterly hand of a very gifted imperial artist, most likely a Kashmiri. Its unique botanical arrangement alternates thick evergreen trees – which clearly suggest Kashmir's mountainous region – with bushes of blossoming clusters aglow in yellow jasmine *(Gelsemium sempervirens)* and, oddly, with an artichoke plant *(Cynara scolymus)*, a plant that has long been cultivated in the Orient. Emitting an intoxicating fragrance, the jasmine is mentioned a few times in Jahangir's *Tuzuk*.[45] The artist's scheme of staging his landscape with the soft folds of overlapping hillocks (an idea taken directly from miniature painting) adds an ingenious note of surreal drama. The larger plants, raised on a knoll, are flanked by smaller cock's-comb and iris plants, all of which are 'backlit' by a magnificently golden-hued ground colour, intensifying the greenness of the leaves and plants and bathing the whole scene in a mystical twilight. The funnel-shaped blossoms of the yellow jasmine (also known as yellow evening flower) seem all expressly placed in an upturned manner. Are they trumpeting the setting of the sun? Whatever the ploy, it is clear that the artist's aim is to pull the viewer into the magic of a fairytale-like experience. The choice of border plants is bizarre considering that, on one hand, we have an edible plant (artichoke), which is, incidentally, also capable of exuding a beautiful purple inflorescence, and the jasmine, which is not only highly odoriferous, but inedible. In this unusual repeat, where *tchi* clouds with flaming wispy tails dash about like comets in the sky, one wonders if there is not a hidden alchemical metaphor or talismanic quality to be understood among this rare mix of gastronomic and toxic plants. It is interesting to point out the obviously Kashmiri nature of the border and the possibly highly stylized Lahori floral nature of the carpet's field. Apart from the close ties of prayer carpets to *kani* prayer mats of Kashmir, the Altman carpet is perhaps the

Plate 18. Palace carpet, border detail, *pashmina,* Kashmir, 17th century.
COLLECTION METROPOLITAN MUSEUM OF ART, BEQUEST OF BENJAMIN ALTMAN, 1913 (14.40.723)

Plate 19. *Palla* detail of botehs, complete shawl, Kashmir, 17th century.
COLLECTION NATIONAL MUSEUM, NEW DELHI

only one that exudes a close stylistic resonance with contemporary shawls of the boteh pattern. There are two *dochallas,* one at the National Museum, Delhi (Plate 19) and the other at the Calico Museum, Ahmedabad,[46] and in each we find botehs raised on hillocks with tiny protrusions, exactly as in the Altman carpet.

The 'Mughal Style' might best be described as India's answer to the Mannerist school of Italian Renaissance art.[47] An excellent example of this style is a shawl from the Shah Jahan era, in a private collection (Plate 20). Its boteh repeat is made up of graceful floral bouquets comprised of roses, carnations, cock's combs, buds and racemes. The bouquets – which sit atop a bed of long undulating fronds, the repetition of which, in itself, produces a brilliant effect of 'unbearable lightness' of flotation – are so delicately arranged that all the blossoms appear to be reaching joyously towards the sun. Although pistils and anthers are absent, this fine weaving nevertheless epitomizes the type of flowers that one finds ornamenting the Taj or any of the other fine contemporary Mughal monuments.

The Muslim love for flowers in India did not begin with the Mughals, but with the Sultans who preceded them, who under Firuz Shah Tughlaq supposedly created some 12,000 gardens around Delhi, as well as a tree-lined road linking Lahore and Agra.[48] With the Mughals came the great decorative heritage of the Persians and by the time of Jahangir we find the crocus, marigold, iris, morning glory and tulip interpolating themselves into the artistic landscape of painting. The tulip achieved great popularity at this time and it is surprising that no shawl has yet been found with this flower. The crocus, perhaps Jahangir's favourite flower, was a frequent decorative meander used in the shawl's *hashias,* a source of fragrant saffron, of intense dye colour and medicinal aphrodisiac (Plate 21). Shawls exhibiting a crocus meander are usually dated to the seventeenth or early eighteenth century. During the Akbar period, the illustration of flowers appeared to be limited to the artist's stereotypical delineation of the petals, stems and leaves. Under Akbar's son, Jahangir, an abrupt awareness of botanical details, such as bracts, floral tubes, sepals and stamens emerged, giving rise to works of art where artists, led by Mansur, fascinated by these phyllotaxic details, created paintings that featured often only a single floral species, graceful and natural.

Jahangir's rich poetic prose, filled with entrancing metaphors and surreal images, reflected his extreme sensitivities to and love for the beauties of his surroundings in Kashmir.

Far left:
Plate 20. *Palla* detail of rare long shawl, Kashmir, 17th century.
PRIVATE COLLECTION

Below:
Plate 21. *Hashia* detail of crocus meander taken from Plate 10.

Left:
Plate 22. 'Lantern' boteh, detail of complete long shawl, Kashmir, Mughal, possibly Jahangir period.
COLLECTION BHARAT KALA BHAWAN, BANARAS

Craft artists were surely seduced by Jahangir's poetic fantasies. The fine, pristine shawl at the Bharat Kala Bhawan (Plate 22), one that I've nicknamed the 'Chinese Lantern' shawl due to the golden specks that 'illuminate' each of the down-turned flowers, could easily have been created to commemorate and immortalize the Emperor's poem:

The garden-nymphs (flowers) were brilliant
Their cheeks shone like lamps;
There were fragrant buds on their stems (or
'under their rind')
Like dark amulets on the arms of the beloved.
The wakeful, ode-rehearsing nightingale
Whetted the desires of wine drinkers;
At each fountain the duck dipped his beak
Like golden scissors cutting silk;
There were flower-carpets and fresh rosebuds,
The wind fanned the lamps of the roses,
The violet braided her locks,
The buds tied a knot in the hearts.[49]

Certain flowers in the west, their symbolism reflected in religious art, were historically associated with salvation. Whereas Jahangir's crocus might otherwise be considered a representation of resurrection and heavenly bliss, in his imperial Shish Mahal it is probably more a source of languorous evenings immersed in blissful opiates. While the styles and stigmas of the crocus provide the aphrodisiacal qualities of the plant, the poppy, or 'herb of joy' as the ancient Sumerians called it in 3000 BC, was more likely the preferred seed pod for the real source of the opiate. Nevertheless, given the qualities of these flowers, it is surprising that there are no known shawls with botehs illustrative of them. A unique fragment in the Kuwait National Museum comes close to the resemblance of a

Plate 23. Rose boteh *palla* fragment, Mughal, 17th century.
Private Collection

crocus flower. The rapier-like leaves and pod shape of the 'blossoms' certainly are characteristics, but the resemblances appear to end here. The poppy flower design was, of course, generally highly employed on carpets and textiles.

By the turn of the seventeenth century, as much as Mughal painting had made a 'thorough assimilation of western pictorial science',[50] it appears that it never really embraced flowers as similes, for example, of power, purity or fertility,[51] as did western painting. In Persian poetical language the red rose (Plate 23) is connected not only with the idea of happiness or joy and love, but likewise with blood and wounds. On the other hand, a peculiar scene that took place during Kashmir's rose blossom season, witnessed by George Forster in 1783, appears to push the definition of 'joy and love' to the extreme. His account is worth quoting:

> *...the rose of Kashmire, which for its brilliancy and delicate odour, has long been proverbial in the east and its essential oil or ottar is held in universal estimation,. The season when the rose first opens into blossom is celebrated with much festivity by the Kashmirians, who resort in crowds to the adjacent gardens and enter into scenes of gaiety and pleasure, rarely known among Asiatic nations. There, all that exterior gravity which constitutes a grand part of the Mohametan character is thrown aside; and the Turk, Arab, and Persian, as if fatigued with exhibiting the serious and guarded deportment of their own country, give licentious scope to their passions.*[52]

Such a unique scene – as in the well-known movie of the bestseller *Perfume* – leaves one wondering if Jahangir, one hundred and fifty years earlier, in all his poems and observations from his many trips to Kashmir, had omitted an important ritual of the Valley.

One of the dilemmas of Indian art is that many historians of the Mughal period tend to place all decorative objects that do not have the typical Shah Jahan floral look, aka 'Mughal Style', into the late seventeenth century or often eighteenth century. The field of Indian art has been in a way stymied by the Emperor's flowers, so that they can't see that his 'clothes' may have already disappeared. Assigning only Mughal style designs to this era is to overlook the simultaneous fashion for designs that may have eschewed floral naturalism. When we look at the great fashionable shawl cone era, which lasted, as we know it, from approximately the early eighteenth century up to about 1825 or so, we find a plethora of various competing patterns that depended not in the least upon the cone. The same reasoning should be applied to Mughal textiles and carpets.

It seems that *kani* decoration begins to appear in Mughal painting only by the second half of the seventeenth century. However, it is obvious by the manner in which flowers were depicted on contemporary shawls that the artist's brush strokes paid little attention to floral detail. A search of the vast body of seventeenth century Indian miniatures in hopes of finding shawl details comparable to those of the great French painters such as Ingres, Baron Gros or David appears to lead only to disappointment. The paintings that do depict the wearing of the *kani* shawl curiously enough come mostly from the Deccan of the second half of the seventeenth century and, although the often crudely drawn flowers they portray impart little to our corpus of botanical knowledge, they nevertheless do exhibit the free spacing so typical of the era (Plate 24). These Deccani shawls also give evidence that only the diminutive end panels *(pallas)* were decorated, leaving the field plain.[53] A further

Plate 24. Shawl fashion in 17th century Mughal India.

Right:
Plate 25. Coloured boteh tracing (detail) of complete Kashmir shawl, 17th century.
COLLECTION MUSEUM OF FINE ARTS, BOSTON, ACC. NO. 45.540

Above left:
Plate 26. Coloured tracing of small fragment, Kashmir, c.17th century, after *The Kashmir Shawl*, J. Irwin, pl. 4.
VICTORIA AND ALBERT MUSEUM, IS.14.1972

Above right:
Plate 27. Coloured tracing of small fragment, Kashmir, c.17th century, after *The Kashmir Shawl*, Irwin, pl. 4.
VICTORIA AND ALBERT MUSEUM, IS.13-1972

Right:
Plate 28. Mughal *dochalla* (detail), 17th century.
TEXTILE MUSEUM, WASHINGTON, D.C.

argument testifying to the freely-spaced flower's sudden appearance in the early seventeenth century is the fact that, before this time, it is not found as ornamentation on architecture.[54]

Given the information in Abul Fazl's chronicles, we know the shawl industry existed long before Akbar, yet little speculation as to what the *kani* shawl may have looked like prior to Jahangir's famous floral 'epiphany' has been submitted. Speculation of this kind is by no means inconsistent with the logic of progressive design development, whatever the medium of artistic expression. Paradoxical as it might seem, of all the renowned collections of Kashmir shawls – and given the fact that it has been strongly argued by some scholars that they derive from an industry in existence for well-nigh two millennia – not one has yet been dated to earlier than the seventeenth century. Except possibly for the well-known 'grotesque' carpets, a similar statement could be said of Mughal carpets.

One of the richest depositories of early, rare and surprisingly pristine Kashmir shawls is found at the Bharat Kala Bhawan, Banaras. However, with few exceptions, these shawls all appear to fall categorically into the seventeenth or eighteenth century period. The Museum of Fine Arts, Boston, possesses a rather extensive collection, yet, apart from one spectacular seventeenth century white *dochalla,* with 'Chinese character' roots (Plate 25), most fall into the late eighteenth to nineteenth century. The late Krishna Riboud, an avid collector with a sharp eye, amassed in the latter part of the twentieth century a fine collection (later bequeathed to the Guimet) and while her acquisitions quickly became a rich research source to be reckoned with, featuring two wonderful seventeenth century fragments, there is nothing earlier in her collection. The Calico Museum is out of the running in this respect and that leaves three remaining museums, all of which own some extremely enigmatic ancient fragments. The Victoria and Albert Museum is one, whose large collection contains some small fragments that were

Plate 29. *Palla* fragment, Kashmir, 17th century or earlier.
KUWAIT NATIONAL MUSEUM: THE AL-SABAH COLLECTION

discovered in the lining of Tipu Sultan's jacket (Plates 26 and 27). Of them, two stand out. One with a sprig (crocus?) pattern on a taupe ground shows a bit of *hashia* similar to that of the Victoria and Albert's often illustrated Mughal fragment of roses. The second tiny piece, more fortunate in its survival, displays a repeat of two shrubs on a spectacular orange-saffron ground replete with its top and bottom *hashias,* thus providing enough information as to its original appearance.

The Textile Museum's well-known collection is graced by an outstandingly soft (possibly *shah tus*) and exotic copper-toned (*feuille morte*) shawl (Plate 28). The huge spacing between the bouquets (or trees) of racemes is secured at the base in a very Persianate style and the unique meander of the *hashias,* with their reciprocating tear-drops, betokens an early age. The National Museum, Kuwait, has several ancient fragments, two of a very early *hashia,* so fine that they handle like the finest silk, and a full *palla* fragment, mentioned above, which is composed of six exotic orange 'flowers' set against a golden yellow ground (Plate 29). The flowers look more like elongated nuts or pea pods but, whatever is the case, there is no question that this fragment evokes a profound sense of antiquity far beyond any known shawl extant. In light of the recent and popular use of radiocarbon dating, one would think that it would be in the best interests of textile history to begin sample testing on these early relics.

Robert Skelton was the first to argue that naturalism of the flowering plant had not made its real debut in Mughal art before Jahangir's visit to Kashmir in March of 1620.[55] So impressed by the overwhelming beauty and variety of flowers from this Himalayan paradise, Jahangir set about describing the Valley in heartfelt wispy poems of a deeply visual and at times olfactory nature, prose that confirmed his keen sensitivities of observation.[56] Mansur, Jahangir's favourite painter of animals and flowers, accompanied him on this trip, and, as a result, produced many beautiful flower paintings that featured the flowering plant in such a predominant way that it marked a complete new genre of botanical style, the likes of which had nothing in common with previous floral imaging.[57] Though only four remain extant, from Jahangir's *Tuzuk* we learn that Mansur painted more than one hundred flowers, which implies that Jahangir intended to create an album cataloguing the Valley's lush flora. It would be difficult to imagine the Valley's shawl industry not responding to the marvels of such an album by recreating at least some of his 'canvas' marvels in *kani* weave.

Previously, flowers were inserted as a minor embellishment in certain parts of the painting. But, with Mansur, flowers became a unique attraction to dominate the tight confines of the miniature and, thus featured, often confront the viewer with dramatic realism in a way not unlike their European herbal counterparts, whence they received their inspiration. A large centrepiece flower was often featured against a stark and sharply contrasting background of highly detailed blossoms and partially opened buds on the verge of unfolding in their inflorescence, highlighting an organic and graceful growth. Such 'Mannerist' images reflected the Indo-European Renaissance of the flowering plant as it shifted from obscurity to stark realism, a shift that could be traced back

Plate 30. 'A Clump of Grass', watercolour, pencil and ink, 1584, after Albrecht Dürer by Fritz Koreny, 1985, fig. 65, p. 187.
PRIVATE COLLECTION

to the seminal drawings of Albrecht Dürer and Leonardo da Vinci. Dürer's sharp focus on the most minute aspects of nature, on commonplace botanical growth, that had long been seen and taken for granted for centuries by artists and people alike, were magnified in the consciousness of man's visual sensitivities (Plate 30).[58] One should be reminded also that the microscope was still an invention a hundred years down the road.

Mansur's meticulous focus had obviously been encouraged by the Imperial ruler's passionate attention to and intimate knowledge of the artistic merits of all of his gifted artists. Jahangir records that he was so totally aware of each painter's inimitable style that he could immediately identify any work put before him. This encouraged progressively recognizable works reflecting the expertise of each of the artists such as Mansur's animal and flowers, Abu'l Hasan's and the incomparable Basan Das' 'imperial' portraits as well as Govardan's holy men, musicians and eccentrics. The beauty, grace and lyricism of many of the extant shawls would lead one to wonder if Jahangir was not equally adept at recognizing the name of the weaver, as well as the shawl artist.

It has been long known that carpet designs over the centuries were so well known to the weavers that popular patterns were actually sung, by the master weaver, for the apprentices to follow with their knotted patterns. This is no less true for the early patterns of the Kashmir shawl. Much of the graceful nature of their patterns alludes to weavers who, imbued with the lyrical poetry of the era, traced out their patterns according to melodic sounds. This begs the almost bizarre question: would it be possible some day in the future to decode the melody itself by unravelling an early Mughal shawl?

It appears that, until the time of Mansur, Indian and Persian artists had not yet found a way for plants to emerge naturally from the soil without hiding the stem's base with large rocks. Mansur also introduced carefully drawn bracts, carpels, floral tubes, sepals and stamens, developing a heightened sense of botanical accuracy. Such details heralded the

Plate 31. Red tulips by Ustad Mansur, Mughal, 1620.
HABIBGANJ LIBRARY, ALIGARH

Plate 32. Martagon Lily by Pierre Vallet. From *Le Jardin du très Chréstian Henri IV*, 1608.
PRIVATE COLLECTION

introduction of a new painting style: creating a miniature solely devoted to the illustration of a single flower species. Obviously, this floral paradigm was to have a strong impact on textile and rug artistry and, as will be discussed further on, what became a particular style carefully modelled on European sources.

Robert Skelton's paper (see above) was the first to discuss Mughal still life painting and its direct inspirational sources from Western engravings. His curiosity was aroused by the similarities of approach between Mansur's picture of a Western Asiatic tulip and the Martagon Lily from Pierre Vallet's *Le Jardin du très Chréstian Henry IV* of 1608, with respect to the artist's approach and especially the inclusion of a hovering butterfly, the use of which was a cliché in European herbals (Plates 31 and 32) – more on this idea of winged insects further on. Vivian Rich greatly expanded on the idea of European herbal influence in her doctoral thesis, coming up with at least four floral miniature paintings positively identified as being copied directly from European sources, with another almost twenty classified as 'most likely copied'.[59]

One of the most important groups of painting for our study can be found in the Dara Shukoh album. Shukoh had refined tastes and a strong penchant for collecting art, similar to his father Shah Jahan. His album, conserved at the British Library, contains, according to Rich, three miniatures that were copied directly from European botanical drawing. The first one, a narcissus, is positively identified as copied from Carolus Clusius' 1576 *Rariorum Aliquot*

Plate 33. Narcissus by Carolus Clusius. From *Rariorum Aliquot Stirpium*, 1576.
PRIVATE COLLECTION

Stirpium, published by Christophe Plantin of Antwerp, the same person who also printed the Royal Polyglot Bible presented to Akbar in 1580 (Plate 33). Sharing the spotlight with Clusius as the most renowned botanist of his time were Dodoens and l'Obel; all three used a common pool of more than two thousand woodcut engravings by Peter van der Borcht (Flemish, 1545-1608). Since a close camaraderie existed between all three scientists, they often shared the same illustrations for their publications.

Floral representation during the period of Akbar was relatively simple, naïve, and in general was based on Persian flora which often included the iris, narcissus, rose and poppy. Under Jahangir the crocus (popular in the *kani* shawl), marigold, morning glory, poppy, rose and tulip took turns in popularity. Adding to the ecological dynamics of nature, Mansur included in the composition both a butterfly and a dragonfly with the Western Asiatic tulip, a flower supposedly not indigenous to India. Quoting Rich, the painting '...establishes the compositional prototype for all succeeding Mughal floral studies'.[60]

Given the predilection of the kingdoms of India for gardens and flowers, the tulip most likely travelled first from Turkey to India before arriving in Europe. Tulips, entering Europe via Turkey, had taken Europe by storm; they were so expensive that fortunes were won or lost in the trading of them. The advent of the tulip engendered a craze for flowers in Europe and was the great impetus that gave rise to the various Flemish art schools of flower studies and the illustrated herbals of Germany and the Netherlands. It was also one of the key influencing factors for Albrecht Dürer (1471-1528) and Leonardo da Vinci's (1452-1519) botanical studies. Carolus Clusius (aka Charles de l'Écluse, 1526-1609) (Plate 34) discovered tulips through his friend, Ogier Ghiselain de Busbecq (1522-1592), the ambassador to the court of Sultan Suleyman I of Turkey. The tulips were planted in the royal gardens which numbered more than sixty and employed a staggering five thousand gardeners.[61] During the reign of Ahmed III (1637-1736), Turkey was the horticultural centre for the Western world. Thus, finding a tulip among the paintings of Mansur is less surprising than one would imagine. Nevertheless, finding tulips on the Kashmir

Right:
Plate 34. Frontispiece (detail) of *Rariorum Aliquot Stirpium,* Carolus Clusius, 1576.
PRIVATE COLLECTION

shawl has, up to now, proven to be elusive.

Horticulture was already an integral part of imperial life and it is known that Akbar called for expert gardeners from Turan and Iran. His governor, Muhammad Quli Afshar, brought in tree grafts from Kabul and was the first to grow sweet cherry in Kashmir, as Jahangir ordered the grafts planted in the imperial gardens.[62] Although the importation of plants and flowers was a practice already in place as early as Akbar's reign, the actual science of floriculture through Mughal painting appeared to be taking root in India. Mansur's studies, inspired by western herbals, represented India's first look into the botanical details that defined angiosperms. In the West, horticulture was already a very serious study and ground-breaking herbal books based on a new science of botanical observation known as phyllotaxy (the study of stem leaves) and phytography (the accurate study of plants) were being published in great numbers; and, without doubt, many of these publications found their way into Indian libraries.

By looking at the many ways artistic foreign influences were adopted by the Mughals, we can better understand the psychology of the craft artist and the rendering of his work. In a positively identified western source found by Ebba Koch in 1982, she describes how the Polyglot Bible, offered to Akbar by the Jesuits, contained two powerful allegorical illustrations and, though such designs may not have necessarily filtered down into textiles, they inevitably had profound effects on the Mughal school of miniature painting (Plate 35).

Plate 35. Polyglot Bible, frontispiece, Christophe Plantin, publisher, 1569-1572.
PRIVATE COLLECTION

Plate 36. Marble balustrade, Red Fort, early 17th century.
PHOTOGRAPH BY THE AUTHOR

Inspired by these illustrations, the artist was able to intelligently incorporate the ethereal and complex symbolism of celestial and metaphysical religious ideas into a powerful set of imperial graphics. This technique 'gave Jahangir and his artist the means to express, in painting, concepts of rulership which had hitherto been formulated only in writing'.[63]

More importantly to our botanical discussion, Koch also writes about the 'vegetabilization programme' of the Imperial Palace buildings by the adaptation of the acanthus-leaf baluster column, a leaf type new to the Mughal repertoire of design (Plate 36). This novel idea was carefully borrowed and altered from a Dürer engraving found on the third page of the Antwerp Polyglot Bible. The new Mughal column (latest appearance, 1637) exhibits a fluted shaft 'sprouting' from a wreath of acanthus leaves that embraces a bulbous vase-like device at the base and while rising upward expands and then gradually contracts to terminate elegantly in a leafy neck which may be seen as the calyx of the capital. Thus, a new and exciting architectural expression was created, as Koch explains, by a 'self-generated dynamism which explores the third dimension'.[64] Although no shawl patterns have been yet been found with such architectural devices, this example of Mughal India's creative ability to adopt and integrate sophisticated ideas within various fields of art is most enlightening. Because of the columns used to support the spandrels, if there is one shawl type most likely to appear with the acanthus, it would be the prayer niche *kani* mats.

The Mughal Emperors' proclivity for exotica and fine works of arts from foreign lands is well known, as attested by their enthusiastic embrace and absorption of Catholic iconography into the school of miniature painting. The close presence of the Portuguese with their established factories at Calicut and Cochin, and the rich depositories of their churches and cathedrals in Goa, combined with Akbar's renowned thirst for exotic paraphernalia, eventually prompted him to dispatch in 1578 one of his agents, Haji Habibullah, to Goa to apprise himself of and acquire examples of the arts and crafts of the Iberian expatriates living in India.[65] Mughal India was populated by merchants, adventurers, explorers and official ambassadors, arriving from all over the globe. The sixteenth century was a time of great European exploration and discovery and, along with the Portuguese trading vessels docking on the Malabar Coast, there were ships arriving on the eastern shores of the subcontinent, off the Coromandel Coast, from China, Indonesia and England. With the advent of the printing press (1440, Germany), and the sudden growth of sea travel including Vasco da Gama's new trade route around the Cape of Good Hope, Europe more than ever was permeating the subcontinent.

Besides the Polyglot Bible which was presented to Akbar, it has been suggested that the Jesuits and other travellers may have carried with them into India European books on botany, including florilegia which were picture books of flowers only, whereas herbals contained important and detailed descriptions of plants and their medicinal properties as well as illustrations. The Jesuit priests were perhaps the first true Europeans to arrive in India. More than just being erudite, they came armed with language and writing skills and with the ability to converse in the dialect of their surroundings. DeNobili, Provenca and Deschi, to name a few, mastered the local vernacular and developed a close rapport with the people. 'The Jesuits were not ordinary travellers since they laboured and lived within the local milieu and were noted for the veracity and correctness of their observations. They were able to read Indian books and studied Indian philosophies'.[66]

As part of his obsessive quest for religious truth, Akbar requested the presence of the Jesuits. Upon their arrival, he was presented with the eight volume Bible printed by Plantin for Philip II of Spain in 1569-1573, as well as other iconic Christian items. During the many years the Jesuits remained at the Mughal court, they had nurtured an intimate contact with the great ruler who acquired an unusual admiration for their intellectual prowess and ability to defend the principal ideas of the Holy Spirit, even over and above those of Islam. Akbar often enjoyed walking arm in arm with the priests and was able to address them in Portuguese, a language his son Prince Murad began learning at the age of thirteen.[67]

With the real possibility hanging in the air of converting one of the most powerful rulers in the Asian world to Christianity, one could only imagine the palpable excitement of the Jesuits as they set up a permanent camp in the court of the Mughal Emperor. They travelled with more than Bibles since the foundation of their learning were based on Western knowledge and science. Besides herbals, they must have been well stocked with books on many subjects. Akbar, of course, ultimately, refused to give in, purportedly excusing himself by saying that he believed neither in miracles nor in monogamy!

In the more elaborate and expensive European florilegia, the illustrations exuded a sharp boldness that epitomized in a way Europe's obsessive scientific mentality for confrontational realism. Their arrival in India must have indeed made a curious impression on the Mughal artists whose aesthetic sensitivities lay rather in the play of rich colours and graceful floral patterns that reflected the poetic mood of Persian literature. Because of the botanicals' widespread influence on textiles, rugs, shawls, architecture, etc., it behoves us to examine them more closely.

As mentioned previously, Rich and Skelton not only established conclusively the herbal influence, but they were appropriately able to point to a few of the actual drawings (woodblocks) from which the Mughal artist copied. This brings us closer to an art form found in the decorative repertoire of the Mughal period and much less anonymous than one would otherwise think. This is not to say that every time we come across a fine floral painting, or a finely woven Kashmir shawl with beautiful flowers, the hand of the European artist can be identified.

The tradition of florilegia originated with Pierre Vallet with his publication in 1608. It contained a rich selection of plants drawn with a dramatic if not powerful realism from the French Royal Gardens. Weighing little and a rather manageable size of about 9 x 14in. (23 x 36cm), Vallet's album confronted the viewer with beautifully drawn, full-blooming flowers, stalks and bulbs in such a way that elicited a visceral reflex of wanting to reach out and

Left:
Plate 37. Pierre Vallet. Frontispiece from *Le Jardin du Roy Très Chréstian, Loys XIII, Roy de France et de Navarre,* 1608.
PRIVATE COLLECTION

Opposite:
Right:
Plate 38. Poppies from *Hortus Eystettensis,* Basilius Besler, 1613.
PRIVATE COLLECTION

Below:
Plate 39. Frontispiece, *Hortus Eystettensis,* Basilius Besler, 1613.
PRIVATE COLLECTION

touch the page. The frontispiece contains a portrait of Vallet and in each corner surrounding his bust are carefully drawn the tools of his trades: embroiderer, painter, draughtsman and weaver (Plate 37). Despite the tradesman-like introduction, every illustration is an explosive macro-shot of a flower the likes of which could not have failed to rivet the attention of the Indian artist. The flowers most illustrated in the book are, for example, the narcissus, iris, hyacinth and peony.[68] Although botanically precise, it is fascinating to note that the illustrations were made for painters, draughtsmen, embroiderers and tapestry weavers, as Vallet himself was a royal gardener and embroiderer to the king.

Although printed only five years after Vallet's book, Basilius Besler's *Hortus Eystettensis* (1613) was the largest single book ever printed. Its monstrous size, weighing perhaps thirty pounds (fourteen kilograms), contains fabulously drawn, detailed engravings almost two feet (sixty centimetres) in height. The flowers are very finely and delicately drawn in a style that goes from Mannerism to Baroque. A glimpse, for example of the dramatically illustrated feathered poppy blossoms, drawn with an uncanny plasticity rendering them almost surreal, is a direct experience with nature itself (Plate 38).

The *Hortus* frontispiece shows a fascinating engraving with a exotic allegorical scene comprised of a naked native being led by the hand of a haloed saint toward the Christian path; a human-faced elephant and lion are also drawn into this charged scene symbolizing the pull of Christianity on all walks of life; a large palm tree dominates the centre field. Given the proselytizing iconography of this book and its tropical scene, and others like it, there is good reason to believe that such herbals were popular on the list of items carried by the Jesuits into India (Plate 39).

The herbals were not printed to be used as entertaining or enlightening reading matter, but served rather as an important source of survival and medical rescue available when travellers found themselves ill and far away from home. They had to be part of one's travelling kit. Since most of the medieval and early botanical gardens were largely composed of herb plants used for medicinal purposes, botanical accuracy was imperative. In sickness, plants had to be identified, descriptions easily understood and medicinal qualities quickly processed for consumption. Many of these books were small and compact in size and published with the idea of travel in mind. One such herbal of extremely compact size was written by Conrad Gesner in about 1559. About this revolutionary 'pocket-book', measuring only 4½ x 2½in. (11.4 x 6.4cm), Greene says 'No botanical treatise having an equal amount of useful matter compressed into so small a compass had ever before been printed'.[69]

Plate 40. Boteh detail of Kashmir shawl fragment, 'a butterfly motif', first half of 17th century.
Musée Guimet, Paris, MA5685A

Because the tradition of florilegia began with Pierre Vallet's floral book in 1608, the possibility exists that the smaller herbal books were the first to find their way into the Mughal courts.[70]

In Mughal miniatures and related textiles and rugs, and especially the many fine contemporary embroideries of Gujarat, hovering butterflies are often depicted as part of the botanico-ecological scene. Despite the fact that no Kashmir shawl has yet been discovered featuring these winged insects per se, there are several early boteh patterns with very curious flowers exhibiting a kind of 'winged' arrangement, something rather un-botanical yet quite fascinating in nature.

Although the interpretation of these curious floral designs does not necessarily lend itself to any immediate source, a perusal of the European herbal pictures and their accompanying phytographic texts may bring some answers (Plate 40).

Since Dioscorides' *Materia Medica,* written 1500 years earlier, none has been more influential in the invention of a new and exciting language used to describe flowers than the German physician and botanist, Valerius Cordus (1515-1544). His celebrated pharmacopoeias and herbals were brilliant achievements at his young age. Cordus' amazing goal – and what made him the inventor of phytography – was to demonstrate that each species of flower could be so exactly described in words that it could be virtually identified alone by its description. It is fascinating to see the glaring differences in language when juxtaposing a description of the same flower by Dioscorides and Cordus. If one were sick and desperately dependent on the search for one flower to get well, Dioscorides's vapid description would certainly not bode well for survival. In Cordus, the descriptive prose bursts with brilliant imagery, making its identification seem easy. Through Cordus' powers of observation one can sense the movement of the plant's growth, witness its various morphological configurations, its colourful hues, taste the bitterness or sweetness of its odour and experience, even sense the kinesthetic effects of swallowing such flavours. Besides his photographic memory of all that Pliny, Theophrastus and Dioscorides had written, Cordus' heightened olfactory, gustatory and tactile sensitivities were gifted abilities that greatly aided him in revolutionizing the world of botany (Plate 41). None of his contemporaries or those that followed, including Dodoens, Tragus, Clusius or l'Obel, to name a few, remained immune to the magnetic pull of Cordus' descriptive powers. Thus Tragus, in observing a wild orchid, describes its various parts as the figure of a wasp or the head and wings of a bird. In orchids, Dodoens begins to see a monk's cowl, a knight's helmet thrown back, a dog or a lizard. In another part of the orchid – and this is perhaps the most significant for our discussion – the figure of a butterfly appears with its wings spread as about to take flight. Cordus developed the term 'papilionaceous' (from the French for butterfly), a term often utilized by succeeding botanists.[71]

Greene, in assessing the historical evolution of botany, and in particular this special language of plant mimicry by these learned men of Renaissance Europe, declares:

> *These are more than curious notes and observations. They cannot have failed to become an incentive to other lovers of flowers and other students of botany, to a minute inspection of the less conspicuous parts of other flowers. They lead in the direction of that close attention to all phases and modifications of floral structure, one ultimate outcome of which was to a discovery of the lesser organs, and another the establishment of a basis for a reform in the classification of the plant world in general.*[72]

Plate 41. Valerius Cordus, German botanist, 1515-1544.

The assumption here is that these exotic flora books, that either entered into the Mughal Imperial libraries or were seen by the Mughal artists, attracted as much attention with their images as with their descriptive texts. Books and libraries were an integral, even intimate, part of the Mughals' residences and their love of books is legendary: In fact, it is known that Humayun always kept his library near at hand, even bringing it into battle with camels laden with book-filled trunks. It can be assumed that most of the herbals and florilegia were only printed in black and white up to the end of the sixteenth century after which hand-coloured copies began to appear. Still the coloured-in copies were usually executed with uninspiring watercolour washes. The Indian artist, with his ingenious techniques for applying mineral and precious gem-dust colours, probably saw a great opportunity to transform these lacklustre images into the sparkling world that was the 'Mughal style'.

Butterflies occurred in only seven herbals printed between 1563 and 1624. According to Rich, out of those that were copied by the Mughal artists, most seem to have been borrowed from Vallet and Van der Passe.[73] The herbals most likely to have actually been available to the Mughal court were those of Carolus Clusius 1601 and l'Obel (1591). It must be remembered that most European books of scientific importance were published in Latin or German. As they made their way to India, the people most likely to have knowledge of Latin and, therefore, capable of translating this classic language, were the learned Jesuit priests.

In discussing the flowers found in these herbals, the question arises as to how much influence the botanist had over those who actually drew the picture of the flowers and those who engraved the woodblock. How much artistic licence the artist infuses into his palette is a moot point and being a gifted artist would not exempt him from being influenced by the scientist who wrote the flower's description, nor would it exempt the engraver from his own interpretation of the flower he cut to the block. In the former the sixteenth century artist probably drew his flowers in situ while in the latter, the woodcutter worked under special conditions, bound by the limitations of his small rectangular woodblock. Thus '...to avoid a rectangular appearance required a distinct effort of will and without this effort he often drew, obsessed by its rectangularity, accommodating his drawing to its form in a way that was unnecessary and far from realistic'.[74] Some botanists required another craftsman to transfer the flower to the wood-block, which more than likely added a further note of varied interpretation to the whole process. Hitherto, no botehs have yet been found exhibiting such rectangularity but, if they were to be, they would most likely be seen in a shawl or textile from the seventeenth century.

Proceeding from our discussion of the derivation of the 'Mughal Style' from European herbals, let us now briefly look at one of the earliest manifestations of this style in contemporary Indian painting. Apart from the tidbits of information found in the *Ain-i-Akbari,* there are no concrete links of any Kashmiri shawl artist working for or at the Imperial court. True, there are many artists with the surnames 'Kashmiri' working at the court atelier, and mentioned by Abul Fazl, but little is known of their lives, and even less is known during this time whether a school of art even existed in Kashmir itself. Of this period no biographical information is known about any Kashmiri artist.

Akbar's rich legacy of court painting, such as the *Hamza-Nama* or the story of Hamza (painted 1564-1579), 1,400 large-scale paintings measuring 20 x 27in. (50.8 x 68.6cm) in seventeen volumes, provides an important starting point for the study of textile design (Plate 42). Although there is no evidence of either the *kani* shawl or of the flowering plant in the *Hamza,* we still have before our eyes a complex corpus of luxuriously patterned textiles, canopies, wall hangings, costumes and rugs providing us with a colourful idea of the fashionable world in which the Mughals were immersed. Unfortunately, nothing in this rich repertoire would lead us to believe that the shawl was decorated with the designs seen by today's evidence extant. A similar statement could be made for the *Akbarnama,* as well.

The shawls one observes in these great works of art, comprised either of waistbands or shoulder mantles, may have no surface embellishment, but the way they are worn and draped most certainly suggests a rich soft material such as a fine *pashmina* or even *shah tus.* Perhaps because most of the decorative stuffs were modelled after those coming from or inspired by Persian trade goods and fashion, the shawl may have been overlooked as a medium for the propagation of such designs. However, with the abrupt change in floral types under Jahangir, the shawl, alongside architecture, painting and carpets, evolved into a natural vehicle for the floral presentation of the new 'Mughal style'.

Another painting under Akbar worth mentioning is titled *A Crisis at Court* (dated

1596-97), by the great master, Basawan. Here we see the central personage wearing a very large, flowing shawl, most likely *shah tus,* with an intensely saturated red dye colour, a colour so strong that the viewer's eye is immediately riveted to the central field of action. Of this painting, Stuart Carey Welch wrote: 'A more accurate view of Mughal court life could not be found... down to the last wine cup... it is an unrivalled source of information on the paraphernalia of Akbar's court'.[75] And yet, shawl patterns are not to be found.

Under Shah Jahan we encounter one of the most sumptuous albums of paintings ever executed, *The Padshahnama,* an illustrated manuscript. This astounding collection of miniatures provides us with images of Shah Jahan's resplendent court, which dazzle us by its endless display of brilliantly coloured textiles and costumes, much more so than in previous miniature painting. If ever there is a place to discover an early missing link in shawl iconography, this was it. It is well known among Indophiles that the principal decoration, the motif par excellence, best associated with Shah Jahan's reign, is the freely spaced, botanically precise, flowering plant. It is seen on the Red Forts in Delhi and Agra, on the Taj Mahal, in miniature painting and in the decorative arts. The debate about how this came to be, how it evolved from being a simple, minor motif to one of singularly large proportions, botanically well defined, often filling the entire page of a miniature painting or the mihrab of a carpet, has been ongoing for the past thirty years. Current theory holds that its sudden jump in importance was an idea that developed during the last decade of Jahangir's reign.

Under Jahangir's reign there was an emphasis on birds, flora and fauna studies, especially after 1620, a date noted as being the first time (Jahangir made altogether thirteen trips to Kashmir) the emperor was able to fulfill a long-standing cherished ambition: a spring sojourn in Kashmir. About this, Skelton exclaims '...he [the emperor] practically went mad with excitement'.[76] It was at this point that Jahangir's passion for botany had, through the likes of the gifted artist Mansur, achieved its greatest legacy. Painting was, besides flora and fauna, more focused on portraiture and the inclusion of western iconographic techniques than the illustration of grandiose epics, as was the case under his father, Akbar. It was this intense veracity of adhering to nature or, in the words of Douglas Barrett, to 'Flemish realism', in the latter years of Jahangir's reign that developed the 'Mughal Style'. The earliest and finest specimens of Mughal shawls certainly display these ideas. While it is quite rare to come across Mughal shawls displaying transitional design motifs of a previous era,

Plate 42. Leaf from the *Hamza-Nama,* c.1565.

this further underscores the importance of understanding the above floral shift; for if it happens in architecture, there is no reason why it shouldn't happen on textiles as well. Although it is not in the scope of this book to discuss the many details involved in this phenomenon, there are several paintings in the *Padshahnama* which best illustrate this abrupt change in floral fashion.

In the painting titled *Jahangir Receives Prince Khurram* (the future Shah Jahan), plain shawls are donned by at least five of the emirs, of which two are wearing shawl wraps decorated with small flowers (Plate 43).[77] It is obvious that Itimadu'd-Daula and Musvai Khan are donning charcoal grey *shah tus* shawls, while the Wazir Khan drapes a cream-coloured wrap and the amir standing to his right wears a peach coloured shawl. In the extreme lower left, just above the artist Balchand, stands another artist, Kishandas, sporting a pistachio coloured shawl. Prince Khurram has just returned from the Mewar Campaign and the ceremony takes place on 20 February 1615. February is a cool month at the Diwan-I'Amm for northern India, which is why we see the amirs wearing warm scarves and shawls, validating the textiles in the painting as being sketched from real life. Before the warm rays of the morning sun, the early hours of northern India's winter required warm garments to fend off the chill during these imperial gatherings, which usually took place at sunrise.

Plate 43. Jahangir receives Prince Khurram on his return from the Mewar Campaign, by Balchand, c.1630.
By permission of the Royal Library, Windsor Castle

The artist himself, Balchand, figures in the lower left-hand corner of the miniature, which means that he was there to witness and record the ceremony. Though the painting is reckoned to have been painted approximately fifteen years after this momentous event, there is little doubt the artists had previously archived all the details necessary in order to faithfully complete the tableau. Turning our attention to the wall decorations behind Jahangir, we notice prominently displayed two square wall insets, each with groups of vases (*chinakhana),* while below are two large wall panels illustrating rows of freely spaced, natural-looking flowers. It is obvious from the latter that apparently a fascination for these single flowers was already in fashion. But wait, do these flowers represent the sudden leap we need to observe? That will come in the painting to follow. What is viewed here is still the Persianate style of flower, that is a rather perfunctory, almost generic flower.[78]

Shifting our sights to the painting by Bichitr titled *Shah Jahan receives his three sons and Asaf Khan during his accession ceremonies* (c.1630, or two years after the ceremony), we encounter a dramatic difference in 'stage setting' (Plate 44).[79] Gone are the Chinese vase boxes and the floral display panels, which were mostly hidden anyway. Instead we have a magnificent floral panel illustrating daffodils (narcissus), carnations and poppies rooted naturally upon hillocks of earth. These tall majestic flowers, symmetrically placed, with their ripe blossoms reaching to a sky filled with wisps of Chinese clouds and hovering butterflies, appear to be trumpeting the joys of the ceremony. They were obviously influenced by, or copied directly from, European florilegium or flower books in which flowers are depicted growing naturally from the earth. Compared with the former miniature where the flowers simply hang in space, here we see hillocks forming the lower register of the wall panel.[80]

Naturally, the throne setting *(jharoka)* and architecture at Ajmer would be different from that in Agra and one might question the verisimilitude of the wall's ornamentation, but, given the actual presence of the artists at these events and Shah Jahan's known fastidiousness, one might also argue in favour of accuracy.[81]

Thus, we have here in these two paintings important evidence for the earliest beginnings of the 'Mughal Style'. The first painting of the event in Ajmer in 1615 was painted about fifteen years later and the second, Agra in 1628, was painted about two years later. Somewhere in between these two ceremonial dates, a period of thirteen years, we might postulate that the 'Mughal Style', at least in architecture, emerged. If we conflate Jahangir's trip in 1620 to Kashmir and the resulting floral studies by Mansur, the emergence of the 'Mughal Style'

can be narrowed down to somewhere between 1620 and 1628. 'Mughal Style' became enshrined as the dominant decorative theme of the Taj Mahal which was constructed from 1632-1653 (Plate 45).

Since few museums can boast having the seventeenth century Mughal Style amongst their collections, studying them by means of the earliest of the Kashmir shawls can indeed present a daunting challenge. Although, as a whole, there are from this period many shawls still in existence, it is, by and large, the ones exhibiting full-blown botehs – bouquets comprised of a variety of flower blossoms, or large bouquets with only a single species – that offer us the most exciting iconography.

In light of our discussion above, the following brief survey of world institutions and private collections in possession of early Mughal floral pieces may prove useful to the reader:

The Textile Museum: two complete shawls
Museum of Fine Arts, Boston: one complete shawl
Metropolitan Museum of Art, New York: two fragments
Henry Art Gallery, Seattle: one fragment
Victoria and Albert Museum, London: one complete shawl, three fragments
Al-Sabah Museum, Kuwait: one fragment
Calico Museum, Ahmedabad: two complete shawls, one fragment
Musée du Guimet, Paris: four fragments
Bharat Kala Bhawan, Varanasi: eight complete shawls
Fondazione Antonio Ratti, Como: one complete shawl
Jagdish and Kamla Mittal Museum of Indian Art, Hyderabad: one fragment
National Museum, New Delhi: two complete pieces
Berlin, private collection: one fragment
David Collection, Copenhagen: one fragment
Neutrogena private collection: one fragment
Author's collection: one fragment.
Crafts Museum, New Delhi, one fragment

Plate 45. Marble dado, Taj Mahal, Agra.
PHOTOGRAPH BY THE AUTHOR (1980)

All told, we come up with approximately thirty-five seventeenth century shawls, two of which are identical pieces. Extremely few are in private collections. If we turn our attention to non-bouquet weavings, i.e. those with small floral sprigs, the number could quite possibly rise dramatically. However, this doesn't solve the riddle of various other pieces which, in the past, have been attributed to the early eighteenth century, and could be attributed to the seventeenth century. So far research is such that we are not yet at this point. This would especially hold true for many of the *patkas* designs. Although this may change when radio-carbon dating is eventually put to use, it can be easily stated that seventeenth century shawls are an extremely rare species indeed.

Our ideas about the early beginnings of the cone, or curvilinear boteh, have been shaken up by recently discovered Zand paintings. We now know that the cone began much earlier than anybody would have previously thought, by at least thirty years. Because there are cones exhibiting seventeenth century transitional design devices, it is surely not inconceivable that they were in fashion by the end of the seventeenth century. This remains to be studied as more material evidence and paintings are uncovered, and as more scholars delve into these unanswered questions.

Opposite:
Plate 44. Shah Jahan receives his three sons, by Bichitr, c.1630.
BY PERMISSION OF THE ROYAL LIBRARY, WINDSOR CASTLE

Chapter 4

The Development of the Sikh Style

The hallmark of the art of Maharaja Ranjit Singh is thus its truthfulness. It is of the earthly earth. In spite of the import of some of the painters from the Pahari courts, the abundance of portraiture shows how almost everyone, including the Maharaja, was in search of an identity in their new exalted status, which they had acquired from modest origins in the villages of the Punjab plains. Thus, every expression under the patronage of Ranjit Singh and his nobles, shows a vitalist urge for freedom to open out to life, and more life, in the midst of things of beauty which may please the eyes, make the heart glow and intensify the emotions.

Mulk Raj Anand[82]

'Truthfulness' and the 'vitalist urge for freedom to open out to life' are indeed poignant observations as expressed in Mulk Raj's eloquently defined hallmark of Sikh art, and they apply equally to the dramatic change in emerging shawl patterns at the beginning of the century. For many years shawl design reflected the taste of the various international markets to which the weaver responded slavishly. However, this was no longer the case, at least in the particular style that we are dealing with here, for it appears that artists were now breaking with the past and with this newly found creative emancipation they discovered a truthfulness through the creative assimilation of their own emerging cultural tradition. Just as Sikh patterns represented an indigenous and outstanding facet of Himalayan/Punjabi art, so too did miniature painting of the region, before the arrival of the Sikh, achieve moments of prominence. In the mid-seventeenth century, for example, the fine Basohli style of painting seemed to emerge, devoid of any crudely incipient beginnings, to become one of the most dramatically innovative styles in Indian art history, as well as a benchmark of excellence, against which all the other schools of arts were measured. A century later brought the fabulous paintings from the state of Guler, whose post-Mughal style is attributed to the master, Nainsukh. Finally, in another leap in creativity, though this time in shawl artistry, an exciting style was to reach its peak under Maharaja Ranjit Singh. Like Kangra painting, which leaps with feelings of mystery and bliss, the new Sikh patterns reach out to us on a mystical, subconscious level. Their unleashed exuberance of playful geometry or arches, and circles, suffuses these graphic swirls with a kinetic energy that cannot help but evoke feelings of mysticism and awe.

Opposite:
Palla detail of WM28 (see page 159). Kashmir long shawl.
Foreshadowing the Art Deco era by a century, this dramatic scene captures a rare ethereal moment, showcasing a *naqqash's* creative talent with unbounding energy. It is rare to find a *palla* design with no repeat. Sikh period, c.1835.
COURTESY, NATIONAL MUSEUM, NEW DELHI, NO. 59.395

Above and detail opposite:
WM5. Kashmir square shawl *(rumal)*
A curious 'propeller' effect, due to the jagged edges of the centre's 'blade' elements, emerges from a riot of tendrils and leaf forms. *Rumals* almost always had separate centres sewn in, often of a very different pattern or no pattern at all. Although the centre is composed of a square and eight smaller 'propeller' tip pieces, the *naqqash* has employed the entire shawl 'canvas' to create a brilliantly conceived work of art. Late Sikh period, c.1850.
COLLECTION SAMUEL JOSEFOWITZ

Above and detail opposite:
WM6. Kashmir long shawl (detail)
Like tightly packed penguins, tall botehs line the *palla* of this colourful *dochalla* with an overlay of smaller floating botehs. The lower register contains a repeat of fan devices with spiky protrusions creating an Art Deco atmosphere. The U-shaped devices with their curled-end tips appear to be a further stylization of the recurve bow, as seen in WM 14, page 104. The intense chromatic range is a triumph in the art of dyeing. Sikh period, c.1840. 135 x 54in. (343 x 137cm).

Museum of Art, Rhode Island School of Design. Museum Collection, acc. no. 78-192-2. Photograph by Erik Gould

Plate 46. Golden Temple, Amritsar.
PHOTOGRAPH BY THE AUTHOR (1980)

They are the visual record of a culture. In perspective, when the Kashmir shawl is weighed against the narrow, domestic market of Indian miniature painting, we arrive at a formidably powerful vehicle for the international dissemination of a highly sought after fashion that resonated in all parts of the elite world.

In light of these new Sikh patterns, and before addressing some of the essential elements that may have engendered them, let us take a brief look at some of the events leading up to Sikh hegemony, followed by a reflective glance at eighteenth century Pahari painting whose gifted artists and influential patron-rajas energized the creative fabric of this adjacent region. Following this will be a discussion of a few of the unique European mercenary characters who settled in the region. Until recently, Sikh art, in general, has really not been viewed by Indian art historians as significant, often taken as a crude derivative of the Mughal School. To rectify this stigma or lack of a clear definition, several major exhibitions of Sikh art have begun to cause scholars to reassess historical events and artefacts of the period which have heretofore been either overlooked or unappreciated.[83]

With the decline of the Mughal Empire, the imperial authority of Delhi disbanded, leaving the hill states to their own autonomies and giving rise towards the end of the eighteenth century to the ambitions of two ethnographic groups: the Sikh *misls* and the Pahari rajas. By dint of rivalries with the British and the Afghans, Sikh power matured during the eighteenth century into a formidable force. The Sikh religion was founded by Guru Nanak, who was born in a small village near Lahore in 1496. Although Nanak grew up in a traditional Hindu family, his intense spiritual inquisitiveness continually brought him into contact with men of all faiths. Once, while bathing in a river, he experienced a moment of divine revelation whereby he proclaimed 'there is no Hindu, there is no Mussalman'. Thus he set out on a mission, which was to last twenty-five years, of teaching the Brotherhood of Man. His peregrinations took him to Ceylon, Ladakh, Tibet, Mecca, Medina and Baghdad, places where he witnessed first-hand the intolerance, narrow mindedness and inane rituals that eventually impelled him to form his own caste-free religion.

A succession of nine gurus followed, ending with Guru Gobind Singh (1666-1708) who founded the Khalsa, composed many poems, and declared the Holy Granth as the last and abiding guru. In response to the spread of Mughal imperial hegemony, which threatened the Sikh religion and cherished homeland, the Punjab, Sikhism was moulded into a fierce military sect. From then on a true Sikh (disciple) was baptized with sweet water (*amrit*) stirred by a double-edged sword, and adopted the Khalsa (pure), where his commitment to Sikhism was reinforced by the wearing of breeches, his unshorn hair and beard, by carrying a wooden comb, an iron bracelet and a sword (*kuchacha, kesh, kungha, kara* and *kirpan*, respectively). The turban, though not specifically a part of the Khalsa, eventually became a symbol of Sikh commitment to the Gurus. Amritsar, a small town about forty miles (sixty-four kilometres) due west of Lahore, became the site of the Golden Temple, built by the fifth Guru, Arjun Dev (1563-1606) (Plate 46). Pilgrims who visit the Temple today circumambulate the exterior and as they leave the temple are handed a mix of semolina and honey which is taken in cupped hands and eaten, not only as a form of *prasad* (blessed food) but as a symbol of the breaking of caste.

The tenth Guru, Gobind Singh, a true warrior,

declared the end of guruship and that Sikhism should be perpetuated from then on through the *Adi Granth* (Plate 47). The book, containing devotional songs from revered Hindu and Islamic saints, is composed of about 6,000 hymns of the Sikh Gurus. Sikhism is therefore both a faith and a community born of and identified with the Punjab; and such was the nature of the religious and warring environment from which Ranjit Singh emerged to become Punjab's great military leader. The second half of the eighteenth century saw the Sikh organizing into twelve loosely grouped *misls,* each with its own leader and locality and each vying with the other to gain power. At the young age of twelve, Ranjit Singh rose to the head of the Sukerchakia *misl* and, by the time he was twenty, captured and ruled over Lahore and Amritsar. He was crowned Maharaja in Lahore in 1801

Thus, the Sikh religion, born in the Punjab where Persian was widely spoken, developed in an environment in which the cultural fabric was interwoven with the seamless and pious lineage of the ten great Gurus. Indeed, many Sikh spiritual concepts had been drawn from Sufi teachings. Valuable Sikh coins were stamped with Persian couplets, reflecting the continued heritage of Indo-Persian bonds.[84] This active period is marked by exciting growth within the provinces that eventually became controlled by Ranjit Singh and, later on, it was stimulated in some ways by the driving energies of Ranjit Singh's European officers, General Jean-François Allard, General Jean-Baptist Ventura, Paolo di Avitable and General Claude Auguste Court, who arrived in India on the charismatic coat-tails of Napoleon Bonaparte's huge military achievements. According to Lafont and Schmitz, 'As soon as Sikh power in Lahore was consolidated into a political unity, there was a blossoming of arts and architecture. There was a frenetic building activity in the two capital cities of Lahore and Amritsar for almost forty years'.[85] Ranjit Singh's appetite for wall decoration ran unabated as he continually sought artists to decorate his official buildings, palaces and temples, where fresco artists especially were needed. Moorcroft wrote that he had sent to Lahore artists from Kashmir to work on the ceilings of the Baradari of Shalimar.[86] By 1823. only forty artists remained in Kashmir.

Although outside the suzerainty of Ranjit Singh, but just as important for our understanding of the artistic environment, was the building craze taking place in the Cis-Sutlej area of Patiala. Relatively new as a princely

Plate 47. Reading of the *Adi Granth,* Golden Temple, Amritsar.
PHOTOGRAPH BY THE AUTHOR (1980)

state, having been founded only in 1763 by Maharaja Alla Singh, Patiala quickly developed into one of the most thriving cultural cities in all of India. It had once been described as a 'fairy world on earth'. During the reign of Karam Singh (1798-1845), architects came from all over to assist in great building ventures, where mural painting, art, music, literature and poetry all flourished in a peaceful atmosphere of princely fashion and royal pageantry.[87] The state became the principal Sikh power to the east of the Sutlej. Delhi, despite the waning of the once great empire, still remained the showcase of Mughal architecture, a bastion of great wealth: 'The streets are not mere streets, they are like the album of a painter', according to one poet. Dalrymple described the city as 'the epitome of an elegant Mughal metropolis'.[88]

It has been generally thought that Sikh influence on the Kashmir shawl quickly evolved at the time of Ranjit Singh's takeover of Kashmir in 1819. It is important to note that the shawl industry was already a well-oiled machine, run by mercantile agents whose international activities did not grind to a halt each time the political winds of change brought Srinagar under a new ruler. In this regard, Forster, who visited Kashmir in 1782-3, notes that the Sikhs kept up:

> *an extensive and valuable commerce which had been extended to distant quarters of India, particularly to the provinces of Bangal and Bihar where many Sikh merchants of opulence at this time reside. Merchants of every nation or sect who may introduce a traffick into their territories, or are established under their government, experience a full protection, and enjoy commercial privileges in common with their own subject.*[89]

One can easily assume that such 'traffick' included shawls, although Forster does not specifically mention them in his assessment of commerce. Nevertheless, he didn't hesitate to detail the terrible cruelty of the then Durrani governor, Asad Khan, whose oppressive rule, combined with the marauding bands of pirates from conterminous states, reduced '...the commerce of Kashmir to a declining and languid state'.[90] Forster implies that the Sikh merchants had figured out a way to transport goods securely by circumventing the troubled Punjab, a region which since 1739 had become a veritable free-for-all battleground between Marathas, Afghans, Sikhs and the British.

Kashmir under the Sikhs or under the Afghans has no recorded census, thus we have little idea of the number of Sikhs actually living in the Valley, either before or after Ranjit Singh. One reference submits the figure of 2,000 in 1812, but this number appears to apply mainly to agricultural workers. In another, Sikh soldiers are brought in by an Afghan governor in the mid-eighteenth century; how many, we do not know. We do know that around 1830 the overall population was close to 800,000.[91]

These numbers tell us how little the physical Sikh presence was felt or seen in Kashmir and, from a Sikh point of view, forces us, in a way, to look outside the Valley for the commercial manipulation of the industry. The proximity of Lahore and the surrounding towns and villages, where weaving ateliers were most likely established, must have made it easier to carry on business as usual, outside the purview of Afghan politics.[92] The purchase of materials and supplies could have been made, albeit clandestinely, in Leh, which was the usual source of the wool, and the shawl washing could also have been done in one of the nearby effluent rivers of the valley (Plate 48).[93]

While within Srinagar, depending on the various ruling powers and the severity of the tax on their shawls, and considering the oppressive work conditions, one might assume that the more affluent *karkhandars* (shawl weaving workshops) remained immune to the vicissitudes of change, which they most likely did, by dint of either their local political connections or their direct ties with the Lahore Durbar. Quality shawls produced by these weaving ateliers were often under the protection of the various sovereign clients for whom the work was being performed and, since their cost was already steep, the imposition of any higher taxes would not have been a deterrent to production. Indeed, the quest for quality shawls moved Burnes to remark, after listening to the grumbling of the shawl merchants, that good articles were now only to be procured by commissioning them from the Valley.[94]

Until the discovery of a series of Indian paintings, there was no clear idea of the social dynamics within a Sikh-owned *karkhandar*. The paintings, eight altogether, had been exhibited in London in 1988, but they were sold and immediately disappeared into a private and anonymous collection. Each is filled with the detailed steps of shawl production in what is obviously a well-to-do Sikh, family-run, shawl business in a palatial home. More importantly, they show Sikhs and Kashmiri working closely together (Plates 48 and 54). The shawls depicted are detailed as well and are of the late Dogra period. Indeed, the paintings, executed on an unusually large scale, have been attributed to a commission for the Universal Exhibition of 1867, Paris. The style, of smooth, soft pastel colours and an inimitable serenity, shows remarkable influence from the Pahari region and is reminiscent of the many paintings by Nainsukh. Toby Falk suggested that 'the most reputable artists in Lahore would have been employed'.[95] Each face is distinct and modelled with a meditative yet focused expression; the folds and wraps of the costumes are done with exactitude and all implements required in the production of the shawl have been illustrated. The paintings are captivating documents of a busy family at work and the production processes they illustrate well confirm those detailed in Moorcroft's account of 1822. Certainly, little has changed in forty-five years.

The late eighteenth century saw instituted in Kashmir an oppressive tax system, called 'Dag Shawl'. It is no wonder that the number of looms dropped dramatically in Kashmir, as noted by Forster who claims that the number under the Mughals was 40,000 but during his visit there in 1783 he approximated only 16,000.[96] So, what happened to the 24,000 looms? Calculating three weavers per loom, a better question might be: what happened to the 72,000 weavers?! It is most likely they were absorbed by the surrounding towns and

Plate 48. Shawl washing, painting, possibly Lahore, c.1867, after Kyburg exhibition catalogue, 1988, London.

WM7. Kashmir long shawl (detail)
Again, we encounter 'phantom' botehs' which really add little to a pattern already supercharged with an undecipherable language of graphic swirls. In the lower register is a scalloped wave of spiky extensions that rise over a curving trefoil pattern. Similarly, in the above register is a spear-like trefoil pattern highlighted with hanging 'necklaces'. In fact so much of the design is overrun by tendrils drifting in all directions that attempting a precise description becomes a daunting task.
COLLECTION TEXTILE MUSEUM, 1965_19_2

villages in the Punjab; they shifted to Amritsar and Lahore, Ludhiana, Lucknow, Patiala. The timing was right for the weavers to move in safety since the Afghan raids were over and, as noted by Forster above, a relative calm reigned over the region. From another source, however, we discover that by the end of the century the number of weavers had quickly grown to 54,000.[97] Although Sharma states that 'Kashmir was ruled like a large prison and no one was allowed to leave the valley without passport or payment', one wonders if this rule, in the time of devastating floods, earthquakes and famine, was not often broken.[98]

It was not until Ranjit Singh assumed control over Kashmir that major diversions of shawl weavers, and especially of the *pashmina* wool itself, became an issue of high intrigue. Since shawl weaving was the most profitable industry in the entire region, it is no wonder that manufactories were springing up all over. In 1809 Kangra came under Ranjit's suzerainty, governed by his *nizam*, the affable and fair Desa Singh Majithia, whose warm personality drew the admiration of his subjects and eventually attracted Rajput artists towards Sikh patronage.[99] Sikh officers were installed in the various regions where Sikh communities settled and built estates. Raja Gulab Singh and Desa Singh Majithia were quite busy establishing their own business empires of shawl weaving, building cities and collecting tribute; the former established his shops in Amritsar and Nurpur, the latter in the Hill State

region of Kot Kangra where, substantially, he had already launched one hundred weaving shops.[100] Under the rule of Sansar Chand (1775-1823) Kangra painting flourished and conceivably Desa Singh, in pursuing his shawl venture in which much depended upon having good *naqqashs* (artists), was seizing upon its renowned pool of artistic talent. The polity of the above situation begs the question: what were these ministers doing by diverting an excellent source of Ranjit Singh's revenue, i.e. the *pashmina* and the weavers, to their own pockets? Although it is not within the scope of this monograph to explore the full dynamics of this interesting situation, suffice it to say that part of the intrigue is due to Gulab Singh's brothers (Suchet and Dhyan) who appear to have offered a buffer zone of opportunity in these ventures.[101] However, one should not overlook that, by this time of Hill State settlement, the English had secured direct access to *pashmina* through their recently acquired Northern territories contiguous with Nepal. Amritsar, fuelling its wool industry from Tibet and Bukhara, had become home for thousands of *kani* shops, which, of course, meant an active market for the *naqqash*.

Facilitating connections between the Hill States and Lahore was the Ravi River and perhaps it was the romantic confluence of this nautical connection that brought together General Allard and his future wife, Bannou Pan Dei, daughter of the chief of Chamba, whom he married in Lahore in 1826 (Plate 49). The

Plate 49. General Jean-François Allard and his family, Lahore, 1838, gouache and gold on paper, 8⅛ x 10½in. (20.6 x 26.9cm).
COURTESY OF THE ARTHUR M SACKLER MUSEUM, HARVARD UNIVERSITY ART MUSEUM, 443.1983

Opposite:
Plate 50. Raja Raj Singh of Chamba with his wazir and infant son, Jit Singh, Chamba, ascribed to Ranjha, son of Nainsukh, c.1779.
COLLECTION JAGDISH AND KAMLA MITTAL MUSEUM, HYDERABAD

Right:
Plate 51. Embroidered *rumal* (detail). Sikh Sardar sitting on curved-arm chair. This type of arm chair was a ubiquitous piece of furniture in Sikh period painting. c.1840.
COLLECTION CHET GATSBY

final link in cementing Rajput-Lahore relations was the marriage of Ranjit Singh to Sansar Chand's (Plate 50) two daughters. With Sikh 'gentrification' of the region, realignment in local artist's patronage and the establishment of new shawl-weaving ateliers, this dynamic shift in demographics, unlike in Kashmir, may represent an important element in evaluating the artistic impulses which most certainly resonated with the expansion of the incipient new shawl motifs around 1820.

Previously mention was made of the sudden arrival of new artistic styles, as in Basohli painting, but now a particular Guler style came to be defined by characteristics that could be due only to Sikh patronage. The royal state umbrella with a bent handle, held aloft by an attendee, the slender and curved arms of the Sikh chair (Plate 51) and the ubiquitous shield which every Sikh warrior was required to wear became veritable adjuncts to the Guler painting repertoire. In the words of Archer, Sikh patronage '…encouraged [the Guler artists] to adjust their styles to Sikh taste, to incorporate new devices, and thus, to create an art that was vividly Sikh'.[102] Archer explains that any apprehensions towards the new Sikh rule were 'mollified' by the arresting kindness of the likes of Desa Singh Majithia and his successor son, Lehna. This atmosphere created a warmth

Plate 52. Sikh Sardar (possibly Desa Singh Majithia) presiding at a wedding reception, gouache, Guler, c.1815-1820.
VICTORIA AND ALBERT MUSEUM I.S. 153-1952

between the local artists and their new Sikh masters to the extent that they felt enticed to travel to the Punjab plains.[103] Kashmir, itself, after its Sikh annexation, may have been a promising destination as well, as Moorcroft writes about an artist he met in Srinagar, who worked under Sansar Chand (see below).

The Victoria and Albert Museum has a painting that purportedly shows Desa Singh Majithia (d.1832) presiding at a wedding reception (Plate 52). To the sound of music, a stool, spinning wheel and baskets (items which Archer describes as 'conventional equipment for a bride') are being ceremoniously carried into the large reception room. Although the painting has yet to be positively confirmed as Desa Singh's wedding, the 'equipment' therein may be either of Sikh, Hindu or simply Pahari tradition. Whatever be the case, given the sensitive nature of the Kashmiri shawl artist to his regional clients, these are all items to bear in mind when scrutinizing shawl patterns. The few shawls that appear in the painting are of solid colour, most likely plain *pashmina*. In fact, except for the striped *dhurrie*, nothing else in the painting – costumes, turbans, shields, walls, etc. – is decorated with any pattern. However, the finely modelled and expressive features of each of the more than fifty Sikh characters in the scene attest to the work of a gifted Guler artist and underscore the warm creative atmosphere between Rajput and Sikh.

WM8. Kashmir long shawl (detail)
As graphic patterns intensified during the Sikh period, faintly outlined botehs, almost phantom-like, became less dominant.
Sikh period, c.1835.
PRIVATE COLLECTION

Hailed as the 'only honest man in Lahore' by one account and *Hasmuddaula* or 'Sword of the State' by another, Desa Singh's son, Lehna Singh Majithia, took over his father's position as *nizam* of the Kangra Hills. Besides the excellent reputation Lehna Singh enjoyed by his generosity and kindness towards his subjects, he possessed talented abilities in mechanical engineering and invention, with deep interests in astronomy and mathematics. He not only applied his skills to improving weaponry; he also invented a clock which showed the hour, day and month and phases of the moon as well.[104] No doubt he had left behind a large archive of sketches. Whether Lehna's engineering talents, or his *Hasmuddaula* sobriquet, found their way into shawl designs, or some unknown artist saw fit, under other creative impulses from a totally foreign domain, to attempt a dramatic shift away from the standard buta patterns, is not known. What is known is that these complex

Opposite:
Plate 53. Sansar Chand, Maharaja of Kangra, Kangra school, c.1800-1825.
COURTESY OF MORGAN LIBRARY, M.1035.11

geometric patterns indeed emerged suddenly to become extremely popular among the Sikhs. One measure of the resounding success of Sikh hegemony in the Hill States is the way in which local Rajput artists, from 1828 onward, began portraying their new rulers in paintings – a radical development since, under Sansar Chand (Plate 53), Sikh subjects were 'boycotted'. Greatly adding to this important shift in artistic sensitivities was the wedding of Ranjit Singh to the Gaddan ranis (see above).

Srinagar may have been ruled by the Sikhs, but no one can say they were a presence there, culturally speaking. During their rule Kashmir was administered by a succession of ten governors, some Hindu, some Sikh. Their main focus was to make sure that Lahore received its due from the rich source of revenues the productive Valley was capable of providing. At times contingents of Sikh soldiers were required to quell Muslim uprisings and to enforce taxation, monies of which were constantly needed to finance the warring conflicts that incessantly occupied the expansion of Sikh hegemony. Thus it would appear that, given the nature of Sikh sovereignty over Srinagar, and the demographics of the inhabitants, the Valley itself did not represent a fertile breeding ground for Sikh culture to grow. There are times when it may help to view Kashmir as one big factory. The whole Sikh political structure was centred around Ranjit Singh's court in Lahore – in fact he himself had never set foot in Kashmir – and often it may have been impossible for the Sikhs themselves to personally oversee their own shawl production. But we can probably infer from Jacquemont's observations that unrivalled quality was still being produced in the Valley when he wrote 'several Noble Sikh that imitate the magnificence of Ranjit Singh by having their little courts, have in Kashmir, each an agent to oversee the weaving of the shawls they make each year'.[105]

By the time Kashmir came under Sikh rule it was evident, as attested by Moorcroft, that the shawl represented one of the biggest industries in the world, reaching out further and further to international markets. Just as in Europe when Jacquard shawl designing reached its peak, and artists responsible for their designs became known throughout the continent, so too, one would assume, the Kashmiri artist became known for his patterns, though perhaps on a lesser, domestic scale. While the term 'artist' is a Western concept, usually denoting a person who makes paintings or sculpture, in the Orient the term 'artist' per se does not exist. In India the term 'craftsman', or one possessing a specific manual dexterity, would probably be better suited as a job description. Often objects that were once classified as crafts are now celebrated as works of art and the Kashmir shawl is a case in point.

Little or nothing is known of the actual craftsmen whose wonderful and minutely detailed shawl patterns, in Moorcroft's words, 'could only have been executed in Britain by miniature painters'.[106] According to Srivastava, two categories of Punjabi 'artists' existed, *naqqashas* and *musawirs,* and each worked independently of the other, within his own style and method. The former would have been equally versatile at decorating pages of calligraphy, illuminating or illustrating Islamic, Hindu or Sikh manuscripts, or embellishing letters or important documents. The latter would have been responsible for painting portraits and capturing historic moments in the lives of his patrons. *Naqqash* is someone who makes a *naqsha,* which is Farsi for drawing, design, plan or portrait. It therefore defines a wide range of artistic activities, including flower painting and textile design.[107] Since *naqqash* is the same title as that used in Kashmir for shawl-pattern drawer, it would not be illogical to assume that the Punjabi *naqqash* also applied himself to shawl patterns when necessary or commissioned. Moorcroft recorded only twenty-five *naqqash* remaining in 1823, and such a low number reflects three things: one, that the number of looms was steadily shrinking from a high of 18,000 in 1800 to only 8,000 in 1823; two, the

Plate 54. *Naqqashs* at work, painting, possibly Lahore, c.1867, after Kyburg exhibition catalogue, 1988, London.

figure may be indicative of the *naqqash's* (Plate 54) exceptionally valued services in the Punjab where employment became increasingly available; and three, the eerie penumbra that still lingered from the famine of 1813.

Since artists plied their trades in various mediums such as manuscript, miniature, wall, textile and lacquer painting, to name a few, it behoves us, in light of the bleak information about shawl artists, to briefly explore those who, indeed, made a name for themselves within the Punjab and Hill regions. Examining the various artistic movements in the surrounding areas of Kashmir may shed further light on shawl artistry. The craftsman's versatility might allow us to visualize him sitting and sketching out a group of flowers for his patron's new Kashmir shawls. Furthermore, these sketches would have been sent to Kashmir (as the French did, years later) and translated into the secret shawl-code language of the *talim guru*, while the *tarah guru*, or colouring master, for the specific warps and wefts, would have been responsible for conjuring up his magical colours.

Despite the unsettling politics of the Punjab, the Hill States and Kashmir, draughtsmen and painters, all of whom came from families where such professions were a long-held tradition, were able to thrive by honing their skills in various techniques of painting and ornamentation, migrating from one city to the next. Because of the endless upheavals in the princely kingdoms, this was only possible toward the end of the eighteenth century, as artists, in order to survive, had gone from a retained status to freelancing professional. Underlining this push toward migration is a unique, heart-rending, early nineteenth century letter to Raja Sansar Chand, from an obviously down and out artist pleading for sustenance. The letter represents the only known writings of any Indian artist.[108]

Drawing on rare Urdu, Punjabi and Persian references as sources, Srivastava offers, along with genealogical tables, innumerable names of artists and the artists' families, their area of expertise, and the temples, darbars and bazaars, etc. where they worked. Unfortunately, few dates are given, and some of his source material may be open to question. Nevertheless, we learn that it was the Chughtai family (originally from Kabul and settled in Lahore), of which some members had worked at the Mughal court, that reigned supreme before and after Ranjit Singh and from which the illustrious Imam Bakhsh descended. The family of Kehar Singh, which was settled in Lahore and Amritsar, was the second most influential artist family; Bhai Kishan Singh, a member of this family, was sent by Sher Singh (son of Ranjit Singh) to do a portrait of Dost Muhammad (ruled Afghanistan c.1826-1839). Kehar Singh, Kishan Singh, Bishan Singh and Kapur Singh were all artists whose abilities brought them to the courts of the Punjab and Hill States, including Purkhu of Kangra, who plied his trade in Lahore in the art circles of Imam Bakhsh and Kehar Singh.[109]

Artists saw in Ranjit Singh a man of empathy and kindness and one who listened attentively to the needs of his people (Plate 55). Attesting to this is a letter from the Maharaja himself, confirming the small *zamindar* of the Kangra painter, Nikka. The letter's perfunctory wording implies a long history of patronage; certainly Nikka was not the only painter to achieve *zamindar* status among the Sikhs.[110] In the words of B.N. Goswamy, 'the sheer quantum of [art] work done in the Punjab must have been impressive'.[111] In commissioning works of art, besides the Maharaja, the powerful Sandhanwalia *sardars,* who had close familial bonds to the Maharaja, as well as the noble Dogra brothers Dhyan Singh and Suchet Singh of Jammu, were also actively engaged; the Dogra brothers' connection with painting goes back purportedly over a century.[112] The role of the French generals in the service of the Maharaja will be discussed further on.

Prior to the late eighteenth century, works of art indubitably attributed to Kashmir, in almost any medium, are virtually nonexistent and this is especially true of the huge number of religious and secular manuscripts that were produced then that to this day go undated and unattributed. Abul Fazl, in his chronicles, mentions the names of five Kashmiri Muslim artists who worked at the Mughal court, but provides us with no other information about them. The only true Kashmir painting known during this time dates far back to the eleventh century, to the fabulous murals found at the *gompas,* Alchi, Ladakh, for example.[113] Few shawls were actually embellished with the types of flowers found in painting.

The hill state of Basohli is one area where both artistic creativity and innovation fused to

Plate 55. Portrait of Ranjit Singh at Rupar in 1831.
Private Collection. Photograph courtesy of Jean-Marie Lafont

Plate 56. *Patka*, 18th century.
COLLECTION BHARAT KALA BHAWAN, BANARAS

Plate 57. *Patka*, 18th century.
COLLECTION BHARAT KALA BHAWAN, BANARAS

Opposite:
WM9. Kashmir long shawl (detail)
An unusual pattern is created from overlapping mihrabs and striped arches in which the 'phantom' botehs are almost superfluous. Sikh period, c.1835.
PRIVATE COLLECTION

form a great new and refreshing style, lending itself as an excellent case in point to sharpen our observations of *kani* weavings and fuel our imagination to reach beyond the urban confines of Srinagar's *karkhandars*. The Basohli style spread to many of the other states and eventually developed into a conventional form that persisted throughout the foothills of the Western Himalayas right up to the nineteenth century. The style has been traced to the artistically gifted Kashmiri Brahmin family of Pandit Seu Raina who, according to Randhawa, had supposedly fled Kashmir during the fearful period of Aurangzeb's proselytizing and later settled in Guler. The Kashmiri Brahmins traditionally prefix their names with Pandit. In the case of the Seu family, the term Raina refers to a Kashmiri sub-caste.[114] Pandit Seu's two sons, Manaku and Nainsukh, were two of the greatest exponents of this style that spread throughout the Pahari principalities of Jasrota, Guler, Jammu, Chamba, Noorpur and Kangra. Their grandchildren continued the painting tradition.

In the later part of the seventeenth century Basohli became known for an exciting innovative style where, in Pratapaditya Pal's words, the use of such dazzling colours as 'hot yellows or fiery oranges' and other passionate, enigmatic colours were used to express the inimical style that defined the beauty of Basohli painting. Pal submits that the Basohli style was due to a single artist who was conscious of the Mughal style of detailed ornamentation, architecture and elegance, yet eschewed the 'Mughal concern for perspective, observation of facts, psychological insight and naturalism'.[115] Yet the power of emotion is none the less achieved through a conceptual rhythm of form and passion for colour. Observations such as these resonate with the way we look at *kani* weavings of this period. Obviously not all seventeenth century shawls conformed to the high Mughal idiom of slender and grace but reflected the various regional styles and tastes of the Pahari courts, as well as the remoter cosmopolitan regions of the Deccan, Hyderabad, Bengal and, of course, Delhi. The sack of Delhi by Nadir Shah in 1739 may have had something to do with the change of artistic climate that engendered such dramatic changes in painting style. Although perhaps not as dramatic, the colour palette within the *kani* weaving industry of the late eighteenth century, it seems, also experienced a change towards more intense coloration (Plates 56 and 57). Although knowledge of the various regional styles and techniques of Indian painting may eventually become useful, drawing conclusions according to colour palette alone could only be

Plate 58. Mian Mukund Dev of Jasrota riding through a meadow, by Nainsukh, c.1754, gouache and gold on paper, 11¾ x 17¾in. (30 x 45cm.
VICTORIA AND ALBERT MUSEUM. IS 7-1973

speculative. Whatever is the cause of such an innovative style, whether it was due to the initiative of one or several artists working together, or due to a revival of artistic energies following the devastation of Nadir Shah, the Kashmir shawl as a sensitive artistic vehicle of changing fashion can, it seems, often be weighed to a degree against the rise and fall of political and social events.

From the eighteenth century one prolific artist working in the Pahari hill states who particularly stands out is Nainsukh (fl.1730-1775). Perhaps the most famous post-Mughal painter of all, he carefully recorded with his delicate brush the humdrum quotidian and quiet rituals of his great patron, Balwant Singh (1724-1763). The gifted Nainsukh appears to have revelled in the juxtaposition of bold colours against a serene, if not dreamy, background of large plain washes of light hues, a technique which seemed to vivify the characters he painted. Although his earlier works depict plain shawls, Nainsukh invested time in carefully detailing floral designs in other textile objects, such as summer carpets, tents and saddles. In *Balwant Singh Offering Homage to Radha and Krishna Enthroned,* illustrated in Goswamy's *Nainsukh of Guler,* one finds a niche wall, dado and throne all elaborately decorated with flowers.[116] It appears that it is only later on that Nainsukh begins to draw simple and albeit indecipherably adumbrated *buti-palla* shawls (Plate 58).

In another fine painting Nainsukh's patron, Balwant Singh, is presented wearing a finely detailed Chinese Mandarin robe with rank badge, profusely ornamented with dragons and cloudbands. The exoticism and novelty of such a foreign costume obviously not only captured his patron's curiosity but Nainsukh's as well, for the costume may have represented an exchange of gifts between a Chinese dignitary and Balwant Singh.[117] Since it is extremely rare to come across a Kashmir shawl woven with motifs of Chinese influence, Balwant Singh's possible contact with items from the Far East indeed brings up some interesting speculations about trade with, for example, China.

However, the point to bring out here is that the intensity of Nainsukh's minute details of the Mandarin robe did not appear to match his curiosity for the colourful and minute floral details of the Kashmir shawl (Plate 59). His attention, it seems, was drawn more to the sculptural rather than the floral elements of the soft folds of the Kashmir shawl. Thus, Balwant Singh is depicted donning a magnificent saffron shawl (Plate 60). Its unusual twists and turns were rendered such that it imbues Balwant's stature with a regal air, capturing the viewer's eye and creating a brilliant flamboyance. Nainsukh may have promoted a shawl fashion unknowingly. One thing we learn from Nainsukh's shawls is that he illustrates them with diminutive *pallas,* a format indicative of the early eighteenth century. Yet, why does Nainsukh pay so little heed to the shawl's design? Has the ubiquitous presence of a textile, woven so close to home, numbed his appreciation? Such perfunctory attention to details here does not seem representative of an artist family whose roots (as initially thought) may have harked back to Kashmir. Indeed, Goswamy argues that, based on the strength of 'inscriptional and oral evidence', Pandit Seu's family origins can now be placed squarely in Guler.[118] Besides his long years working for Balwant Singh, Goswamy notes that Nainsukh's talents had him working also for various influential Sikh governors of the Punjab.

Do Nainsukh's paintings reveal an artist who may have lent his *'naqqash'* talents to shawl designs, or was he only working on portraits and genre scenes? If so, with a glance at the future, will a day come when we could speculate about which shawl pattern may have come from such and such an artist? Given the paucity of information at the moment, this may seem an insurmountable hurdle. Not long ago, however, few people knew that Akbar's artists borrowed from Flemish engravings or that Jahangir's artists copied flowers from herbals, which designs, in turn, could be traced to the Frenchmen, Carolus Clusius or Pierre Vallet.

Nainsukh's older brother, Manaku, also painted very much in the same style albeit his colour palette seemed to differ slightly whereby he often juxtaposed stark, lustrous, primary colours with intense tones to create a striking image whose overall effect was dream-like as in Gauguin's Tahitian paintings. The power Manaku achieved thus was expressive of an emotional texture that easily transcended the subject matter, uplifting the work to a high spiritual plane.[119] One of his most famous paintings – and the only one bearing his signature – provides us with a sense of how the artist was able to play with reality and illusion through his blend of surreal shapes, magical lighting and rich chromatic tones. Who can say whether this great artistic talent

Below left:
Plate 59. Balwant Singh in Chinese robe, by Nainsukh, gouache on paper, c.1750, 9½ x 6in. (24.2 x 15cm), after B.N. Goswamy, *Nainsukh of Guler,* pl. 42.

Below right:
Plate 60. Balwant Singh donning a saffron Kashmir shawl, by Nainsukh. c.1750-55, after B.N. Goswamy, *Nainsukh of Guler,* pl. 183.

did not spill over into such *kani* masterpieces as the Bharat Kala Bhawan's *dochalla* (Plate 61).

Many of Nainsukh's paintings were of a devotional character and thus less reliable to textile observation, though often his characters were colourfully dressed in stripes and prints; there was, it seems, much less attention to making the shawl any defining feature of his work. Nevertheless, many of the fine and rare Mughal shawls, contemporaneous with Manaku's era (early eighteenth century), especially the pieces conserved in the Bharat Kala Bhawan, exhibit such strikingly rich colour tones and large, surreal, flower blossoms – given the frail stems supporting them – that it is difficult not to be tempted into believing that the magic of his genius had, somehow, in times past intersected with the art of the shawl (Plates 62 and 63). Although perhaps less illustrious in renown, the Pandit Seu family continued its artist endeavours into the nineteenth century via Nainsukh's three grandsons, Gokal, Harku and Chhajju, the last of whom purportedly worked at the court of Lahore.

Left:
Top:
Plate 61. Detail of Kashmir long shawl, c.1750.
COLLECTION BHARAT KALA BHAWAN, BANARAS

Centre:
Plate 62. Shoulder mantle, detail of complete shawl. Kashmir, 17th century.
COLLECTION BHARAT KALA BHAWAN, BANARAS

Below:
Plate 63. Shoulder mantle, detail of complete shawl. Kashmir, 17th century.
COLLECTION BHARAT KALA BHAWAN, BANARAS

Opposite:
WM10. Kashmir long shawl
Shawls such as this one, with its tall stalks and snaking vine elements, may have been the prototypes arriving in Europe that inspired Antony Berrus, the Parisian shawl artist, to launch his jungle foliage type patterns during his extremely fecund period of 1848-1850. Given the early French presence in Srinagar, however, this remains a fine point of uncertainty for further research. Sikh period, c.1840.
PRIVATE COLLECTION

Perhaps the most important observation to be learned through the examination of Pahari painting is that not only do we learn little of eighteenth century shawl patterns, but clues foreshadowing the bold graphic style which was to become the mainstay of the Sikh period are absent. In fact, despite the increased prevalence of the depiction of shawls in Indian paintings of the second half of the eighteenth century, a general survey of regional painting styles offers little information that might be helpful in assessing the development of the Sikh style. This increase is most likely due to the freeing up of markets in the Hill States, as a result of the Mughal Empire's disintegration.

Nevertheless, from the region of Kotah (Rajasthan) we learn through works on paper conserved in the Kotah Royal Collection that local artists were active in producing styles for the production of textiles and shawls. In a recent publication by Stuart Carey Welch one encounters an interesting and colourful illustration of a boteh pattern from the royal collection of Kotah.[120] It is a painting on paper and, although it is undated, its style is typical of those patterns woven in Kashmir during the eighteenth century. Since the painting is part of the Kotah Royal Collection, one can assume that the pattern was created by court artists working directly for the *maharao* kings. Kotah had been an important centre for painting during the sixteenth and seventeenth centuries. Working under Maharao Bhin Singh and later Maharao Umed Singh I, Sheikh Taju made a name for himself during the first half of the 18th century as the 'Master of Elephants'. But artists in general who worked there undertook all kinds of projects including portraits, hunts, Hindu epics, even military maps.

Kotah's next flowering of art seems not to have appeared again until the early part of the nineteenth century. Consequently, the date of the boteh's pattern in the painting, which is probably too démodé to be assigned to the latter period, fits easily into the types of botehs in style during the mid- to late eighteenth century (Plate 64). The size of the buta, 12¾ x 7⅞in. (32.3 x 20cm), although quite large, does not exceed the types of butas found on known shawls of the late eighteenth century. The painting's paper is grainy, unlacquered and appears not to be of any special quality, ruling out a possible Kashmiri provenance; the colour palette is atypical, having little in common with the colours of Kashmir. However, the most distinct features are the detailing and shading of the flowers, which seem to burst forth effusively with a bright and gay flowing movement. The person responsible for assembling this fine floral bouquet had to be an artist with a sharp eye for nature, for the image he created exudes a palpable sense of plasticity. Among the easily recognizable crocuses, primroses, and zinnias, other distinct botanical features are apparent, such as the carefully delineated sepals, calyxes and perianths. Particularly unique are the anemones with their finely drawn corollas and large drooping sepals. This boteh is something one might associate with European artistry, perhaps to be found in the atelier of Isabey; and, indeed, one could speculate as to whether it wasn't altogether painted by someone from the Company School.[121] Kotah painting is known for the energetic depiction of dense leafy nature and, in fact, there is at least one artist whose style has been compared to that of the French painter Henri (le Douanier) Rousseau.[122]

For the moment the above painting is the only work on paper known prior to those which Moorcroft sent back to England. It serves to highlight the importance of shawl patterns being created by artists who lived far removed from the weaving ateliers of Kashmir. Other beautiful works on paper, such as designs for textiles, are conserved by the Kotah Royal Collection, attesting to the notion that serious attention was given to create customized fabrics and dress accessories in a manner becoming the royalty of Kotah Rajputs.[123]

An earlier attempt to identify a particular design repertoire of patterns through the socio-economic history of Afghanistan's domination of Kashmir resulted only in identifying various shapes and motifs that bore little resemblance to any concrete expression of cultural sensitivity towards Kashmir's north-west frontier neighbours. During this period it appears that the cone shape matured to enclose an ever increasing multi-floral concoction of mosaic-like petals, often with a vase supporting a spray of flowers which were carefully arranged in a distinct radial fashion. Though quite beautiful and colourful, something was missing, perhaps a warmth, leaving the viewer indifferent. On the other hand, the culture of the Mughals is indisputably associated with the flowering plant (Mughal Style) and from its creative application to the period arts we are able to grasp a feeling of poetic sensitivity and grace, of play and amusement; their shawls embodied these emotional states. Turning towards the Sikh period, however, something totally new developed: a creation not only in fabulous designs, but also the full utilization of the shawl's surface in which these designs were able to romp and play and spread their wings, so to speak. There was an onslaught of architectonic and symbolist ideas which rose to dominance under Maharaja Ranjit Singh, engendering a general movement away from naturalism. The sharp curvilinearity of these patterns, the multiple concentricity of the regimented floral arrangements, the shield, hook vine and incipient zoomorphic motifs, to name a few – all these are just some of the interesting devices clearly developing immediately following Ranjit's takeover of Kashmir. Perhaps there is no better statement that more epitomizes and better reflects the creative exploration of such new designs as when Jacquemont recorded in his diary an entry about the insatiable curiosity of Ranjit Singh:

> *I have spent a couple of hours on several occasions conversing with Ranjit... His conversation is a nightmare. He is almost the first inquisitive Indian I have seen, but his curiosity makes up for the apathy of his whole nation. He asked me 100,000 questions about India, the English, Europe, Bonaparte, this world, in general, and the other one, hell and paradise, the soul, god, the devil and a 1000 things besides'.*[124]

Plate 64. Boteh painting, late 18th century, watercolour, 12¾ x 7⅞in. (32.3 x 20cm), after *Gods, Kings, and Tigers*, S.C. Welch, p. 204.
RAO MADHO SINGH TRUST MUSEUM, FORT KOTAH

This incisive inquisitiveness which Jacquemont experienced had no doubt filtered down to shawl artistry in which a specific sector of Kashmir's school of art, perhaps the avant-garde, felt inspired to turn away from the old style that simply repeated a series of identical botehs across the shawl's extremity.

WM11. Kashmir long shawl (detail)
Arguably one of the greatest *kani* weavings of mid-19th century Kashmir, artistically this shawl pushes the limits of the art form to vertiginous heights. In 1997 I wrote: 'Rare are shawl designs that fuse pattern movements of both the central field and end panels to create a complete overall design. The completeness found here is expressed with explosive power through the cosmic-like mandala of the shawl's stunning and unique central field, a field that reflects the strong continuous cultures which surround the Valley of Kashmir: Hinduism, Islam, and Buddhism'. *Dochallas* were always woven in pairs and recently the sister to this one was discovered (Joan Hart Collection). Late Sikh period, c.1850.
TAPI COLLECTION OF PRAFUL AND SHILPA SHAH, SURAT

Plate 65. General Jean-François Allard wearing Commander of the Legion of Honour medal, awarded by Louis Philippe, signed 'Court, 1837', by Joseph-Désiré Court, 1837, after *Maharaja Ranjit Singh*... by Jean-Marie Lafont.

The explosion of new designs was a phenomenon that predated the Jacquard loom's engineering advances that had eventually enlarged the design repeats.[125] It was this crucial innovation of new designs and enlarged *kani*-weave surface that offered up an identifying stamp to Sikh culture and gave the Kashmir shawl its defining characteristics as a newly minted art form on the Indian subcontinent. It is mainly on the long shawl that Sikh patterns found their highest expression. These 'tapestry' shawls, like the plainer ones before them, were also made in pairs *(dochallas)*. The finest pieces would have been woven with a minimum number of seams. The end panels *(pallas),* beginning from the added fringe gates right up to where the shawl's central design starts, would be of one loomed segment. The central square panel, often rectangular on the earliest pieces, is *kani* woven of one piece though, at times, it might be of plain fabric or contain finely embroidered *kunj* botehs. These central panels were usually surrounded by four or more joined segments of *kani* material which invariably reflect a similar design and coloration to that used in the *palla*.

On some occasions, the *palla* might be composed of two panels joined by an invisible seam, but generally this is not an indication of sacrifice in quality. Only in shawls of the Dogra period do we begin to encounter the 'patchwork' shawl – a shawl pieced together by the *rafugars,* often with hundreds of pieces. Shawls with *palla* designs that overflow into the central panel suggest that the artist carefully mapped out his creation using some kind of cartoon, and not the *talim*. It is with these spill-over patterns that we often encounter artistic conceptions of the highest calibre. Square shawls *(rumals)* also represented a vehicle for the dissemination of the Sikh artistry, albeit on a lesser scale for obvious reasons of limited size. Both mediums, square and long, it appears, were used in the creation of the many Sikh design devices discussed in this book, such as temples *(gurdwaras)* and other architectural motifs, decorated boats and those enigmatic leafy medallions or garlands.

Thus the maximum number of *kani* segments of a quintessentially pieced Sikh shawl would be of the order of five, not counting the two long *hashias* which run end to end lengthways, which are invariably sewn on: two end panels, the centre, and the two narrow panels flanking the centre. The *hashias,* always woven with silk warp foundation, must mirror the pattern of the transversal all-*pashmina hashias,* in order for the shawl to maintain its superior status. A shawl of three segments only implies that the entire centre had been woven in one piece, a rare but not unknown occurrence. Otherwise we come across perfectly respectable shawls with seven *kani* segments, the *pallas* in two pieces, the central field framed by two panels and the remaining two segment *palla,* not counting the *hashias*.[126]

Often one of the giveaways to the

recognition of a Sikh period shawl is the unembroidered, solid colour fringe (made up of about four different colours) attached to both ends of the shawl. However, one should be aware that fringes could have been changed over the years. Among shawl aficionados, the general consensus has been that embroidered fringes began to appear after the Universal Exhibition of 1851, but this should be weighed very prudently, only when comparing all the other iconographic information a shawl of this period has to offer.

The Sikh Kashmir shawl style during the reign of Maharaja Ranjit Singh cannot be fully understood without knowledge of the foreign expatriates who diligently served under the monarch. The following will discuss some of the key areas out of which inspiring design ideas possibly grew and eventually found resonance with the shawl artists. While a seemingly endless stream of designs emerged during this period, some of which actually depict the ideas discussed, I remain quite confident others have yet to be discovered.

Coincidentally, General Jean-François Allard and William Moorcroft both arrived in the Kashmir-Lahore region in 1822 – one a military man and the other a veterinarian – two occidentals doing their own thing without the recognition of the other, yet both somehow involved in the shawl business, one supporting the industry and attempting to improve it, the other spying on it. One can assume that it was not long after Allard's arrival in Lahore that he became involved in the business of shawls, especially given its lucrative trade. We learn of Allard's direct and intimate involvement with the shawl industry during his trip to Paris in 1835, where he had been appointed by Louis Philippe Political Agent of the French Government at the Court of Lahore.[127] While this title may seem to have an aura of secrecy to it, Allard's family life in Kashmir and allegiance to Ranjit Singh was unassailable.

Thus it was that twenty years before the great Parisian artist Antony Berrus honed his dense verdant zoomorphic shawl style, another striking French character bedecked in glorious Napoleonic military attire arrived at the doorstep of India's last great and powerful Maharaja. A former captain of the 7th Regiment of Hussars (Old Guard) and aide-de-camp of the notorious Maréchal Brune, General Allard must have cut a dazzling figure as he rode through the gates of Lahore mounted on horseback (Plate 65).[128] Allard arrived in Lahore in 1822 with his Italian comrade-in-arms General Jean-Baptist Ventura (Plate 66), and soon after Ranjit Singh put them to work, forming a 10,000 to 15,000 strong special army known as the The Royal Brigade, or *Fauj-i-khas*, that became the spearhead of the French army.[129] Allard's responsibility was to protect the southern border of Ranjit Singh's territories known as the *cis-Sutlej*, a term connoting 'beyond the Sutlej', describing the southern portion of the Punjab controlled by the British consisting of an area of principalities stretching

Plate 66. General Ventura, oil on canvas, c.1838, after *Maharaja Ranjit Singh...*, by Jean-Marie Lafont.

WM12. Kashmir long shawl (detail)
This celebratory pattern represents another fine example of the many 'Diwali' shawls found in various museums. Whether the fan-like floral blossoms, bobbing here and there like rockets exploding in the sky, are actual pyrotechnic sprays is not important. What matters is the general feeling one senses of a shawl woven for a very special occasion. Sikh period, c.1835. 52.5 x 130in. (133 x 330cm).
TAPI COLLECTION OF PRAFUL AND SHILPA SHAH, SURAT. 1566 / S1-135

Opposite:
WM13. Kashmir long shawl (see detail on page 12)
Very finely woven, this masterpiece stimulates the visual senses as much by its rich warm colours as by its novel pattern of a stacked array of large sweeping arches (rainbows?) overlaid with equally large horseshoe-shaped vines and tendrils. Sikh Period, c.1835.
TAPI COLLECTION OF PRAFUL AND SHILPA SHAH, SURAT. ACC #. 97.1419 -S1-75

Right:
Plate 67. The Cross of the Legion of Honour, First Empire (1804-1814).
By permission of the Royal Museum of the Armed Forces and of Military History, Brussels

Far right:
Plate 68. The Cross of the Order of Spain, 1809-1811.
By permission of the Royal Museum of the Armed Forces and of Military History, Brussels

from the Jamuna to the Sutlej. Sikh chieftains in this area were protected by the British. The expatriates Allard, Ventura and their soon-to-arrive French cohorts, driven by their Napoleonic aura, were living a fascinating and exceptional military lifestyle. Napoleon's Hussars, famous as the elite and most fearsome of cavalry troops, wielded a reputation as the most colourfully attired branch of the French army. Judging from the portraits of Allard and Ventura, and given their exalted station in life, one could easily assume that these were officers who knew how to dress and they surely took full advantage of it. A huge effort went into assuring that the elite troops were bedecked with the proper uniforms; for orders of cuirasses made to French specifications, manufacturers received orders as far away as Kliegenthal, Saxony.[130]

Allard sported a stunning white beard that hung down in two points, causing more than one writer, including Jacquemont, to remark that it 'increases the importance which he enjoys' and exalted his status as 'chief of the little French community'.[131] Supposedly he always wore his medal of the Legion of Honour (awarded 27 January 1814), which was the most coveted and honoured decoration of France, awarded only to those who achieved gallantry in action (Plate 67 and WM14, page 104).[132] Further, he received the decoration the Order of Spain (Plate 68) on 15 March 1812 for his valorous service in Napoleon's campaigns. The Hussar's uniform consisted of a tail-less braided jacket known as a *dolman*. It was elaborately decorated with rows of gold braids (frogging) and chevroned sleeve badges symbolizing the corps d'elite, epaulettes of red silk with aiguillettes and the whole bannered across the chest with a large bright scarlet silk ribbon. Add to this resplendent scene Allard's medals of the Legion of Honour, La Croix de Guerre and his tall shako fur hat with plume, and we arrive at a mesmerizing image of a man who suddenly found himself in perhaps one of the most exciting and exotic places on earth.

As for costumes worn by the Sikh officers, Soltykoff thought they made a queer sight: 'They wear patriarchal beards and uniforms of satin, velvet or clothing of gold … as for the cut, it has been fixed by the late General Allard and is the same in all regiments. It is the French uniform modified to Sikh taste'.[133] Indeed, figurative embroidered shawls of the period depict a myriad of personages in European costume, reflecting the visual impact

Opposite:
Detail of WM14 (see page 104).
Note the similarities of this detail's center star and the forked wings of the Legion of Honor medal.

WM14. Kashmir long shawl (detail)
In this fine, richly dyed shawl, we find cypress trees and hillocks surrounding an intense saffron centre – a celebration of Kashmir's nature. The three scalloped medallions pointing towards the eight pointed star centres represent in a way an iconic symbol of the *Khalsa* Punjab. Sikh period, 1830.
Private Collection

Plate 69. Embroidered *rumal* (detail of WM15, page 108-109.), c.1850.
COLLECTION CHET GATSBY

of military rank, file and accoutrements on the Kashmiri shawl artist (Plate 69).

Impressed with Allard's military decorations, Ranjit Singh ordered the manufacture of a new medal known as the 'Order of Ranjit Singh' which consisted of a large trefoil whose coin centre contained his profile with the aureole of the sun's rays, while each of the leaves bore inscriptions in Arabic. Opposing full-sized bulls (Punjab symbolism) with heads lowered fill the spaces in between the top leaves while the bottom space is occupied by an eagle (symbol of Napoleon and, by extension, the Revolution). The two lower leaves and eagle

Right:
Plate 70. Medal of the Order of Ranjit Singh, instituted by Ranjit Singh, c.1825, after *Piety and Splendour,* B.N. Goswamy, p. 187.
SHEESH MAHAL MEDAL GALLERY, PATIALA

Far right:
Plate 71. Bright Star of the Punjab, instituted by Ranjit Singh in 1837, gold and enamel, set with diamonds and emeralds, after *Piety and Splendour* by B.N. Goswamy.
SHEESH MAHAL MEDAL GALLERY, PATIALA

Below:
Plate 72. Napoleon I, on the coronation throne, by Ingres.
MUSÉE DE L'ARMÉE, PARIS

are underlined by a large unsheathed sabre. The whole is affixed to a large sunburst forming a second class badge (Plate 70). The third class badge was essentially the same thing only without the large sunburst. Unquestionably these medals were bestowed for meritorious service on the *Fauj-i-khas troops.*[134]

The effect of Allard's wearing the Cross of the Legion of Honour should not be underestimated. While he was in Persia Abbas Mirza, prince and younger son of Fath Ali Shah, was so awestruck seeing the coveted cross pinned to Allard's breast that he immediately asked him to join his army as colonel and military instructor![135] The 'Bright Star of Punjab' medal, instituted in 1837, was composed of a large Maltese cross with four tendrils within the interstices and the centre featuring a portrait of Ranjit Singh (Plate 71).

Ingres' famous painting of Napoleon's coronation (1804), engravings of which surely made their way around the globe, clearly show Napoleon on the imperial throne with the eight pointed cleft-star of honour on his chest (Plate 72). It is interesting to note that, when King Louis XVIII regained control of France in 1814, Napoleon's creation of the Medal of Honour was never questioned. By that time 50,000 medals had been awarded! Thus the omnipresent mélange of French military uniform paraphernalia and neo-classical style must have created a rich ambiance to which indigenous artists could not have remained immune.

Equally, one should not discount another coronation, that of King George IV (19 July 1821); there is a painting in which he is depicted with his military cross of honour. A discussion of coronations would be incomplete without that of Ranjit Singh, which took place, albeit much less regally, in Lahore in 1801, two years after his capture of the city.

Another item, also highly visible, should not be overlooked: the Napoleonic flag (Plate 73). It would not be unreasonable to believe that flag mementos were carried with the Frenchmen during their peripatetic escapades through the Orient, or that they had flags made to reflect the adoption of their new Indo-French surroundings. While sojourning in Lahore, Jacquemont, in a letter to his father, recounts how popular Napoleon's flag was in the Punjab and that it was due to Allard who, eight years previously, had, in fact, adopted it to the armies under his command.[136] In France, the flag poles had been topped by eagles and the flags themselves were decorated in the four corners with bees and laurel wreaths encircling

Plate 73. The Napoleonic flag.

a bugle. Baron Hugel, visiting the Allard house in 1836, noted that 'The eagle and Napoleon's flag are displayed on every wall'.[137]

The antique market, over the past few decades, has seen the appearance of several curious shawls whose patterns were woven obviously with boat or boat-like motifs. These motifs are not the normal *shikaras* found on Lake Dal (Plates 74 and 75) today. They are usually big arching hulls (no doubt stylized) bedecked with fluttering flags, indicating that they were woven in commemoration of a particular event. Kashmir is a Venice-like land of water with a majestic backdrop of some of the highest mountains in the world, the Karakorum. Hundreds of streams gush down

Plate 74. 'Monshee Bagh', Commissioner's boat, photograph by Samuel Bourne, 1864, after *Picturesque Views...*, Rafael Dedo Gadebusch (ed.), fig. 3, Hatje Cantz, Germany, 2007.

WM15. Square shawl, embroidered (detail) Whether the elegance and grace of these colourfully costumed angels derive from the creative pen of Imam Bakhsh Lahori, from a descendent of Nainsukh, from another artist associated either with the court of Lahore or from the highly developed school of art in Kangra, is beside the point. The fact is, this elaborately embroidered *rumal* is obviously from a gifted artist. It is interesting to learn that many of these embroideries served as vehicles for the illustration of the great epic poem the *Shahnameh of Firdausi,* in which, among other mythical creatures, angels played an active role; that Muhammad received his first revelation through the Archangel Gabriel is well known from the Koran. Given the numerous and fine embroidered known shawls in various museums and private collections, it is quite clear that this *rumal* format was the ultimate 'canvas' in which consummate artists and embroiderers were able to join forces in demonstrating their talents, c.1840. See Plates 51 and 69 for further details.
COLLECTION CHET GATSBY

Plate 75. Sunset over Dal Lake.
PHOTOGRAPH BY THE AUTHOR

into a valley lush with a renowned beauty of wild flowers, former imperial gardens, floating shops, markets, and boat navigation. François Bernier observed: 'From these mountains an infinity of streams and wells from every side...come finally to reassemble and form a very beautiful river carrying boats as large as our Seine [does]'.[138]

For short distances and 'taxi service' the *shikaras,* with its spring seats and often fancy curtains, is the most popular of the known boats. The *parinda* or 'flyer', no longer in use, was a sleek, fast, long boat designed to be rowed by a team of forty to fifty paddlers (Plate 74). Two kinds of barges, the *bahat* and the *war,* were designed to haul cargoes up to 1,000 *maunds* and 400 *maun*ds respectively. A large prow and a stern with two rooms, in which the boatman and his family lived, defined the *bahat's* shape; while the cargo hold, for storing grain, was covered with a thatched roof. By far the commonest of the larger boats is the flat bottomed *dunga,* 50-60ft. (15-18m) in length and 9ft. (2.75m) in girth, with a sloping roof of matting. These were capable of hauling upwards of 2,000 *maunds.*

In the Mughal era, boats had become a virtual way of life, an indispensable means for the merchant's transportation of goods. Akbar, always a man of innovation and improvement, 'disliked the shape of the boats on the Jhelum, ordered the construction of a thousand doubled-storied boats on the Bengal model and soon there was a floating city on water'.[139] During the time of Zain-ul-Abidin (r.1420-1470) specially designed sailboats plied the fresh waters of Kashmir.[140] During Mughal times Lahore and Allahabad were actually shipbuilding centres where large vessels were launched and sailed by river to the coast.[141] Jahangir speaks of almost 6,000 boats, and more than 7,000 boatmen working in the city itself and its surrounding villages. Such enormous numbers bespeak of an amazing culture that thrived on water. Today one would be hard pressed to visualize such a scene. Over a century ago (around 1836) Baron Hugel writes, about his meeting with the then Governor of Kashmir, of being picked up by the '...state boat, an unshapely affair, sixty or seventy feet long and only six feet wide and manned by thirty rowers, the seat was at the upper end and covered with Kashmir shawls, or pashmina'. This description is strongly

reminiscent of those boat-like images seen woven in the Kashmir shawls, which indeed seem 'unshapely'. The *kani*-woven boats appear as double-enders with a kind of superstructure at either end. Thus the bow and the stern may be the seating area described by the Baron, who appeared impressed by the very large vessels navigating the rivers (Plates 76 and 77).[142]

Above:
Plate 76. Boat detail of *kani rumal* (detail of WM22, page 127).
COLLECTION FONDAZIONE ANTONIO RATTI, COMO

Left:
Plate 77. Boat detail of *kani rumal* (detail of WM21, page 126).
COLLECTION FONDAZIONE ANTONIO RATTI, COMO

One possible explanation, and perhaps the most plausible, for the appearance of these strange boats seen now and then in shawls, could be from Ranjit Singh's funeral:

The Maharaja's body was placed on a decorated bier in a shape like a ship. It was wrought with gold, and the sails and flags were made of the richest silk, embroidered with gold. The vessel was placed on a board upon which the body of the Maharaja lay, and was carried by a number of men. Thousands of people accompanied the funeral, and the procession moved slowly from the interior of the fortress towards the funeral pile, where originally existed a small but beautiful garden.'[143]

It was a 'grim scene of awful grandeur' whereby four of the Maharaja's Ranis and seven of his slave-girls mounted the funeral pyre to be reduced in only seconds to ashes.[144] Although Archer says little else about the boat, one might assume – although this custom appears highly unusual for funeral ceremonies in India – that the boat is there as a vehicle to carry the deceased's soul soon to set out on its journey across the oceans of the netherworld.[145]

At the same time, the idea of the boat underscores the cultural importance of and dependence on the region's waterways to the local population (Plate 78). Fortunately, the British Museum owns an anonymous Kangra painting depicting this funeral scene, which was probably executed soon after the event. In the lower left-hand corner is a type of structure 'in the shape of a ship' with flags, or rather pennants, which are often seen on the boat structures woven into shawls (Plate 79 and WM16, page 115). While the arching superstructure dripping with garlands has yet to be found woven into *kani* designs, in between the boat's flag poles can be seen a curious chevron pattern, a pattern which often does shows up in Sikh *hashia* designs.

Although the dramatic centre fields of two spectacular and rare *rumals* in the Ratti collection (WM 21 and 22, pages 126 and 127) are drawn featuring a large arching-hulled boat (albeit stylized) with centre superstructures, it is not until we come to the Tapi Collection that

Right:
Plate 78. View of Dal Lake, Srinagar, November, 1980.

Opposite:
Plate 79. *Samadhi* (funeral) of Ranjit Singh (1780-1839), gouache, Kangra, c.1840.
British Museum, 1925-4-6-03

Detail of WM17 (see page 116).

a truly remarkable *kani* shawl appears. It is a finely woven Sikh shawl with a repetition of woven boat designs both large and small. Its superstructure is bedecked with a dazzling display of flags fluttering in the wind and its sharply curved hull is shown supporting a kind of platform (or bier) also with a chevron pattern, stretching clear across the deck, very similar to the boat in the Kangra painting. Below the staggered array of flags is a bizarre red undulating pattern which one can best describe as 'roaring flames'. Clearly, this shawl is a strikingly rare weaving, commemorating the *Samadhi* of Maharaja Ranjit Singh (WM16)

A few decades ago a very interesting shawl came on the market, the design of which depicted the clear outline of daggers, highlighted against two large perfectly round objects which could probably be taken for shields. The two daggers stand, leaning slightly on either side of what appears to be a large quiver filled with arrows fanned out in clusters. The dagger or *khanjar* is one of the five requisites of the Khalsa or Sikh Brotherhood. During this era it was curved, sharpened on both ends, carried in a sheath and stuck in one's belt or cummerbund. In those daggers seen woven here one can clearly distinguish the identifying characteristics of the quillon, hilt and pommel; and, by the exact symmetry of their finial outlines, one can visualize even the head of a horse (WM17).

Opposite above and detail below:
WM16. Kashmir long shawl
This weaving, known as the 'Ranjit Singh *samadhi* shawl', is arguably one of the most exciting shawls to have been recently discovered. The image of a boat (see detail) is undeniably similar to that found in a painting (see Plate 79) first published by Archer *(Paintings of the Sikhs)*. The exacting minutiae of the design and the fineness of the *kani* weave are executed with phenomenal dexterity in what is truly a rare historical document. The talent of the Kashmiri industry, as exhibited in this masterpiece, represents the unsurpassable heights to which the *kani* art had developed. Sikh period, c.1842.
Tapi Collection of Praful and Shilpa Shah, Surat

Above and detail opposite:
WM17. Kashmir long shawl (detail)
In this unique shawl are found not only symbols of the *Khalsa* (Sikh Brotherhood) such as daggers, but also shields, quivers, bows and arrows. Further, each of the three pairs of white-outlined, bent-tip botehs is divided above by a downward pointed arrow, which the artist has illustrated, with its carefully drawn fletching and sharply pointed head. The arching waves of the 'vibrating string' give the impression of an arrow just released from its powerful recurve bow. This may in fact be an illustration of the symbolic ideas expressed in the *Sri Guru Granth Sahib:* 'The pursuit of virtue is my bow and arrow, my quiver, sword and scabbard' or 'Take aim with the arrow of Truth, and shoot down sin' (page 16, line 17/page 15, line 9). The artist in juxtaposing bold, split-leaf, arabesque strapwork, and tripartite domes against this backdrop of weaponry has created a rare document of Sikh Punjabi culture. Sikh period, c.1830.
COLLECTION WOLFGANG WITTROCK

WM18. Kashmir long shawl (detail)
The juxtaposition of sharply contrasting primary colours and well-spaced cursive and geometric elements, unencumbered by floral overfill, provide a delightful levity and playfulness to a dramatic bold pattern. The design features a row of boats across the lower register. The boat appears to be a later rendition of that found in Ranjit Singh's Samadhi event. Sikh period, c.1840.
COLLECTION TINA AND NIRMAL MATTOO

WM19. Kashmir long shawl (see pages 122-123 for detail)
In this spectacular shawl we find a variation of the bow and arrow theme set against pendulous flowers suggesting a 'Diwali' celebration. The cursive lines of the drawn bows bisect scalloped spandrels of the Islamic mihrab arches, expressing a unique pattern.
A pattern of such complexity and elegance could only have been derived from a gifted artist imbued with a talent for expressing geometry within a harmonic framework of symphonic proportions. Sikh period, c.1835.
COLLECTION INDU PUNJ. PHOTOGRAPH SUNIL JAIN

WM20. Kashmir long shawl (detail)
The compartmentalized *palla* is what became known in France as the 'harlequin' shawl. Here the artist has employed this theme to illustrate a kind of fireworks display of 'exploding' flowers. The shawl's unique centre, a tour-de-force in creativity, is arguably one of the most elaborate and elegantly drawn patterns known among pieces of this era. This shawl most likely derived from the same weaving atelier as WM19 (page 120). Sikh period, c.1835.

Collection Indu Punj. Photograph Sunil Jain

Above:
Plate 80. A group of swords by Nainsukh. c.1760-1765, after B.N. Goswamy, *Nainsukh of Guler*, Pl. 84.
PRIVATE COLLECTION

This prompts the question: who owned daggers with horse-head finials, or were they a common occurrence?

Obviously the symbolism of the *khanjar* is one of power and strength and over time it has been utilized as decoration on flags and other heraldic devices, especially among the Arab countries (the flag of Oman, for example). It is often seen in both Qajar and Indian portraits of dignitaries. A study of a group of seven colourful swords (Plate 80) was painted (1760-65) by Nainsukh, in which he meticulously detailed their quillons, hilts and pommels, and also their finials, replete with tassels.[146] These could have been in the private collection of his patron, Balwant Singh. One could easily imagine a shawl with these motifs being offered up as tribute to or commissioned by a ruler with a passion for swords or daggers. The Sikh passion for arms led Soltykoff to remark that they were, in general, armed to the teeth: bows and arrows, shields, swords and lighted matchlocks.[147] It also appears that it was a Sikh custom – perhaps symbolizing a right of passage – for travellers crossing the Sutlej to be presented with a bow '...and two bags of money...'.[148] Imam Bakhsh, in one of his finely illustrated manuscripts of the day, depicts a man on horseback with a bow and arrows, and many of the contemporaneous Sikh paintings, especially those of the staunchly militant Guru Gobind Singh, feature the bow and arrows with religious symbolic intensity. Archer submits that bow and arrows represented emblems of state.

Although arriving after the demise of Ranjit Singh, the pomp and glitter of the Sikh culture was also observed by the traveller, Prince Alexis Soltykoff, who, mesmerized by his awesome surroundings, may have unknowingly shed light on the origins of some of the enigmatic shawl patterns encountered during this period. The Prince went on to win high honours for the many grisaille drawings he made while in Kashmir (c.1843) and in India but, unfortunately for our study of the shawl, his artistic sensitivities were bent more on monochromatic character studies rather than on detailing the colourful play of textiles that infused the local culture. In his masterful sketch, 'Cavalcade of Sikh Chieftains' (Plate 81), which depicts Dhyan Singh galloping on his horse, one discovers the Prince's highly sensitive eye to physiognomy; however, the many textiles he depicted became lost in the light washes of his *im-kalam* (half-pen technique). The Prince describes with wonder an ethereal experience:

> *The other day we were invited to pass the evening with the King (Sher Singh) whose palace is in a fortress at the other end of the city. The king received us in the open, in the midst of his warriors, in the moonlight in a vast courtyard, surrounded by vast, crenellated walls. There were thirty magnificent horses there, covered with precious stones and illuminated by torches and by a kind of Bengal fire which cast a blue light from the tops of the walls. I might mention that the Punjabis are famous for their fireworks. Seen thus the white horses, with their emerald ornaments, seemed like*

Below:
Plate 81. 'Cavalcade of Sikh Chieftains', drawing by Prince Alexis Soltykoff, c.1843, after *Indian Scenes and Characters...*, London, 1858.

dream figures, while the black ones, with their ruby decorations looked like specters from the Inferno, in the dim torch light.[149]

Spoken like the true artist, traveller and writer he was, Soltykoff paints us a surreal picture of a fabulous evening and he goes on at length to explain the Punjabis' love of fireworks, the origins of which date back, at least in Kashmir, to the period of Zain-ul-Abidin.[150] The explosive firework-like patterns noted on some of the Sikh shawls now become clear and logical; it confirms that the artists were not confined as hermits in their ateliers as one might have thought, but, on the contrary, were actively seeking new creative ideas that reflected on and mirrored contemporary culture, ideas that were a direct response to people, places and events of the day.

A particularly curious item that seems to have been adopted by the Sikh shawl 'canvas' was the quoit, a flat piece of steel, very thin, with edges highly sharpened, shaped as a lunar crescent with sharply pointed tips (Plate 82). It was part of the Akali tribe's menacing accoutrements which were forever being brandished at a moment's notice and could be employed as very deadly weapons which caused Soltykoff to observe: '...the Akalis, some of whom formed part of the royal escort, wear in their turbans sharp steel quoits which they can throw to a considerable distance, and which will break a head or slit a stomach open, in a word, which are weapons'.[151]

The Akalis, a tribe of religious fanatics, whose '...fanaticism borders on insanity', were notorious for their unmitigated ferocity and reputation as acting for the Sikh as the death squad.[152] With this notoriety, and as guardians of Amritsar, where they mostly resided, even Ranjit Singh was tactful enough to give them a wide berth. To this day one is apt to spot them in all their menacing paraphernalia wandering around the Golden Temple. The fact that this symbol found its way into the Sikh repertoire of designs (for example WM24, page 131) is perhaps consistent with the searching eyes of the shawl artisans who remained sensitive to their surrounding culture.

Plate 82. A Sikh *Akali* with quoit headdress, from *The Costumes of the People of India,* Captain W.W. Hooper and Surgeon G. Western, 1860-70, albumen print, 7⅜ x 4¾in. (18.6 x 12.2cm). VICTORIA AND ALBERT MUSEUM, NO. 0932:5

Above:
WM21. Kashmir square shawl *(rumal)*
Four tall botehs, enclosing small temples on a stunning red ground, dash toward a lotus centre with a cog-wheel vine surround. In the border we find laurel wreaths, which perhaps were inspired by the Legion of Honour medals adopted by Maharaja Ranjit Singh for his army. The two large boats were ideas also borrowed from Ranjit's Samadhi. Sikh period, c.1840.
COLLECTION FONDAZIONE ANTONIO RATTI, COMO

Opposite:
WM22. Kashmir square shawl (detail)
During the 19th century the peacock, India's national bird, was often featured on shawls and was very popular as a motif on *rumals*. However, as a bird whose symbolism extends to love and romance (especially in Indian painting), its bold depiction may also signify a marriage shawl. Here we find that the boat has become stylized, resembling more a building or *gurdwara* than anything nautical. Sikh period, c.1845.
COLLECTION FONDAZIONE ANTONIO RATTI, COMO

The residence of the Napoleonic Generals was obviously a showcase of lavish expatriate living, attracting visitors from around the globe. In the minds of an occidental, steeped in Victorian attitudes, it would be hard to imagine a setting more awe inspiring: Allard, married to a Chamba princess; Ventura, doted on by fifty slave women; a dream world with an unending stream of curious visitors composed of men of science, doctors, princes, writers and intellectuals; a Lahore *darbar* glittering in a colourful swirl of bejewelled characters mounted on horses draped in finely embroidered textiles and shawls.

The importance of the Sikh Court is underlined by Archer's list of 'Records and First Impressions by Early Travelers', which begins with Jacquemont and ends with Emily Eden.[153] The Court of Maharaja Ranjit Singh, indubitably visited by many others who came and went, anonymously, became a magnet for many Soldiers of Fortune.

While in Anarkali, Jacquemont had visited the residence shared by Allard and Ventura and recorded that they:

> *...live together in a huge house, half European and half Persian, built by them on the ruins of a Mughal palace...the rooms are decorated magnificently. The walls and ceilings are covered with mirrors in a gilt setting, or paintings or arabesques etc; everywhere Persian and Kashmir carpets of great beauty, furnishing of velvet, hangings of silk and brocade, etc.*[154]

The point is that throughout the important residences of Lahore, the admixture of European and Indian architecture, design had become an integral part of the military elite's daily lives and, by proximity, a pervading influence within the artistic community of the Himalayan valley. It is no wonder that, during this period of such intense and even radical developments, shawl patterns took off in new directions.

Alexander Burnes, visiting Lahore in 1832, made a curious observation about Ranjit Singh's Sumun Boorj Palace where, impressed by the ceiling and wall decorations, he remarked that their architectural beauty owed much to the genius of a European artist. It is unfortunate that Burnes did not elaborate on who this painter was, since the remark begs the question of whether the Generals had in their midst a western artist. Perhaps Burnes simply thought that the paintings, which had been copied by Indian natives from imported illustrations, were actually done by Europeans.[155] Describing General Ventura's house in 1836, Baron von Hugel wrote:

> *General Ventura's house, built by himself and though not of great size, combines the splendour of the East with the comfort of an European residence. On the walls of the entrance Hall, before the range of pillars on the first storey, was portrayed the reception of the two French officers at the court of Ranjit Singh, consisting of several thousand figures. The second room is adorned with a profusion of small mirrors in gilded frames, which have an excellent effect; the third is a large hall extending the entire width of the house and terminating in the sleeping apartments.*[156]

Given such activity in the decorative arts, it is obvious that the French generals under Ranjit Singh had engaged a bevy of artists.

Another traveller, William Barr, a young English lieutenant, wrote in his diary in 1839 his impressions of the mural paintings he had seen when visiting the Generals' residence. He described one area of the painted frescoes as the 'Painted Chamber' where the two generals were portrayed as engaged in battle scenes. In his naïve expressiveness, he exclaims that he was not fooled by the ridiculously skewed perspectives of upended cannons and airborne cavalry and was aghast to believe that the Generals would find this type of work ornamental. Barr, whose visit must have taken place within weeks of Allard's death (January 1839), further observes that:

> *in the room where we dined there was a portrait of General Allard....He wore at the time it was taken, a uniform similar to that of our horse-artillery, and was decorated with two orders, one the 'Legion of Honour', the other, the 'Bright Star of the Panjab', lately instituted by Ranjit Singh'.*[157]

One can only wonder at the impression such lavish decor must have made on our English guest, not to mention that he was dining in the home of two decorated generals who fought in the Napoleonic Wars.[158] Unfortunately, none of the fine frescos that served to glorify the residences remain today. Lafont and Schmitz believe that these particular frescos' themes as

Opposite:
WM23. Kashmir long shawl (detail)
Criss-crossing, tall, bent-tip botehs bob across a 'sky' filled with exploding fireworks, perhaps in celebration of Diwali, India's Festival of Lights. Sikh period, c.1845.
Museum of Fine Arts, Boston. Gift of Dr. Ananda K. Coomaraswamy, 34.170

Above left:
Plate 83. Page from *Recueil des décorations intérieurs…*, Charles Percier, Paris, 1812.

Above right:
Plate 84. Page from *Recueil des décorations intérieurs…*, Charles Percier, Paris, 1812.

described by the various nineteenth century travellers bear a direct correlation to Imam Bakhsh's works on paper and that Bakhsh may have come from a family of traditional fresco painters from Lahore.[159]

Given the showcase residence of the Generals and the impact of their Napoleonic charisma, the intense curiosity of the Sikhs for exotic items, the design geometry of the medals would have simply been another impetus towards the adoption and assimilation of 'exotic' art forms. Unlike the Mughal era, which was, in many ways, defined by the charm of the flowering plant, the decorative art of the Sikhs was, as submitted by Mulk Raj, a medium in constant search of identity; Sikh art lacked something that could serve its culture with a unifying symbol. There is no doubt that such a symbol had already tacitly developed within the architectonic patterns of the Kashmir shawl.

In more painted frescos in other buildings we find imaged the Imperial eagle and Napoleon's flag and figures of soldiers who served under Allard: lancers, dragoons and foot soldiers; Allard, himself, dressed in cuirass and Persian cap and Ventura in the costume of Sabreur de Wagram; Court in naval uniform and Avitable carrying Akbar's sword.

One is very tempted to believe that Allard and Ventura, having both established themselves and luxuriously comfortable in their decorated residences, although not exposed on a daily basis, were not completely isolated from the rich repertoire of the Empire decor that was sweeping over Europe. Like the success Napoleon had achieved on the battlefield, his architect, Charles Percier, and decorator, Leonard Fontaine, in creating the Empire style had achieved a similar triumph in the fine residences and palaces of the well-to-do. Their joint publication in 1801 and 1812, *Recueil de Décorations Intérieures* (Plates 83 and 84), which established the fundamental vocabulary for the Empire style of architecture and home decoration, became extremely influential and had many printings.[160] A direct result of Napoleon's Egyptian campaigns, it was a style, of course, that had germinated under the periods known as Directoire and Consulate (1795-1803) and then again under Napoleon's reign (1804-1815). Whether Allard or Ventura were in possession of such a useful and highly published book is not clear; that they spared no expense in lavishing the finest decorations of the region to construct their comfortable residences, basically from scratch, is indisputable. As for decorating their home with fine French fabrics and articles of European origin, this apparently presented little problem, as attested by Burnes in 1832.[161] The point of this discussion of French fabric and fashionable decoration should be weighed against several of the suspicious looking French patterns, albeit

WM24. Kashmir long shawl (detail)
Quoits, stars, temples *(gurdwaras?)* and lotuses are just a few of the many interesting design devices coming together to form what is a very powerful graphic image. This *palla* design is almost identical to a tracing by Chavant. Sikh period, c.1830.
COLLECTION BHARAT KALA BHAWAN, VARANASI, NO. 1273

on a subtle scale, found in the Kashmir shawl woven around the turn of the century.

Allard's visit to Paris must have been quite frenetic, if not exciting. Surely the highlight of his sojourn was his audience with King Louis Philippe who appointed him 'Political Agent to the Court of Lahore'. Later he was to meet scores of people requesting favours from him, including the Parisian shawl manufacturers who were expressing their discontent over the quality of the shawls arriving from Kashmir. Between Kashmir, Lahore and Calcutta, Allard and Ventura traded in shawls via the Palmer Bank in Calcutta with the help of Captain Wade, the English political agent in charge of Punjab relations.[162] Through close ties and family members travelling between Calcutta and France, Allard and Court managed their shawl trade: 'Mefredi and Falcon' acted as 'Allard's business managers [as well as] Mazar, Court's nephew and chargé d'affaires of his maternal uncle'.[163]

Thus it could be assumed that Allard and Ventura were established in the trade of shawls well before Allard's trip to France. Allard was indeed carrying tremendous responsibilities: having allegiances to two potentates, training an elite corps of Indian troops, fending off marauding attacks on Ranjit Singh's territories, overseeing his building projects, family, etc. He passed away only a few years after his return to the Punjab.

WM25. Kashmir long shawl (detail) Although it is possible to identify the lobed arches, eight-pointed stars and understand the Indu-Islamic nature of the pattern, the overall effect, with the mountainous sprays of leafy fronds and phantom botehs, remains a mystery. Sikh period, c.1830.
PRIVATE COLLECTION

William Moorcroft

Moorcroft's eight shawl gouaches, sent back to England in 1823, provide an important reference and source for boteh patterns prevalent at the time of his sojourn in Kashmir. In the first half of the nineteenth century and earlier, these coloured shawl drawings represent the only existing contemporaneous shawl art work. With the recent discovery of new Zand paintings, proving that the curvilinear boteh harks back much earlier than anyone hitherto expected, three of these gouaches, commissioned by Persian nobles, assume greater resonance.[164] The fool's cap, the aigrette, the hooked vine, the phallic or spear-like cypress and the lotus-like rose were a few of the developing motifs found within these images that became hallmarks of the Sikh period.[165] The circumstances in which Moorcroft acquired the drawings and their significance to the British industry is important. That Moorcroft happened to be in Srinagar at the time of the shawls' completion was a simple coincidence. Through a memorandum found in Moorcroft's papers, we learn that he engaged an artist to copy the patterns off the already woven shawls. This, of course, tells us that only the *talims* were available, and no one had previously bothered to commit their patterns to coloured drawings.

The eight drawings were part of a group of thirty-four designs dispatched to England.[166] Three were commissioned by a Russian noble, two by a Persian shah, one by a Persian individual and the remaining two were unsigned and destined for 'Hindoostan'. Since English taste for Kashmir shawls was more than likely very receptive to fresh and exciting designs, these drawings quite possibly had a spirited impact on English shawl fashion. They were beautifully executed, delicately painted and, to protect them from the elements, varnished to a sheen. Surely, at the time, they were considered exotic and precious works of art in themselves, containing fashion ideas for other countries besides Russia, Persia and 'Hindoostan'. Hopefully, one day, the mystery of the twenty-six lost drawings will be solved, in order to shed much needed light on contemporaneous patterns and possibly provide us with further clues as to the early beginnings of Sikh period motifs.

Plate 85. *Dochalla* (detail of long shawl). This *palla* detail approximates very closely the types of designs which Moorcroft sent back to England in 1823.
JOAN HART COLLECTION

Opposite:
WM26. Kashmir long shawl (half detail, see other detail on page 28)
From the amazing complexity of interlocking motifs emerges an awesome pattern of architectural wizardry.
Sikh period, c. 1830.
COURTESY, NATIONAL MUSEUM, NEW DELHI. PHOTOGRAPH BY SUNIL JAIN

The Metropolitan Museum of Art acquired these eight drawings (all signed by Moorcroft) in 1962 and a year later they were written up by Caroline Karpinski in the MET's journal (Plate 86).[167] In her attempt to critique the cone patterns destined for Persia, Karpinski observed a 'lyrical linear emphasis' – a style drawn from Persian miniature painting, which contrasted with those destined for 'Hindoostan' bearing a style of 'fat, more naturalistically painted flower bunches'. Of course, observations such as these, based on so few of the remaining lot of paintings, could only be highly speculative. Yet, brief as they were, Karpinski's remarks were prescient and offered the first hint of a multifaceted school of shawl design. The 'lyrical linear emphasis' makes up for the lack of modelling and shading and, therefore, any floral plasticity which the artist may have wanted to impart to the distinctive mosaic petals and flattened circles. The question remains as to whether this linear emphasis was indeed limiting, in the sense that the artist avoided depicting large petal flowers and therefore focused on, for example, zinnias, gerberas, primroses and chrysanthemums – all blossoms defined by tiny petals, lending themselves more easily to the weaver's loom technique of *kani* weaving. Large swatches of colour would have been easier and less time consuming to weave, but obviously labour was so cheap that the complexity of the pattern was insignificant to the final cost of the shawl. The question of plasticity and shading in *kani* weaving was actually resolved in France during the early efforts of the French to produce their own *kani* shawls (see Chapter 5, Kashmiri Manuscripts, page 182 for further discussion of this). The motifs mentioned above demonstrate the shift away from Afghan stereotypes towards

Plate 86. Indian painting of boteh, gouache on paper, varnished, written on reverse: 'Pherozee (Turquoise colour), No. 23, By order of Mahummud Azeem Khan', from Moorcroft's shawls patterns dispatched to England in 1823.
Metropolitan Museum of Art. 62.600.235 (8)

an indigenous Indian style that was not immune to its Sikh environment.

Moorcroft's published notes on lacquer work in Kashmir and his first-hand account of how the shawl artist created his work appear to be the only detailed recorded accounts of such processes. In describing his personal experience of observing the shawl artist, our famous entrepreneur records:

> *These artists employ neither chalk nor lead pencil, nor compasses, but with an eye of great accuracy and with a hand sure of its work, present at once to lay on their colours and execute the design with a fidelity and dispatch that with difficulty could be equalled and could not, I conceive, be surpassed by the ablest artists of Europe.*

Moorcroft adds:

> *In the course of a half a day and a night, an artist belonging to Raja Sunsar Chund (Sansar Chand) from drawings of mine, made two copies of patterns for his master which with difficulty, I could distinguish from the originals. Such could only have been executed in Britain by miniature painters and at heavy expense on account of the minuteness of the details of the flowers and the great variety of the colours, yet this artist's wages did not cost fifteen roupees a month.*[168]

It is possible that this Kangra artist was already known by Moorcroft since he had visited Sansar Chand before his arrival in Kashmir. At that time Moorcroft wrote of the munificent patron: 'He is fond of drawing, employs several artists who execute the minute parts with great fidelity, but are almost wholly ignorant of perspective. His collection of drawings is very great'.[169] One can only speculate over the number of visiting artists from other Indian regions who sojourned in Kashmir. Obviously here the new alliance in 1809 (both dictatorial and matrimonial) struck between Sansar Chand and Ranjit Singh had possibly stirred up a new exchange of artistic interactions in the Kashmir-Lahore-Hill States nexus. There is no doubt that the downfall (1809) of Sansar Chand, a raja whose obsession for painting was matched only by his resolute devotion to his caste origins, resulted in the dispersal of many of his artists.

In this particular section of his voluminous manuscript, Moorcroft seems to encounter one frustration after another in procuring an artist to accompany him in his travels and to assist him in recording the clothing, dress, implements and various other native folk articles – all items which he thought Britain could manufacture and sell profitably in 'Tartary' and China. In his first attempt, Moorcroft offered a huge sum of money to one man who worked for the aforementioned Raja, but the artist refused to leave his safe position. Another artist, whose engagement with Moorcroft was completely voluntary, executed a daring nocturnal escape. At the time of his note taking, Moorcroft records that, despite his generous offers to the artists and their families, his success was still very uncertain because all the artists were afraid, due to political unrest, to travel to Bukhara. However, there would not have been a problem in travelling to 'Hindoostan' or even Britain.[170]

While in Srinagar Moorcroft happened to purchase about thirty old fresco paintings which turned out to be for him a treasure trove of rich textile designs, and of which he took great advantage. Engaging local artists, his goal was to produce two to three thousand patterns from these frescos which could be used as chintz designs, perhaps for the Oriental markets. He points out that among his 'employees' was one special artist, Mohammad Joo, who, according to Sharma's thesis, was 'the most intelligent of all the artists in the early phase of Sikh rule'.[171] Such huge quantities of chintz patterns stand out starkly against the puny number of shawl patterns Moorcroft had purchased and sent back to England. 'To the indefatigable Moorcroft', as Irwin asserts, 'obsessed with the idea of making British shawls supreme over all competitors…', one

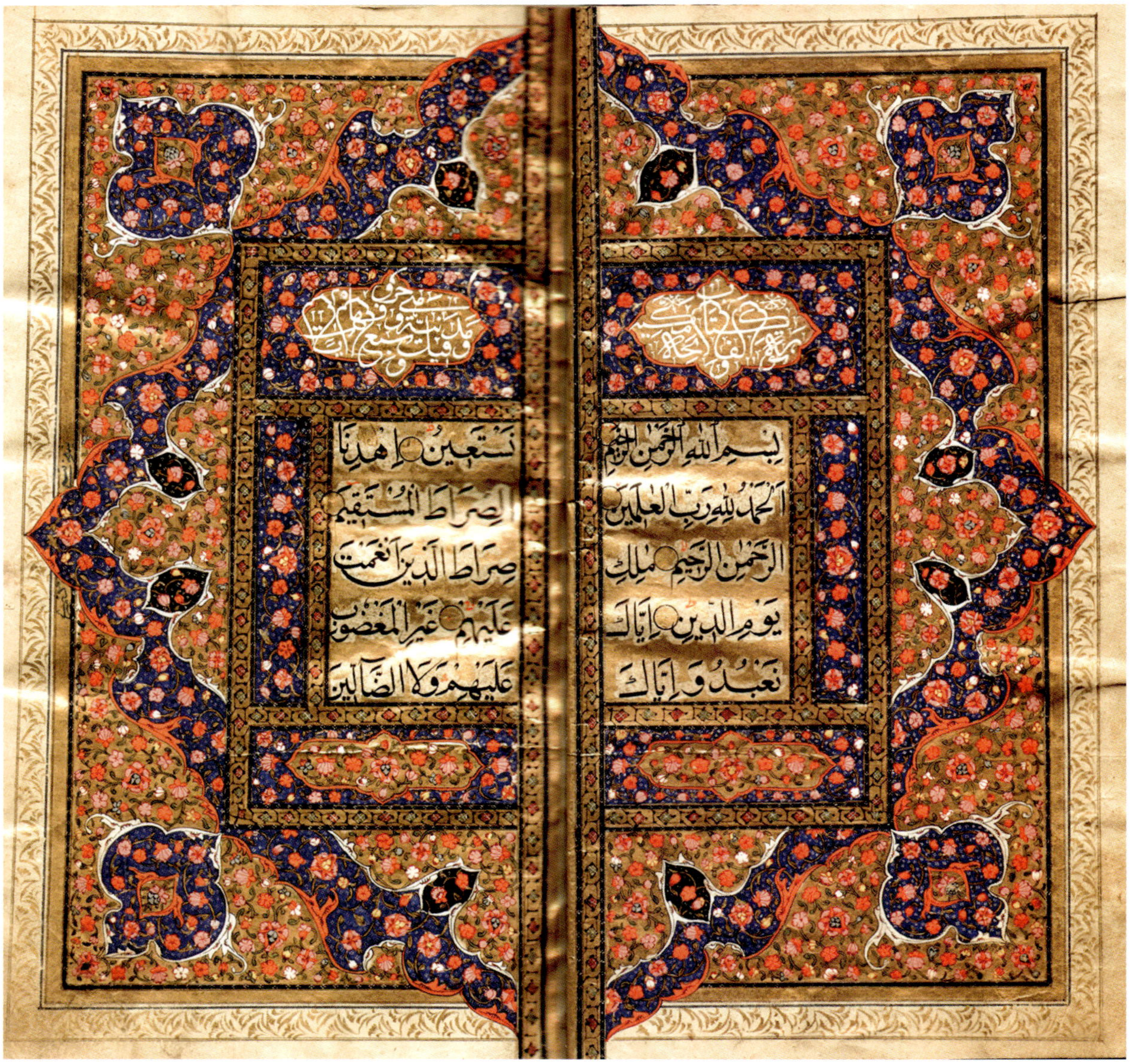

Plate 87. Illuminated bifolio, Islamic manuscript. The colophon reads: 'The writing and illuminating of this book was completed at the capital of Kashmir in the year 1000/1669'.
COURTESY ISRAEL MUSEUM, JERUSALEM, 814.69

finds it hard to believe in his shipment of only thirty-four shawl drawings to England.[172]

Moorcroft's sharp eye also recorded the various steps with which workers of papier-mâché lacquered pen-boxes plied their trade. Besides the variety and elegance of the painting, he was very impressed by the brilliant colours and beautiful varnish. He goes on to describe the metallic ground colours and the different pigments of cochineal, kermis insect, ultramarine from Yarkand, white lead from Russia and verdigris from Surat, or possibly from Britain, and to further detail the various sources of varnish. The fine brushes were made from the hair of the shawl-wool goat and the 'pencils' from cat fur. The process of ornamenting or 'embossing' parts of the painting is also discussed by Moorcroft. Before the arrival of the Sikh, this craft must have been one of the largest and busiest in Srinagar, considering that upwards of 1,200 natives moved about in *palkees* (palanquins) all worked in papier-mâché.[173]

One is curious to learn that Moorcroft employed ten manuscript copyists to churn out *Rajataranginis, Nilmat Purans* and *Vrihat Kathas,* but, despite this close contact with the artisans, he mentions nothing about manuscript painting or lacquer book-binding.[174] Moorcroft's faithful dedication to his country's quest for new ideas of trade, commerce, science and art – to the extent that he often put his life in danger – was so great that it would be hard to imagine anything escaping his tireless and constant investigations of industrious endeavours. His

Christian leanings certainly were not a hindrance to his scientific dedication since he was of the type that '...took all things and all men on their merits without prejudice, certain there was something to be learned from all'. Given the rough, rugged and pestilential surroundings in which he worked and the amount of investigating, writing and doctoring he performed, his accomplishments are simply staggering. It should be recalled that, as a doctor in Kashmir, Moorcroft quickly acquired a reputation as a great healer and was often treating upwards of some '300 poor wretches in a single day'.[175]

Arriving in Srinagar about a decade later, Jacquemont, on the other hand, observed between 700 to 800 manuscript copyists, transcribing and illuminating pages in colour and in gold, by order only, of the Koran or *Shahnameh,* plus a small number of other books.[176] He points out that almost a generation earlier, under the kings of Kabul, the business of making books was much greater. Although few Kashmiris spoke Arabic, trade was brisk with colourful gold manuscripts selling for the highest price.[177] It was often the custom for religious manuscripts to be illustrated with a beautifully gilded double page with a graphic pattern, sometimes with split-leaf arabesques and floral infill or with a kind of heavy strap-work Islamic pattern coloured in with burnished lapis lazuli and gold outlining (Plate 87). Here there is no doubt that some of these typically Islamic designs were incorporated into the Kashmir shawl. Barbara Schmitz has noted that, in comparison to Srinagar, in Lahore 'the tastes of the book buyers were much more catholic'.[178] Besides the usual religious items such as the Korans and *Shahnamehs,* the Lahori scribes were busy copying and illustrating historical, scientific and cosmological books. The list included books on Persian literature, and poetry, Hindu classics, animal husbandry, military training and sex manuals. Although it seems that both the secular and sacred in this capital of the Sikh Kingdom coexisted, in fact such was not the case, for example, in Amritsar, where 'the religion of Nanak admits no rivals...'.[179]

Although Jacquemont noted many hundreds of copyists, their gold work fetching a premium, his observations leave us uninformed as to the distinctive characteristics that set the Kashmiri manuscripts apart from those made in other countries. The most often used colour is bright orange, and then purple and pink; gold and the rich blue of lapis lazuli were polished smooth with agate stone for the brilliantly illuminated pages of bifolios. An interesting phenomenon that appears to develop at the turn of the nineteenth century, however, is the creation of a 'white outline' style (Plate 88). Flower petals are delineated with white; this is often seen in contemporaneous lacquer binding. Whether the style originated from shawl or lacquer artists is not clear but it is known that the opening up of new markets in Central Asia often necessitated a shift in colour palette: the khans and emirs commissioned shawls with dark colours, often deep reds, blues or blacks as ground colours. This exerted new efforts on the part of the *tarah guru* to better contrast his flowers. This idea is seen in the well-known

Plate 88. Kashmir long shawl (detail), illustrating the use of 'white outlining'.
BHARAT KALA BHAWAN, BANARAS

pashmina prayer carpet at the Metropolitan Museum of Art (Plate 89), an excellent and rare example of an Indian carpet reflecting a shawl *naqqash's* contribution. The flat radial flowers and precisely regimented racemes show floral styles (with white outlining) that are found in contemporaneous shawl patterns popular at the end of the eighteenth to early nineteenth century.

The flowers found in lacquer painting most associated with that of the Kashmir shawl style derived from the industry of religious manuscripts and papier-mâché craft items such as the very popular pen boxes *(kalamkars)*. Finely painted flowers of Kashmiri crafts, outside lacquer, appear to be virtually nonexistent. The problem one has in studying manuscript sources of the late eighteenth or early nineteenth century is that they are for the most part undated.[180] The boteh seems not to appear in any Kashmiri lacquer works prior to c.1800. This fact supports the idea that the curvilinear boteh was still limited to shawls and had not made its way into the mainstream of Indian painting, as it had about a generation earlier in Iran. Curiously, in order to find interesting dated lacquer pieces, one has to turn outside this time frame. In doing so, one would be hard pressed to find any comparison between a lacquer floral style equal to that of the floral style of the shawl, as lacquer works are, for the most part, meticulously drawn in a very realistic manner.

We know from Moorcroft's observation in Srinagar that the artist was capable of drawing directly on to the paper and quickly finishing, freehand-style, a completed buta painting. So it doesn't seem possible that the mosaic style evolved by the transfer from a natural drawing first. Yet in one of Moorcroft's drawings one can see the extent to which naturalism can take form, given the artist's rendition that restricted him to *kani* penmanship. Despite the flattening of the flowers and their chaotic mélange, one can see a concerted effort by the hand of the artist to carefully delineate each flower and stem, to create a wonderful pattern which, according to Moorcroft, had been already woven as a shawl (Plate 90).

Opposite:
Plate 89. Prayer carpet, *pashmina*, late 18th century, Kashmir.
Metropolitan Museum of Art. Gift of Joseph V. McMullan, 1970 (1970.302.7)

Left:
Plate 90. Indian painting of boteh, gouache, from Moorcroft's shawl patterns dispatched to England in 1823.
Metropolitan Museum of Art. 62.600.235

If a *tarah* guru was normally employed, then obviously the *naqqash* had only to hand over to the weavers his completed black and white sketch, who in turn placed it on the loom to keep it in view as they manipulated the *tojis* (small sticks of wood wrapped with *pashmina* in various colours). Weavers always worked on the reverse side of the shawl, so without crawling underneath the loom to see the developing fabric, there was no way to observe the pattern, except by the sketch. At the start of weaving, the *tarah* guru's job was to call out the appropriate colours for the weavers, and for the *talim* guru as well, who dutifully recorded

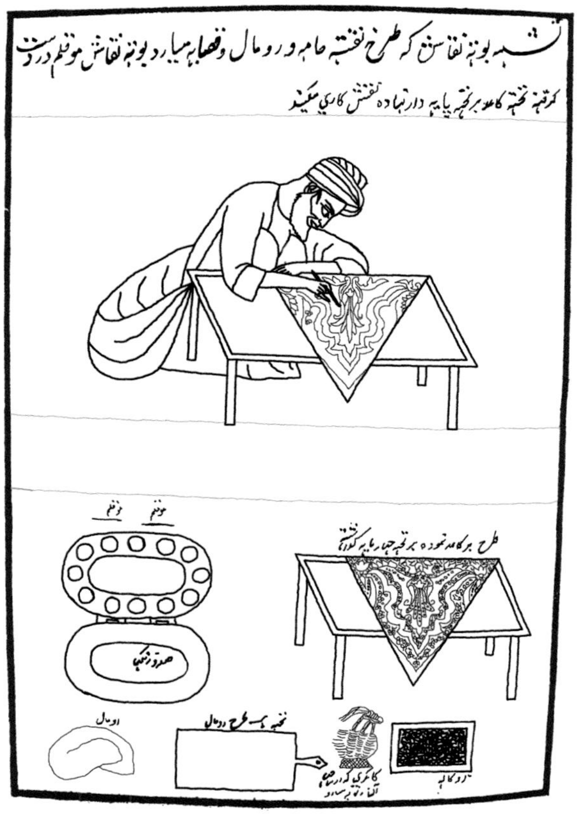

Above:
Plate 91. *Naqqash* at work (tracing), after J. Irwin, *The Kashmir Shawl*, 1973, fig. 2.

Opposite:
Plate 92. The Court of Lahore by August Schoefft, 1855.
PHOTOGRAPH COURTESY OF JEAN-MARIE LAFONT

the warp number and weft colours into his secret code on a card (*talim*). Although it was the *naqqash* (pattern drawer) who earned the most, the colour caller's work appeared to be no less demanding, for he obviously had to call upon long experience which enabled him to choose his colours well, according to the complexity of the design, which he did on an ad hoc basis. The *tarah* guru could be expected to know from memory about four or five designs. A new or exceptional pattern may have required the careful attention of both *naqqash* and colour guru to assure that the fabric and *talim* were wrought successfully.[181] For a row of eighteenth century botehs, where the flowers were arranged either symmetrically or asymmetrically around the boteh's central axis, it must have been a challenge to achieve the right harmony. With the arrival of the expansive Sikh patterned shawls and seamless panels, which were often quite large, one can only wonder how these weaving gurus were able to record, if at all, such an amazing amount of warp/weft/colour information on to the *talim*.

According to Moorcroft's notes, we come up with anywhere from thirty to forty *naqqashs* remaining in Srinagar.[182] However, another reference notes that by the end of Sikh rule only six or seven families were actively engaged in this field.[183] Sharma estimates the number of *naqqashs* in Srinagar at around thirty, and about one hundred colour callers and twenty *talim* gurus, during the time of Moorcroft's visit – a credible number, given the difficulty he had in trying to employ an artist for his travels.[184] This number may have something to do with the shift to complex patterns beginning to develop at this time, where it was impossible to call out or even recall the colours for such complex designs.[185] One might surmise that it was only the simpler boteh patterns which required the use of the colour callers while the more complex designs were patterns that had already been coloured in. This is obviously evident in the mid-nineteenth century painting illustrated by Irwin which depicts a *naqqash* leaning intensely over a table upon which he is tracing out a Dogra pattern on a triangular piece of paper. The pattern is clearly one destined to serve in the making of a patchwork type shawl, one comprised of many pieces, each sewn in with an invisible stitch. In the painting's lower register, we see the artist's colour kit, completed drawing and other paraphernalia of his trade (Plate 91).

August Schoefft

The magnetic pull of Lahore with its colourful and charismatic reputation and its multi-ethnic spectrum of warriors, costumes and foreign intrigues must have represented an undeniable attraction to artists, not least among whom was the gifted Austro-Hungarian artist, August Schoefft. For the study of Sikh period shawls, Schoefft's presence in Lahore in 1841 provides us with important elements in our study. He was lucky enough to be witness to one of the most colourful events to take place in India in the nineteenth century. Through his sharp powers of observation and retention of detail he was able to recreate, ten years later while in St. Petersburg, an oil painting of the glittering Lahore court scene held at the marble Baradari (Plate 92).

Plate 93. The Baradari in 1980.
PHOTOGRAPH BY THE AUTHOR (1981)

Of the magnificent sweep of scintillating characters that people his painting, Aijazuddin remarks: 'Schoefft resurrected on one canvas the self-destructive lemming-like policies of the ruling sardars and presented their darbar as a fiery meteor, glowing for a final moment before it exploded into fragments'.[186]

'Glowing fiery meteor' would also be a very apt observation of the distinctly visible and fabulous shawl patterns depicted in this chef-d'oeuvre, which Schoefft had most likely detailed with meticulous care in his preliminary sketches. But as much as his skill could capture with 'astonishing quickness' the likenesses of people, one might still find it difficult to understand how, ten years later. he was able to replicate a complicated shawl pattern in his oil painting. To answer this, one could point out that Kashmir shawls were often exchanged for services rendered. Schoefft's work in portraiture for Maharaja Sher Singh and the various principals of the court were, in my opinion, rewarded by the very shawls that figure in his paintings and which he more than likely packed up with him as treasured souvenirs upon leaving Lahore after a year of residence.

The twenty-nine year old artist took imaginative artistic licence in sketching the Baradari or audience hall of the Lahore Fort. To begin with, the Baradari's facade actually contains five scalloped-spandrel *mihrab* arches (Plates 92 and 93) instead of the three he painted. In doing this, he was able to broaden the openings, enabling the placement on stage under the arches of his numerous characters. He then lifted the height of the structure and rotated it outward, making an oblique angle with the Lahore Gate. This created a noble and awesome edifice giving increased power to an already charged scene. Carefully incorporated into this architectural ploy, Schoefft found an ingenious way to suspend three magnificent

Kashmiri shawls whose initial purpose would have been to block the strong rays of the sun in such a way that they could easily be raised or lowered. The widening of the arches allowed him to fully unfurl the shawls within, completely filling the columned spandrels, and at the same time making the shawl's width appear unusually large. Schoefft obviously had many choices of textiles and shawls to choose from, and it was not by chance that his final choice was a type of shawl most enjoyed by the Sikhs.

On the surface, one might be a little surprised that our European artist, whose education was most likely steeped in the classic and most popular French tradition of painting, did not succumb to those types of shawl patterns which often figured in the paintings by the great Napoleonic artists such as Baron Gros, Ingres, and David; in other words, these were the long diaphanous *dochallas* with mostly plain fields of *pashmina* and *pallas* decorated with simply botehs, a design which certainly would have simplified his painting. Schoefft would have none of it. This scene of Oriental pageantry he was capturing was not only a unique moment in time but also an important statement of Sikh fashion. While the shawl pattern he had chosen was not only one that epitomized those motifs that were extremely popular for the Sikhs, its particularly convoluted style was also a symbolic statement reflecting on the thrilling atmosphere unfolding in the almost one hundred people that animated his canvas. In Aijazuddin's examination of Schoefft's painting and the various religious groups that made up Ranjit Singh's kingdom, Aijazuddin astutely pointed out that:

> *He deliberately composed his picture to reflect the paradox inherent in the Sikh kingdom, the contradictory circumstances under which devout Muslims and practising Hindus served a Sikh Maharaja with a devotion that the Sikhs themselves could not rival. The loyalty of these communities, though, remained, like some sacred thread of friendship, attached to his person only.*[187]

Plate 94. Wall mural inside and on the back wall of the Baradari. This is the only period wall decoration in Lahore found with botehs. The design is reminiscent of Islamicate *sarlauhs* seen in illuminated manuscripts and, as such, highlights the links of Islamic art with the Sikh Khalsa. PHOTOGRAPH BY THE AUTHOR (1981)

While the 'sacred thread' was perhaps not a defined part of the woven shawls that Schoefft had carefully chosen for his masterpiece, the powerful effect of their convoluted designs dangling just above the monarch's head indeed appeared to have been religiously embraced by the congregating Sikh warriors.

To produce this effect, our young artist had chosen two richly ornamented shawls whose centres contained large open areas of plain *pashmina* surrounded by busy floral infill. It is obvious that both shawls are very similar in design; in fact, in all probability they are indeed a matching pair *(dochallas),* though the far one appears to have a tan ground colour while the one more in focus, and closer to the viewer, shows a lighter ground than the former, an effect which may be due to Schoefft's lighting effects. The latter one has a *palla* filled with a swirling display of multicoloured interlacing snake-like motifs that seem to be constantly in a state of motion, mirroring, in a way, the scene of the milling crowd below. With fairly large scale designs there are also several shawls which serve as saddles for two horses, while a few people in the crowd appear to be dashingly draped in Kashmir shawls.

Thus through the eyes of the gifted Schoefft we learn, by his ability to capture faces, costumes and textiles, so much more about the Sikh culture, yet, as a result, through a nostalgic longing, we also bemoan the many more rich tableaux he could have created, had he arrived in Lahore only a few years earlier.

Imam Bakhsh Lahori

Except that he descended from the Chughtai family, claiming roots from Kabul, little is known of Imam Bakhsh Lahori's biography. While there appears to be no direct link of Bakhsh to shawl weaving, since so little else is known about artists working in the region his artistic activities merit examination. Bakhsh's talents first became known in Europe in 1862, through his signed illustrations in a book of La Fontaine's fables, commissioned through Allard during his brief sojourn in Paris in 1835 by Félix Feuillet de Conches, a foreign affairs

Plate 95. General Court's residence at Lahore, by Imam Bakhsh Lahori, c.1835.
Musée National des Arts Asiatiques, Guimet, Paris

official with the government of France.[188] However, Bakhsh's reputation had already been firmly established in India even before his illustrations reached Europe. Before they were dispatched abroad, many important people within the Allard coterie had enjoyed the opportunity to admire their fine execution and charm. It is interesting that Bakhsh most certainly had drawn inspiration for his illustrations from the library of General Allard, where the latter had kept a copy of Akbar's *Tutinama*, adding supporting evidence that Allard was directly involved in the transfer of artistic ideas to the local artists, and that his shawl manufacturing ventures might also have been closely intertwined with his own aesthetic sensibilities. Lafont avers that Bakhsh 'used many details [of the *Tutinama*] for his own paintings'.[189] It is known, for example, that both Generals were in possession of a French military manual *(manuel d'infanterie)* in which they invested a great amount of attention in seeing to its Persian translation and lavish illustration by the painter, Imam Bakhsh, in 1825.[190] With the defeat (1803) of the French by the British in the Ganga-Jumna *doab,* many of those already trained in the French military system sought employment in the Sikh army. The military manual could easily have found its way to Lahore during this time or, more likely, with the arrival in 1813 of Ganga Ram, the former *diwan* of Bourquien, who, along with his son arriving a year later, was engaged by Ranjit Singh to take charge of his army units and artillery.[191]

Imam Bakhsh had to be the busiest artist working in the Punjab, finding time to paint frescos, creating fifty-nine masterpiece illustrations for Feuillet, producing ninety colourful illustrations of people, places and events while travelling with General Court (Plate 95) for his 1200 page Memoir, not to mention his contribution to numerous other book and manuscript projects. Bakhsh's talents were drawn upon also by the Transylvanian mercenary, Dr. Martin Honigberger, who had arrived in Lahore in 1829, to illustrate his autobiography *Thirty Five Years in the East,* published in 1835 (Plate 96). Add to this workload portraits of the nobility and military officers and it becomes hard to believe that Bakhsh did not surround himself with a coterie of other gifted apprentice artists.[192] Close to a hundred manuscripts illustrated in his style can be found in institutions throughout India and Europe. His prolific works continued throughout the nineteenth century to be heavily copied and illustrated in many publications. According to Lafont and Schmitz, Imam Bakhsh's 'contribution to the art of the Punjab is equal to or exceeds any by Pahari artists… Lahore itself had given birth to an active school of miniature painting'.[193]

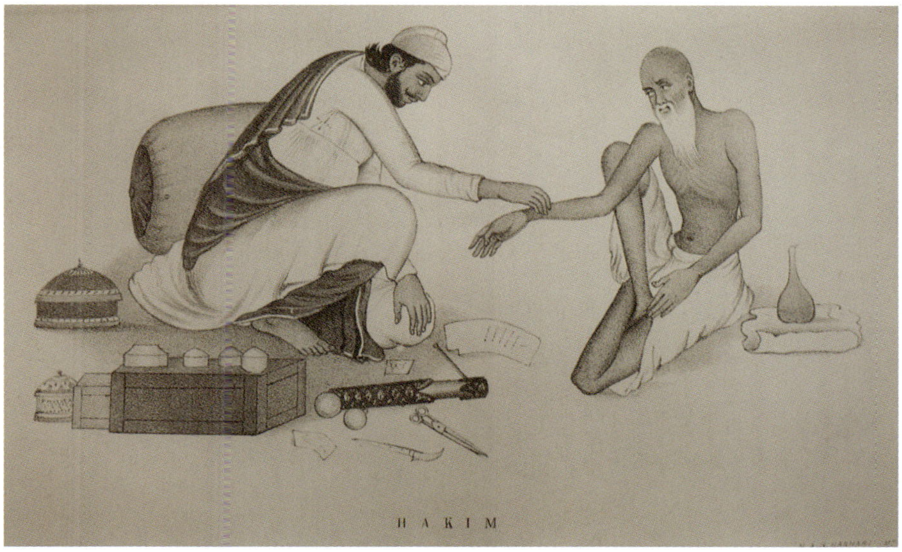

Plate 96. Medicine man, by Imam Bakhsh Lahori, after Honigberger's *Thirty Five Years in the East.*

As perhaps the pre-eminent talent in the Punjab, Bakhsh must have equally worked on many artistic projects under Ranjit Singh. We learn from Vigne that the latter had commissioned two shawls, at the sum of 50,000 rupees, to illustrate his battle victories, of which one was supposedly completed.[194] Pictorial shawls woven in the *kani* technique are extremely rare. They represent valuable insights into the working aesthetics of the shawl artists. On occasion one comes across a *kani* shawl with various objects, or human and animal figures (for example, the Shikarga shawls, Plate 121), but if the pattern has to do with a major pictorial subject, such as the map of Srinagar, or Persian literature narratives, or, in this case, battle victories, the embellishing technique would have most certainly been

Plate 97. Painting illustration by Imam Bakhsh Lahori, 1837-39, 'Phébus and Borée' from Jean de la Fontaine's *Fables*.
COURTESY MUSÉE JEAN DE LA FONTAINE, CHÂTEAU THIERRY

done in embroidery and usually in a *rumal* format. Such work would not have been undertaken by the ordinary Kashmiri *naqqash* who created designs for *kani* weavings but it would have fallen into the hands of a more worldly artist, possessing the vision and intellectual capacity to tackle complex and expensive projects.

Perhaps, it is not such a coincidence that, corresponding to this period, an unusual number of map shawls have been found. Being able to tackle large projects such as map making certainly would have been within the multi-talented realm of the *musavvir* Bakhsh and his atelier. With the jockeying for power and land during the early years of the nineteenth century, among the Sikhs of Lahore, the Gurkhas to the East, the princes of the Hill States, the British of the Cis-Sutlej and, last, but not least, Raja Gulab Singh of Jammu, the political map of India was being carved up faster than map makers could put compass to paper. One of the duties of the Ranjit Singh's *nizam,* Desa Singh Majithia, who was dispatched to the Kangra fort, was to make a survey of the Hill States. Oddly enough, Delhi too was experiencing a topographical phenomenon whereby local monuments were suddenly attracting renewed interest by the late Mughal nobility as well as by the English residents and the local artists themselves, many of whom came from Agra.[195]

Scattered in various collections, at present we know of a dozen finely embroidered shawls with fabulously animated scenes of courting, pageantry, celebration, processions, marching soldiers, mythology, etc, whose designs have hitherto experienced little study. One thing stands out among every embroidered shawl of merit: the concept of *horror vacui*, where the need to embellish every nook and cranny of a design becomes obsessive. Bakhsh was capable of understanding and articulating the fables of La Fontaine into fascinating and colourful dreamy images of a surreal world in which lissome animals converse, horses and lions assume anthropomorphic qualities, while overhead Greco-Roman chariots fly through the skies (Plate 97).

If Bakhsh was a talented animal painter, he was no less gifted in his representation of the human characters who peopled his world of painting. La Fontaine's fables provided him with a unique outlet to express a creativity that transcended the normal working projects which were commissioned of him, insofar as he was able to place himself in a fantasy world where exact likenesses were not required and also where he could easily articulate design ideas which he had obviously assimilated from foreign sources, such as the eighteenth century frigate shown in the 'L'huitre et les Plaideurs' (Plate 98) or in 'Le renard et les raisins' where he paints a 'charmille', an elegant leafy grape-laden arbor. or, as previously stated, a mixture

Left:
Plate 98. Painting illustration by Imam Bakhsh Lahori, 1837-39, 'The Oyster and the Arguers' from Jean de la Fontaine's *Fables*.
COURTESY MUSÉE JEAN DE LA FONTAINE, CHÂTEAU THIERRY

Below:
Plate 99. Painting illustration by Imam Bakhsh Lahori, 1837-1839. 'The Love of Mars and Venus' from Jean de La Fontaine's *Fables*.
COURTESY MUSÉE JEAN DE LA FONTAINE, CHÂTEAU THIERRY

of Indian and Greco-Roman elements in 'Phébus et Borée'. In his 'L'homme et la couleuvre' ('The Man and the Snake') one encounters a pavilion with a roof made of bamboo with a Far-Eastern look.[196] Some of Bakhsh's designs, either through his possible shawl endeavours or paintings, may have found their way into European shawls, since Parisian artists were constantly searching for novelty in the marketing of their Jacquard loomed products.[197] In his 'The Love of Mars and Venus' (Plate 99) we not only encounter Bakhsh's love of winged creatures, so often found in the fine Kashmiri *rumal* embroideries of the period (WM15, page 109), but also the Sikh chair with its slender curved arms, which Archer points out as a typical characteristic (among others) of Guler painting. One does wonder if Bakhsh's atelier apprentices were on hand to detail many of his paintings, given that so many of the animals were not drawn from nature but imagined or copied from other idealized sources. For example, one finds tigers sporting bizarre manes, wolves resembling foxes, vultures resembling falcons, etc.

At present about two hundred works of art are known to exist by Bakhsh, providing a

Left:
Plate 100. Embroidered *rumal* (detail), Kashmir, c.1840.
TEXTILE MUSEUM, WASHINGTON, D.C. ACC. NO. 6.258

Below:
Plate 101. Miniature painting by Imam Bakhsh Lahori.
NEW YORK PUBLIC LIBRARY SPENCER, INDO-PERS. MS. 19

substantial corpus of reference material for future research. A sumptuously embroidered shawl (Plate 100) at the Textile Museum appears to show off this similar *quissa* or fairytale world of playfulness and fantasy.[198] The handsome white steed, reminiscent of Ranjit Singh's beloved horse, Layla, is captured in full gallop, mounted by a richly dressed Sikh in striped silks, while birds scoot above (something typically Bakhsh) and a playful mermaid-body winged angel flees a barking dog by leaping into the night air. In the same shawl, flanking the other side of three well-dressed characters of dubious stations in life, marching with raised sticks or perhaps swords, is a wonderfully rendered green horse and colourful rider. One can discern the horse's teeth and also a slight patch of white on the horse's face, a detail often applied to Bakhsh's horses. A complete discussion of this *rumal* will be left for future study. The few details covered here from this amazing shawl, filled with hundreds of human characters and animals, was done to highlight the characteristics of design which could only have

Plate 102. Painting illustration by Imam Bakhsh Lahori, 1837-39, 'The Horse and the Fox' from Jean de la Fontaine's *Fables*.
Courtesy Musée Jean de la Fontaine, Château Thierry

come from the pen of a consummate artist, certainly an artist capable of parading people and animals in a bizarre world of unabashed fantasy. Burnes experienced this fantasy first hand in 1831. While riding next to Ranjit Singh on a sports outing, he was obviously impressed by the 'elegant saddle-cloth of the richest embroidery, ornamented in its border by almost every beast and bird which the sportsman calls his own'.[199]

Among the fine miniatures coming from the hand of this illustrious artist is the Spencer manuscript at the New York Public Library.[200] Ten finely executed paintings provide us with a few further inimitable characteristics to the artist. They also bespeak of an artist who was, earlier on, influenced by artistic conventions of the Pahari school – to wit, the angularity of the pools or streams of water or flocks of birds sailing high on the horizon (Plate 101) – while the Lahori school is apparent in the artist's way of showing only the tops of heads of soldiers with their bodies hidden behind hills of vivid blue, purple or fiery orange. Bakhsh's hills, usually of solid washes of colour, were often dappled with tiny mounds of soil from which sprigs of grass would squeak out from all sides. For those seeking to pursue his equestrian studies vis-à-vis shawls, besides the three brilliantly illuminated *sarlauh* folios found in the manuscript, five of the nine miniatures contain horses (Plate 102).

Fine shawl embroidery seems to have

Plate 103. Embroidered *rumal* (detail), map of Srinagar, c.1850.
VICTORIA AND ALBERT MUSEUM, LONDON

Plate 104. Embroidered *rumal* (detail), shawl of Maharaja Gulab Singh, embroidered by Sayyad Joo, Jammu, dated 1852, *pashmina*.
COURTESY GOVERNMENT MUSEUM AND ARTS GALLERY, CHANDIGARH

Plate 105. Elaborately embroidered *rumal* (detail) with hundreds of people and animals. c.1850.
PRIVATE COLLECTION

reached a high point of virtuosity in Kashmir in the mid-nineteenth century, as attested by several magnificent extant specimens in public and private collections. The Victoria and Albert Museum's map *rumal,* arguably one of the most fine needle-worked shawls ever executed, is more than likely a reflection of the traverse or route surveys which the British undertook during the eighteenth century in India (Plate 103). The exploration of new territories and unknown districts demanded the services of professional map makers whose expertise was at the time limited to observations of the 'picturesque as an aesthetic convention'.[201] Although these maps were not accurate, they possessed a fine descriptive quality. By 1800 British map making in India was superseded by the new and precise geometrical system that was based on triangulation, known as trigonometric surveying.[202] The Victoria and Albert Museum's embroidered map is perhaps, on one hand, a strong antidotal statement of a return to the lost aestheticism of the earlier maps whose narrative and artistically colourful qualities often imbued them with an irresistible charm. On the other hand, it may indicate a subtle conflict with British colonial rule whose legitimacy in India had gained the high ground through the adoption of this map making science that 'would not only result in India's progress but would also improve geodesy'.[203] The new maps coming from the 'Geographical and Geometric Survey Department' of the British Army were devoid of this aestheticism. Whether Imam Bakhsh actually had a hand in the artistic development of these fabulous map shawls is unknown. The study of Bakhsh's architectural drawings, as well as those of his Indian contemporaries, may in the future shed further light on a subject about which very little is known.[204]

A truly historic, embroidered *rumal* at the Government Museum and Art Gallery in Chandigarh is dated to 1852 and had been created as a gift for Maharaja Gulab Singh (Plate 104). Of this *rumal* B.N. Goswamy notes in his description:

> *This justly admired piece, most richly embroidered, on a light green ground, features thus hundreds of figures; kings and warriors; musicians, courtiers and attendants. Whole scenes are envisioned, the designer undoubtedly drawing his inspiration from illustrations of the celebrated texts [Shahnameh, Sikandar nameh] that he must have known from manuscripts.*[205]

Included with the date is the name of the Sayyad Joo, who calls himself the *rafugar,* a resident of the *chakla* of Jammu in the land of Kashmir. What is very interesting is that there is no mention of the artist. Given that *naqqashs* were supposedly the highest paid, this is curious indeed. Unlike the Chandigarh shawl, so many of these super fine embroidered *rumals* have not been signed and remain completely anonymous, such as the one from an anonymous collection, in Plate 105. A serious study of all the great known embroidered *rumals* is an area that needs to be

Plate 106. Chamba *rumal,* embroidered, late 19th century.
COLLECTION BHARANY

addressed. Elaborate *rumals* such as these, with complex narrative patterns replete with a wealth of architectural elements, military costumes, headgear, textiles, animal and equine drawings, etc., provide a rich corpus of material for future scholars in this field.

Creating patterns for the Chamba embroidered *rumals,* which might be viewed as a cousin to the embroidered shawls described in this section, also required artists in possession of a good knowledge of Hindu mythology. Chamba *rumals* were square pieces of very fine cotton which were embroidered in polychrome silks (Plate 106). They depicted scenes from the Hindu epics, Krishna and Radha, etc., and it appears that the most important historic period of their craft was during the eighteenth century, otherwise known as the 'Chamba Palace' period. Nainsukh had two sons, Ranjha and Nikka, of whom the former worked for Raja Raj Singh (r. 1764-94) of Chamba, for almost twenty years. Ranjha's art preference favoured large symmetrical paintings crowded with figures. Perhaps his progeny carried this idiom into the embroideries for which Chamba was famous. Of the history of these embroideries, however, extremely little is known, save that the best designs were created by court artists drawing directly on the cloth and then later embroidered by women. After the decline of imperial Delhi, Mughal artists arrived in Chamba and Basohli, where the region became known for the quality of its painting.[206] Thus one must entertain the possibility of these embroideries being made by former court artists who also may have had a hand in shawl patterns.

Fleury Chavant and Jean Rey, Revisited

The Sikhs took control of Kashmir in 1819 and, soon after, a dramatically new shawl fashion developed in three ways. First, the pattern began taking over a significant portion of the shawl's surface, causing the *palla* height to be greatly enlarged. Second, freely spaced designs were mostly eliminated in favour of dense and tightly packed floral arrangements– a style that adhered to a *horror vacui* mindset. Thirdly, a particular style, based more on symbols and geometry than natural flowers, evolved.

Because of Europe's obsession with its own development of manufacturing shawls in imitation of those arriving from the source, the literature of the nineteenth century offers us a unique opportunity in assessing the evolution of shawl patterns coming from the Orient. Weaving shawls that took up to at least a year before they were clipped from the loom and delivered to the various cities around the world, at a time when ships took six months to complete their navigation to western ports, created a significant time lag before new shawl styles could win the approval of the European public. Finer shawls with complex and innovative designs and high quality wools, taking up to three years to make, certainly had more of an impact on fashion than the 'garden variety' shawls made for a bourgeois market. Thus, in assessing dated European sources of the development of fashion, as in paintings and engravings, it would not be illogical to declare that its pattern was created at least three years earlier. This would be a conservative estimate, since one is not taking into consideration the time it took to complete a painting or to publish a book. The London company, Girdler, in 1630, commissioned a factory in Lahore for the weaving of a special carpet, measuring 7ft.6in. x 24ft. (2.3m x 7.3m). Although not a particularly finely woven shawl – with a knot count of only 238 knots per square inch – it was completed and delivered four years later.

With this in mind, we return to our discussion of the design changes developed under the Sikhs. Although the following will not address the exact reasons for these changes, as this has been done in depth in the previous chapter, the problem will nevertheless be discussed through an analysis of an important French album of tracings. This album was already discussed at length in my first book over twenty years ago but with the recent discoveries of new pictorial evidence for the shawl in eighteenth century Iran and its role in the development of the international industry itself, it is now possible to review Chavant's album sketches with renewed discrimination.

Fleury Chavant, a French industrial designer, was the first European to publish sketches of dated Kashmiri shawls in his album of 1837 titled *Album du Cachemirien*.[207] The fascinating part of Chavant's rare album is that the tracings he sketched were taken from shawls woven not only in Kashmir, but in Lahore, Isfahan, Kabul and Kandahar, as well. This provides proof that – if we can believe the veracity of Chavant's attributions, and there is no reason to believe otherwise (something which we shall investigate further on) – sophisticated shawls with complex designs were being woven in Afghanistan and Iran. Chavant's album represents an essential key to our study for two crucial reasons: one, because shawl manufacture in Iran and Afghanistan was known hitherto only through written travel accounts, and two, because of the sketches he published. Two have known dates of manufacture, 1825 and 1831, which either foreshadow or, in fact, represent the Sikh period.[208]

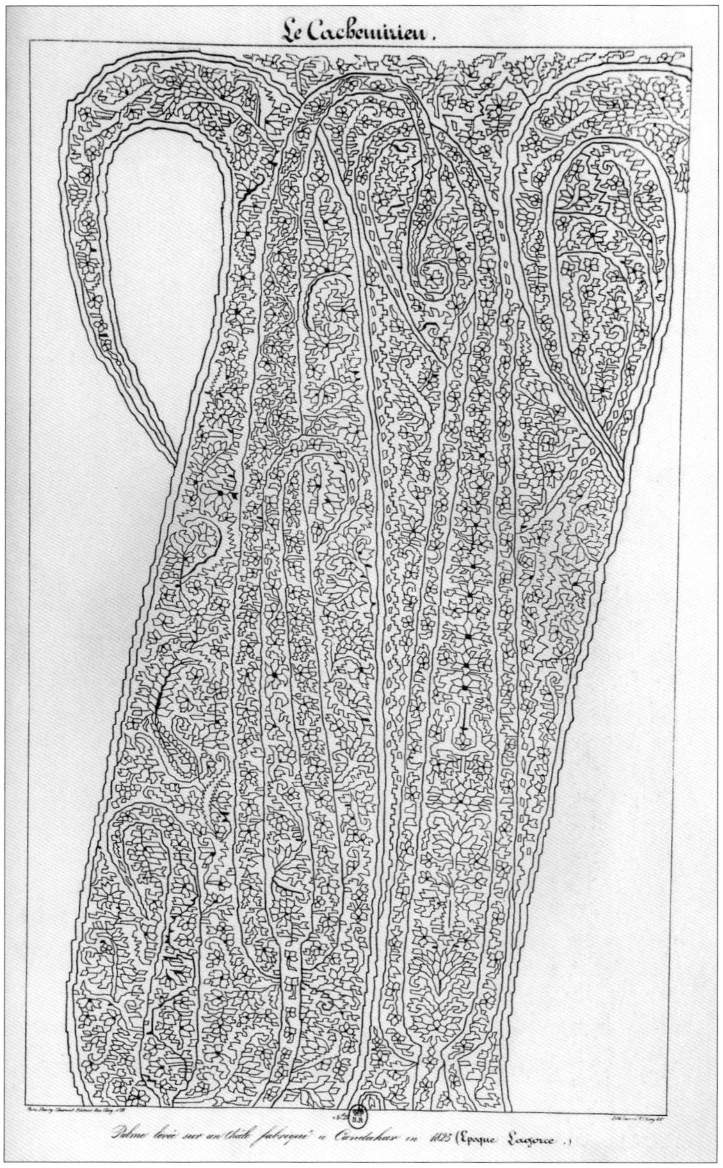

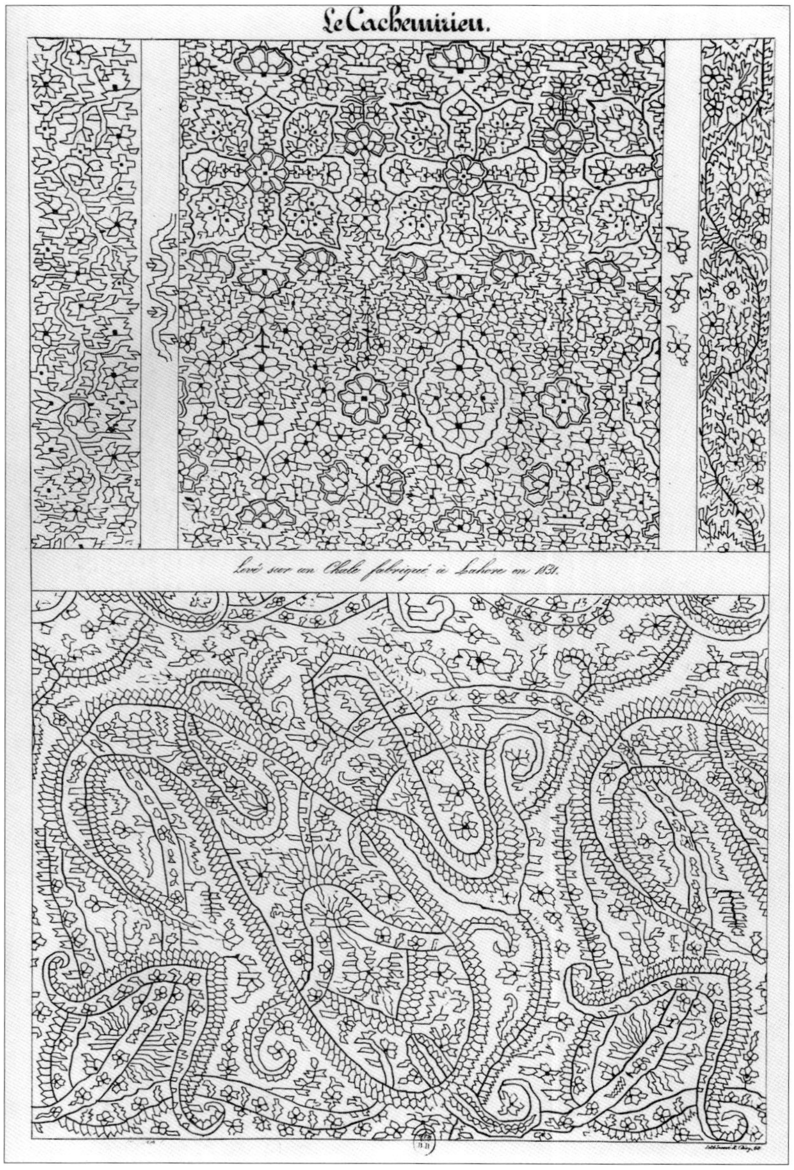

Plate 107 (a-d). Shawl tracings from Chavant's *Album du Cachemirien...*, 1837. National Library, Paris

In the shawl from Kandahar, dated 1825, we find a rather common pattern of tall sharply hooked cones as the main theme, commingling with thinner cones-within-cones, mounted on stems, some with curved delicate and drooping tips (Plate 107a). The floral infill is composed of crudely drawn, nondescript flowers; there are no signs of symbolic curves or geometrics. However, in the sketch of the shawl from Lahore, albeit quite small, dated 1831, we encounter a more exciting symbolic pattern that appears to hint at the architectonic designs that came to define the Sikh period and to suggest that such fashion had already begun (Plate 107b). This sketch, composed of 'leaning' hooked-tip botehs and 'coat-hanger' shapes and swirls, was to achieve enormous success as a repeat pattern, particularly for moon shawls. Although undated, the next important tracing by Chavant, aptly titled 'Le Circeau', defines, by its majestic interplay of circles, eight-pointed lotus stars and triangles, just what the 'mature' Sikh shawl is all about (Plate 107c). In my estimation, this latter shawl was woven some time between 1825 and 1831, given the nature of its sophisticated weave (for comparison, see WM24, page 131). In general, most of the sketches derived from newly created ideas of the late 1820s. This reasoning would keep pace with the discussion of design in Chapter 4. Another Chavant sketch (Plate 107d) may represent the first development of the peacock. Its caption reads 'Design taken from a shawl named the Bird, woven in Tehran'.

Chavant's sketches may have derived from a group of shawls, which had been on exhibit in Paris, sent from India by General Allard after his return to Lahore in 1836. They were exhibited at the Gagelin boutique and the success of the show created a great stir among the Parisian shawl dealers.[209] Therefore, one is easily tempted to opine that the Chavant sketches were the latest fashion to hit Europe. Hence, Chavant's album is significant because of its references to Middle Eastern shawl weaving cities. It is quite possible that prior to its publication European shawl dealers and the general public had no idea that these precious weavings were being manufactured in any place except Kashmir. That complexly woven shawls were woven in Tehran and Kandahar, two cities which are certainly far removed from Kashmir, bespeaks of a well-organized industry that necessarily had been in existence for many years. The big question here is does this mean that the Persian patterns were homegrown? One would have to weigh in the influence of the Persian shawl wallahs who constantly migrated back and forth from Kashmir at least until the Sunni-Shia riots took place in 1831, causing the expulsion of between two and three hundred Persian from the valley.[210] Monochrome sketches such as these, of course, indicate neither the subtlety of the weave nor the beauty of the colours, so we can neither corroborate nor compare Persian colours with those of Kashmir. Many fine examples of the Le Circeau exist today, but the puzzling thing is that they almost all are very finely

Above:
WM27. Jacquard shawl
French shawl with Sikh pattern most likely copied directly from an Indian shawl. The French excelled in replicating with startling exactitude many of the complex patterns coming directly from Srinagar. Despite the small number of ateliers using the *kani* technique (*espouliné*) in Paris during the first few decades of the 19th century, the French had never taken it much beyond simple boteh repeats, similar to the Afghan pattern. The Parisian Jacquard looms, from which this shawl was woven, illustrate France's excellent achievements in superior vegetal dyeing and spinning of *pashmina* wool. Paris, c.1840.
PRIVATE COLLECTION

Opposite:
WM28. Kashmir long shawl
See pages 68-69 for detail and caption

woven, not with any Persian colours or wool, but with typically fine Kashmiri colours and *pashmina* wool (for example, WM24 and WM29, pages 131 and 161).

In light of our discussion of the Chavant sketches, it may be of help to review the comments of the Parisian shawl manufacturer, Jean Rey, who bemoaned the poor quality of shawls arriving from India. Having published *Etude pour servir à l'histoire du châle,* in 1823, Rey became France's first Kashmir shawl historian and was using his long years of experience in the weaving industry to observe just how the Indian shawls were pieced together. He correctly submits that 'the most beautiful ones are made up of two pieces' (sewn together by an invisible seam) but, more significantly, it was his observation of the poorer quality ones which may add a critical piece of information to the early beginnings of the Sikh patterned shawl. Rey continues:

> *Most are made up of four to five pieces and at times even the design doesn't hide the repairs. One can say that a shawl is literally composed of pieces and fragments; here, the cones from one end hardly resemble each other: even if they resemble each other in form, they still differ in tint. The corners of a moon shawl will not in any way equal those of the centre medallion, nor will they be brocaded, while the centre is kani woven. The central medallion itself will be composed of two different halves.*[211]

Those familiar with early nineteenth century shawls will immediately recognize just how Rey's comments ring true. The surprising thing is that he places this shoddiness of the Kashmir shawl at such an early date, at a time, obviously for Kashmir, when the political scene was rather turbulent, and when the Afghans were being forced out and Sikh hegemony was taking over, not to mention the great famine of 1813, the lingering effects of which devastated the region, forcing many families to leave the country. Nevertheless, Rey's comments permit us to date many shawls which otherwise would have been erroneously called 'late', due to their 'degenerate' quality, to perhaps as much as a decade earlier. This holds true especially for many of those 'awkward' moon shawls, while those shawls that Rey mentions, composed of four and five pieces, are clearly of the long or square types which normally would have been assigned to the period of 1825 onwards and might now be assigned to somewhere in the second decade of the nineteenth century.

Rey is not talking about the long shawls or *dochallas* with simple boteh repeats, since they were never made in pieces, save for the two or three invisible seams that held them together. Rather, he is clearly speaking about the shoddy piecework indicative of the shift to larger designs that Kashmir was experiencing. Rey's remarks, therefore, add further early proof of an industry gearing up to the new 'tapestry-types' in Sikh designs.

Opposite and detail on pages 162-163:
WM29. Kashmir long shawl (detail). Within this riot of confusing motifs which seem to be thrown together in a jumble, two small peacocks appear in the lower register. This detail for the shawl's end panel illustrates the importance of the quoit as a symbol of Sikh power. Sikh period, c.1840. AUTHOR'S COLLECTION

Chapter 5
Kashmiri Manuscripts

Based on a long Persian tradition, illustrated and illuminated Kashmiri manuscripts possess a remarkably distinct cachet, which derives mainly from their colour palette, floral style and from the way stories and poems were illustrated. As a result these manuscripts represent an important source of iconography, exemplifying an exchange of the artistic ideas of illuminators, painters, lacquerware craftsmen and shawl artists from Persia, Central Asia, the subcontinent and the Himalayan region of Kashmir. The enormous quantity of these manuscripts found in world collections, almost all from the late eighteenth to the early nineteenth century, testifies to their great popularity within both the Muslim and the Hindu communities.

Scholars believe that the style of Kashmiri manuscript painting derives in part from the late seventeenth century in the northern part of the Punjab, while influences from Kashmir's Sultanate period and its intellectual and mercantile connections to Shiraz, where manuscript production reached a peak in the fifteenth to sixteenth centuries, played the most significant role in the formation of the industry in Kashmir. Indeed, the large majority of Kashmiri manuscripts appear to be based on books from this earlier Persian era.[212] If this were the case, and there had been an exchange of artistic ideas between manuscript production and shawl production, it would not be inconceivable to encounter late eighteenth and early nineteenth century shawls with ideas drawn from three centuries earlier. In fact, this may be the case.

Experts in the field of Islamic manuscripts seem to concur that there is little or no evidence of a transitional nature to demonstrate the stylistic evolution of the Kashmiri manuscript prior to the late eighteenth century.[213] Jeremiah Losty, for one, claims that by this time the Kashmiri school of painting had arrived on the scene already fully formed.[214] An interesting comparison to this lacuna, curiously enough, can be found in Kashmir shawl designs of the eighteenth century. We know that the principal pattern on shawls during the late eighteenth century and early nineteenth century was the boteh or buta, curvilinear in shape, filled with flowers and repeated across the width of the shawl ends. One of the most fascinating if not challenging pursuits in the understanding of shawl iconography is the transition from the freely-spaced flowers to the confines of this bulbous buta shape. As in Losty's claim above, evidence of a gradual transition is quite meagre here insofar as it is rare to encounter a natural bouquet of freely-spaced flowers from the eighteenth century. Furthermore, the available evidence is such that we don't find curvilinear butas with 'freely-spaced' flowers in the high Mughal period. As much as this example seems

---

Opposite:
Plate 108. Painting from *Shahnameh*, Rajaur, India, dated 1719.
British Library, add.18804 f.97

Left:
Plate 109. Kashmir shawl, detail of fragment, Afghan period, mid-18th century.
PRIVATE COLLECTION

Opposite, right:
Plate 110. Iris by Muhammad Hadi, Islamic manuscript book cover in papier-mâché, dated 1815, Shiraz, 8 x 4¾in. (20.3 x 12.1cm), after *Lacquer of the Islamic Lands*.
KHALILI COLLECTION FIG. 138

Opposite, far right:
Plate 111. *Gul-bulbul* painting, Islamic manuscript book cover in papier-mâché, 18th century, Iran, after *Lacquer of the Islamic Lands*.
KHALILI COLLECTION

strange, the nearest we come to a transitional piece is a red-ground shawl fragment (Plate 109). Its flowers are obviously of a late Mughal nature, semi-natural in appearance, yet the artist decides to delineate the floral bouquet with a solid curved line, making a bulbous shape. What does this tell us? Perhaps this fragment was woven at a time when this shape was just gaining in popularity; the shawl *naqqash* felt compelled to envelop the buta in the then fashionable curves of the buta. Thus, it hints at the possibility that the curvilinear buta suddenly appeared in fashion..

The lacquer painting method dates purportedly to fifteenth century Herat, from where it spread to Iran, Turkey and Central Asia and, soon after, India. In India the monsoon, lack of collectors, similarity to Persian work and, above all, the lack of dated examples compound the problem of finding good study specimens. Furthermore, Persian and Indian artists shifted back and forth between Iran and India rendering provenance difficult, especially during the seventeenth century when Shiraz was producing massive amounts of manuscripts. One of the important facets in the study of Persian and Kashmiri manuscript books is found in the inimitable charm of their lacquered covers or flyleaves. These covers were usually of papier-mâché, elaborately painted with polychrome flowers and then varnished to a high gloss. For Iran, they represent an indispensable reference source to the study of Zand and Qajar painting, and the decorative arts; for Kashmir, and for the focus of this study, an expanding source of material yet to be fully tapped.

Because study in this field is still in its infancy, lacquer items, notably those signed by well-known artists such as Muhammad Zaman (fl.1649-1704), Ali Ashraf (fl.1740-1756), Muhammad Sadiq (fl.1740s-1790s), Muhammad Baqir (fl.1740s-1800) and Muhammad Hadi (fl.1780-1820) may one day prove to be of critical importance in shawl style identification (Plate 110). One of the most gifted, Sadiq, especially dominated the Zand period.[215] Although little is known of his biography, we do know of his intimate familiarity with early seventeenth century Mughal painting because his signature (along with Hadi's) was found on the border decoration of miniatures captured as booty during Nadir Shah's raid on Delhi in 1739.[216]

In studying lacquer items, one observes a stark contrast in quality between those of Kashmir and the decidedly finer and more detailed ones from Persia, a contrast particularly evident in painted book illustrations. One wonders why this is so when Kashmir was in such close proximity to one of the finest painting regions of India, Pahari, a region renowned for its paintings with emotional vitality and evocative and colourful moods. Why this creative energy never crossed over into the book arts of Kashmir is an enigma.[217]

It is this very lack of vitality which serves as an indicator that manuscript work was more a matter of a churned-out production in an attempt to satisfy a lucrative book market. One cannot help muse over the profiteering similarities of two countries, Kashmir and Persia, each attempting to replicate the other's renowned and inimitable craft: the former, the Persian manuscript and the latter, the shawl. The big difference here, of course, is that as much as the Kashmiri weavers remained anonymous, Persian artists' names, such as Sadiq, Baqir, and Hadi, to name a few, undoubtedly resounded eponymously throughout painting workshops of the Middle East and, most likely, in parts of the subcontinent where Indian patrons, frustrated by lack of book availability due to the warring chaos of North India, may have chosen to order them directly from Shiraz. It is no wonder that Kashmir's book copying industry caught on only towards the end of the eighteenth century.

In fine manuscripts bound in Persia, the cover designs often reflect the format of classical Persian carpets, where one might find, sometimes embossed in leather, a central medallion with extended trefoil designs, as well as corner spandrels with split-leaf arabesques; or, the ubiquitous lacquered papier-mâché covers with charming, natural flowers and birds *(gul-bulbul)* under a highly glossed lacquer surface creating an almost holographic effect — the quintessential hallmark of Persian work, for example, the work of Muhammad Hadi (Plate 111).

WM30. Kashmir square shawl *(rumal)*
Spear-like devices or stalks with flowering tips, as well as clumps of leafy shoots as seen here in the border, became popular design motifs toward the late Sikh period. These designs may have come from artists working in the lacquer and papier-mâché crafts. The centre, bursting with high energy swirling vines, is delightfully softened by the *tarah guru's* (colour caller) perfect use of light pastel colours in the border. Late Sikh period, c.1850.
COLLECTION SAMUEL JOSEFOWITZ

Left:
Plate 112. Floral painting on papier-maché, Islamic manuscript book cover, early 19th century, from a *Shahnameh* by Firdausi.
MINUR 134, STAATSBIBLIOTHEK, BERLIN

Opposite, right:
Plate 113. Floral bouquet on papier-maché, Islamic manuscript book cover, early 19th century, from a *diwan* by Hafiz. The tall, ribbed stem device at the bouquet's base (see also Plates 114 and 115) is a style found within late Afghan period boteh patterns.
MS.OR.OCT 952, STAATSBIBLIOTHEK, BERLIN

Opposite, far right:
Plate 114. Floral bouquet on papier-maché, Islamic manuscript book cover, early 19th century, from a *Shahnameh* by Firdausi
MINUR 14, STAATSBIBLIOTHEK, BERLIN

On the other hand, Kashmiri covers were frequently embellished with a kind of flower garden, an all over design of meandering flower blossoms applied with heavy dabs of paint which rendered a surface slightly embossed under the coats of lacquer (Plate 112). The more expensive covers were finely bound, their lacquered surfaces finished in a sheen of golden flakes. The *doublures*, or inside covers, often reveal a typical spray of Kashmiri styled flowers, with or without a vase, secured at the bottom by a tall ribbed stem device (Plates 113 and 114), or the often seen bulbous 'spear' of flowers set within a prayer niche. Considering the combined efforts of illuminators, illustrators, calligraphers, scribes, lacquer workers and binders, the creation of a fine quality

manuscript often required years. A Russian traveller in Kashmir in the mid-twentieth century writes that:

> *...excellent masters of the manufacture of artistic papier-mâché objects have remained in Kashmir to this day. The art of the papier-mâché object has remained a monopoly of the descendants of the old Persian masters, who live in small isolated colonies in Srinagar. Many of their drawings are imitations of Persian miniatures.*[218]

It is quite possible that these Persian communities of artists left the country at the time of Shah Tahmasp's (1514-1576) shift to strict Shia orthodoxy, when he began to renounce his interest in painting and the arts. Of those who left the most famous were Abul al Samad and Mir Sayyid Ali – two of the imperial Safavid court's most gifted artists – who arrived in India with the then fugitive Humayun to found the Mughal School of painting. There may also have been a small community of the Shahsavan tribe living in Srinagar, headed by a residing Sultan who commissioned and inscribed a Kashmiri manuscript found at the Bibliothèque Nationale.[219] Adamova and Greck submit that 'It would be fair to say that from Kabul to the eastern parts of Uttar Pradesh, and from Central Asia down to the lower ends of Rajasthan, Kashmiri works were known, and were often scripted and painted at the very places that they now are, by itinerant artists'.[220]

Left:
Plate 115. Thick stemmed floral bouquet, Islamic manuscript book cover, papier-mâché, early 19th century, 13⅛ x 7½in. (33.3 x 19.2cm), after *Lacquer of the Islamic Lands.*
KHALILI COLLECTION , P. 255, PL. 210

Below:
Plate 116. Floral painting, Islamic manuscript book cover in papier-mâché, mid-19th century, 7¾ x 4¾in. (19.6 x 12cm), after *Lacquer of the Islamic Lands.*
KHALILI COLLECTION, PAGE 254, PL. 208

Opposite:
Plate 117. Shawl tracing sent by Moorcroft back to England in 1823, written on reverse side 'By order of Shooja ool Moolkh', gouache on paper, 13 x 5in. (33 x 12.7cm).
METROPOLITAN MUSEUM OF ART, NEW YORK. 62.600.235 (1)

The uniqueness of Moorcroft's 1823 gouaches is twofold. Prior to this time no known Kashmiri shawl sketches appear to have survived; they were 'scripted and painted' seemingly by local Kashmiri artists. For this reason, they offer an important reference point for the comparison of floral styles both in shawls and in manuscripts. However, as much as the style of these few sketches resembles that style found in the manuscripts and other crafted items, there is little hint of the architectural style that was soon to follow. One reason may be that the sketches had been drawn from already woven shawls commissioned by foreign potentates whose tastes for fashion were probably not ready for anything avant-garde.

Apart from book covers, we find that prior to the nineteenth century it is rare to encounter Kashmiri manuscripts whose floral embellishments relate directly to that of the shawl boteh style. The stunning 'propeller' *rumal* in WM5, page 70 shows a large border with seven-leaf clusters, each highlighted by a solid colour palmette. This type of leaf cluster (see also WM30, page 168), though not a boteh per se, does show up frequently on early nineteenth century lacquer ware. It appears that it is only well into the nineteenth century that use of the boteh in the actual pages of the manuscript began to appear. A bouquet of flowers arranged in the shape of a cone or buta is not necessarily an indication that it was done by a Kashmiri shawl artist. Eighteenth century shawl design was in its heyday for development of the curvilinear buta, whose bulbous container, often packed with small flowers, evolved tantamount to being Kashmir's national symbol. All indications point to its use only at the end of the eighteenth century and, according to extant evidence, only on manuscript covers and not within the folio pages. Given the huge corpus of manuscripts attributable to the early 1800s, one is quite surprised by the absence of the buta, given its long heritage and already established iconic significance, which reinforces the notion that indeed the bulk of the manuscript industry itself began only at the end of the eighteenth century.

The fine cover in the Khalili collection (Plate 115) is an excellent example of Kashmiri shawl artistry applied to manuscript production. Although it is undated, as most Kashmiri manuscripts are, the cone-like buta is drafted unequivocally using identical flowers found woven into the Kashmir shawl. The roses, irises and marigolds, etc. have that flattened appearance typical of those woven into the *kani* weave. The floral arrangement of the bouquet, including the large stem at the bottom, is a particular style that can be easily identified from late eighteenth and turn-of-the-century shawl butas. In fact, it is almost certain the artist copied directly from an existing shawl pattern. In Plate 116 we see the hand of the shawl artist again at work, but sketching his flowers with a more natural feel. One of the sketches that Moorcroft had made and sent back to England in 1823 offers a similar example of floral work (Plate 117). Floral decoration of manuscripts is suggestive of three schools of artistry at work, both for the

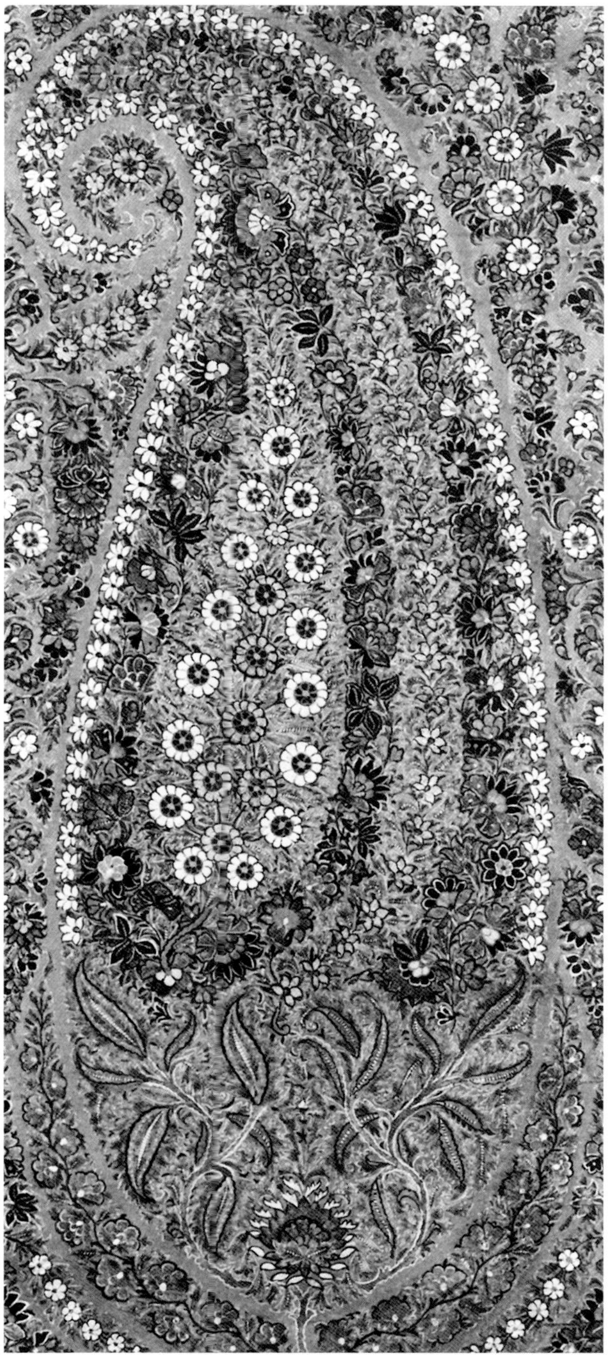

covers and the illustrations including the *unvans* and elaborate bifolio pages within the text: first, from the shawl industry itself; second, a style indigenous to Kashmir but exogenous to shawl workshops; and third, almost completely Persian.

It has been suggested that the cone with its motif of tightly packed flowers may have devolved from the lacquer crafts of bookbinders working in Kashmir at the turn of the nineteenth century.[221] Although it is unclear whether the suggestion referred to the origins of the cone itself or the style of the tightly

Plate 118. Floral boteh, Islamic manuscript book cover, Kashmir, dated 1799, after *Oriental Miniatures of Abu Raihon Beruni* …by A.M. Ismailova, Tashkent.

Plate 119. Islamic manuscript book cover, Kashmir, c.1800, after *The Scent of Flowers…*, p. 14.

packed flowers or both, the idea that floral lacquer artists may have created designs for the Kashmir shawl is an interesting and plausible theory worth exploring. To demonstrate that there was perhaps an exchange of artistic ideas between those artists creating the shawl patterns and those making the lacquer flyleaves, two leaves are submitted as examples relating to those types of patterns which might be found on shawls. In the first, a flyleaf of a Kashmir manuscript dated 1799 – perhaps the earliest known dated flyleaf – we see a large cone beautifully composed of blossoming, identifiable flowers supported by a large stem or column. Violets, primroses, carnations, hibiscus, roses, chrysanthemums and lilies form part of the myriad blossoms that exude a dramatic, if not intoxicating, inflorescence (Plate 118).

One can only marvel at how the artist imparted such life to each of the flowers and at the same time was able to coax them into such a tight, compact cone space. The artist continues his tour-de-force with a floral wreath in the form of a long raceme composed of tiny white lilies. The botanical details are such that one can easily discern, for example, sepals from perianth and anther from pistil, floral minutiae the artist had obviously studied from nature itself. The raceme, with lilies carefully arranged in pairs, and each with its stem and bract clearly attached to a main branch, wraps completely around the cone to barely overlap at the top, leaving a slight drooping curl to the left. Flanking the bottom of the flyleaf are two cat-tail sprays of tiny flowers, a floral device very similar to contemporary shawl-boteh patterns. Sheltering the boteh at the top is a scalloped-spandrel prayer niche with further floral decoration of a nondescript nature. The whole image is nicely framed with a sculptured faux wood appearance.

In the second, from the National Bibliothek of Vienna, again we have a large bouquet, but which lacks the dynamic energy of the former (Plate 119) The floral arrangement is quite formal and symmetrical and the small, mostly white primrose and lily flowers are naturally rendered to form a bulbous spear mounted on a large stem column; the whole is placed within a prayer niche framework. What makes the first flyleaf interesting, other than it being dated, is the wreath with its drooping and trailing edge at the top, which imparts that Kashmir-cone appearance. Otherwise, both images lack the distinctive floral artistry associated with the usual mosaic patterns of the woven shawl. True, in both cases, a flower bouquet is the theme; however, the quality of the rendering of the flowers is so high in the lacquer works that one would be quite reluctant to assume that these types of designs were then transferred to the weaving *talim* and made into shawls. The large mound and floral spear flyleaf on a red ground in Plate 120 is a particularly fine bouquet and again illustrates the dichotomy between *kani* and lacquer floral detailing. Not a single woven boteh extant of the eighteenth to nineteenth century exhibiting such floral perfection has yet been found. Again we can refer to Moorcroft's drawings, but they seem to tell us only how much the pattern degenerated after being woven into the shawl.

Thus, few shawls were actually embellished with the types of flowers found in painting. What often shows up in shawl patterns, however, is the geometric Islamic style of the *sarlauhs* (a cartouche reserved for the customary auspicious and invocatory language) and *unvans* (an illuminated frontispiece seen in Islamic manuscripts) found in manuscript decoration.

Both flyleaves are typical representations of the fine type of lacquerwork done in Kashmir c.1800 and such work became the medium of a great many beautiful and poetic themes, not least among which was the enduring and popular floral theme of the rose and nightingale *(gul-bulbul)*. This theme had also become the leitmotif for the many fine Safavid silks of the seventeenth and eighteenth centuries, expressing the power and pervasiveness of contemporaneous poetry. Why is it then, one may ask, are themes such as these not to be found in the *kani* weaves or, more specifically, that lacquer artists never succeeded in challenging the *kani* weaver to replicate their flowers naturalistically, much as the French had done under Napoleon?[222]

Plate 120. Islamic manuscript book cover in papier-maché, Kashmir, c.1800.
COURTESY ISRAEL MUSEUM, JERUSALEM, 814.69

The idea of beautifully bound volumes with aesthetically pleasing illustrations and illuminations did not appear to be a tradition within the Hindu community. It was not until the eighteenth century, with exposure to the colourful glitter of Persian manuscripts copied by Kashmiri craftsmen, that Hindu patrons took notice and began their own book production, using perhaps the same craftsmen. Although it appears that Kashmiri book craftsmen, who

Left:
Plate 121. Hunting scene or *shikarga* (detail), *dochalla* or long shawl with similar scenes at both ends, Kashmir, c.1750.
COURTESY TAPI COLLECTION OF SHILPA AND PRAFUL SHAH, SURAT

Opposite:
Plate 122. Painting from Saadi's 'Bustan and Gulistan', Kashmir, early 19th century, after *Miniatures from Kashmirian...* by Adamova and Greck, pl. 13.

were Muslims, working on commercial products, were not hindered by their faith by working on Hindu projects, the question may arise as to how much the craftsman's religion affects his work ethic, spiritually. One wonders if, for example, some hindrance could arise from the Shariat laws where the piety of the manuscript posed a restriction, preventing him from venturing into other artistic media which could have been considered an encroachment on the sacred traditions of Islam. However, given the abundance of commercial products these artists worked on – shawls, pen boxes, mirror cases, lacquer book covers, etc., of no particular sectarian significance – it appears that there was little threat of transgressing sumptuary laws. On the other hand, in Amritsar especially I very much doubt if one would have found Sikh artists working on Islamic projects since 'the public practice of the Mohammadan religion is forbidden'.[223]

As noted by Jahangir in his *Tuzuk*, most of the merchants in Kashmir were of Shia denomination, while the craftsmen were Sunni. However, it is known that most of the lacquer artists from Persia were of the Shia sect, as often signalled explicitly in the way they signed their works, invoking the injunction of the Twelfth Imam.[224] Rivalry between the two sects, Simon Digby submits, 'was a factor since the 15th century. Fugitives possibly from Timur, the Shias claim their descent from the Bayhaggi Sayyid; the Sunnis from Sayyid 'Ali Hamadan, with strong ethnic Kashmir ties. The 17th century saw a large upper-class settlement in Kashmir from Iran. Towards the end of the century, there were violent riots between Shia and Sunni in Srinagar'.[225] These sectarian rivalries may have been part of the reason why Kashmiri craftsmen had settled into their own distinct communities, separating one from the other, between Lahore and Srinagar.

As mentioned earlier, it is unlikely that manuscript artists borrowed much from the shawl industry prior to the nineteenth century. On the other hand, shawl artists did borrow from eighteenth century manuscript illustrators, especially for all-over shawl patterns and pictorial designs, with the latter usually found most frequently in embroidery. Some of the finest embroidered shawls were crafted in Kashmir during the mid-nineteenth century. The dynamic imagery and colourful drama that played out in the great Persian epic poems, such as the *Khamsa* of Nizami and the *Shahnameh* of Firdausi, provided a wealth of creative ideas influencing generations of illuminators and illustrators, motivating

Kashmir's gifted embroiderers to display the magical charms of their needlework.

The *amlikar* or embroidered shawl, rather than the *kani* shawl, was the easier to make, since the embroiderer could simply follow the tracings of a pounced pattern supplied by the artist. As a result, a fair number of finely embroidered shawls illustrating Persian literature can be found in institutional collections, most of which are from the mid-nineteenth century. Earlier than this, strangely enough, none has come to light, despite Moorcroft's claim that embroidery on shawls began with a so-called 'Alee Baba' under one of the eighteenth century's Afghan governors (see Ames, *Woven Legends*, note 34). Of those extant, many are languishing on dark shelves in museum collections, unstudied.[226] On the other hand, it is rare to find a *kani* shawl with a significant pictorial pattern. *Kani* weaving is limiting, since the weaver's colour insertions must always be in lock-step to the slanting direction of the 2 x 2 twill, and extremely time consuming and therefore does not offer the weaver the freedom and versatility embroiderers can enjoy. However, there are a few rare exceptions to the rule, and the two eighteenth century Shikarga *kani dochallas* (Plate 121) which I had published in my first book, except for minor variations, appear to have shared the same *talim* pattern.[227] Of significance, though, are the dark and heavily coloured lines, or hillocks, that appear to separate several episodes of an unfolding hunting expedition, which may begin at the bottom of the *palla* to end at the top, in a form of narration. On the bottom stands a frightening looking humanoid figure waving something, possibly a stick or club, and another person mounted on a horse, poking a spear. They appear to be chasing the animals in order to gather them into position for the next scene which is where the noble on the elephant readies himself for the kill, a traditional Mughal hunting technique.

Due to the stylized nature of the woven figures, it becomes, at this point, more difficult to interpret the higher scenes. But the

important thing to be noted is that the shawl artist drew his segmented scenes by borrowing techniques from Persian and Mughal painters. This can be seen in the margins of many of the manuscript pages illustrated in Adamova and Greck's book (Plate 122). The narrow space

reserved for the top register, or horizon, is a typical technique employed by Kashmiri miniature artists. Whether it was a shawl artist who borrowed ideas from book illustrators and painters or a book artist who created the drawings for the shawl weavers is unclear; that artistic techniques from shawl and book illustrators percolated back and forth is undeniable.

Since Kashmir produced mainly Korans, which required the work of calligraphers and illuminators, it is interesting to speculate on whether it was not in Lahore – where during the nineteenth century, a huge variety of books were made – that pictorial shawl designs, both woven and embroidered, were first drawn. Indeed, Lahore and Kashmir represented a tight nexus of interactive exchange in the production and manufacture of crafts and the shared history of these two regions goes back to, at least, early imperial Mughal India, when great quantities of shawls were being woven there. Little has changed since in the demographics of the Kashmiri population in Lahore. Unlike the manuscripts made in Lahore proper, finely wrought *pashmina* shawls and *pashmina* carpets required transportation for washing in the magical waters of the Jhelum River, twenty-one days away. (Jacquemont writes in his letters from India, 1834, that on one occasion he received his mail from Lahore in only three days.) For the production of manuscripts, however, transportation was not an issue, since the Kashmiri craftsmen probably had all the materials they needed right there. Attempting to pin-point their production to one city or the other, therefore, might prove to be an exercise in futility, for the two cities should, in reality, be looked upon as one combined production region.[228] Barely anything is known about any artist in this 'twin city' region until the early part of the nineteenth century when Imam Bakhsh Lahori appears on the scene, to eventually form what must have been a prodigious school of art.[229]

The first serious study of Kashmiri manuscripts was done by two Russian scholars, A. Adamova and T. Greck, in 1983. They address the Leningrad Public Library collection which holds seventeen Kashmiri manuscripts comprised of 545 illustrations, among which is probably the earliest known example from Kashmir, the *Mahbub-al-Qulub,* dated 1699-1700. Its bifolio page contains large strapwork with floral infill patterns that already foreshadow the particular way shawl artists transformed these often dazzling patterns into elaborate *kani* weaves (Plate 123). Except for the slanting calligraphy of the outer border of the Leningrad folio page, the illuminated page of the early nineteenth century manuscript found in the Staatsbibliothek is quite similar in style. Kashmiri manuscripts, in general, are identified by the heavy use of an intense orange on costumes and the frequent use of lavish gold and silver embellishment, giving a glittery appearance to the manuscript; by the combination of rose and pink outlining the figures and the abundance of illustrations closely narrating the surrounding text. Horizons were often relegated to only a narrow wash of colour across the top of a hilly landscape (hence the mountains of the Himalayas), not unlike the *shikargas*. Further important Kashmiri manuscript characteristics, as noted by Nora Titley, in the well-known Rajaur manuscript, are found on later Kashmir works, such as 'single ringlets extending down the sides of the face, the luxuriant beards, the style of architecture, the thrones, fountains and the crowded court and battle scenes.[230] Almost all scholars point to this *Shahnameh* from Rajaur (in the Punjab) dated 1719 as containing incipient elements of the Kashmiri style. After that there is a great void until the end of the eighteenth century.

Opposite:
Plate 123. *Kani* fragment with manuscript-like strapwork, late 18th century.
COLLECTION LAWRENCE KEARNEY

WM31. Kashmir long shawl (detail)
An emerald green centre with a rare pattern comprised of meandering Islamic 'strapwork', a brilliant *palla* design of exceptional beauty, and colours making the whole sparkle are truly the combined elements for an exceptional shawl. Notice the Russian customs stamp in the centre, a country known for purchasing the highest quality Kashmir shawls. Late Sikh, c.1850.
COLLECTION JOAN HART

Above:
Plate 124. Kashmir long shawl (detail of complete *patka*), mid-18th century.
Bharat Kala Bawan, Banaras

Opposite:
Plate 125. Painting from *Shahnameh*, Rajaur, India, dated 1719.
British Library, add.18804 f.97

Decorated almost always with a repetition of the curvilinear buta, shawls of the Afghan period were simplistic in nature.[231] However, beginning in the early part of the eighteenth century, the buta's infill of flowers adopted particular characteristics making them recognizable. At the base we often find a vase with a large amount of flowers. Immediately above the vase one finds a group of flower blossoms arranged in a circular fashion, like spokes on a wheel around a central hub or flower (Plate 124). Several scholars have noted that the depiction of leaves on the trees in manuscript paintings from the early eighteenth century onward are also drawn using a radial technique.[232] The 1719 Rajaur manuscript is a good example (Plate 125). To the far right is a tree, the leaves of which have been arranged concentrically with great precision. It can also be observed from the same painting that the flowers, placed up against the zig-zag wall and also above it, show a very precise spacing between their stems. These stylistic ideas appear to resonate closely with the various floral arrangements found within eighteenth century shawl butas.[233]

In our discussion above, of the two flyleaves and the perfection in floral quality they were able to achieve, we return once again to the lack of such detailed quality found in the *kani* shawl of the eighteenth and nineteenth centuries. Here it is of note to point out France's efforts in this endeavour, to achieve a certain floral naturalness during the Empire period, involving the miniaturist, Isabey. To eschew the 'bizarre and confused designs [botehs] that one sees on foreign [Kashmir] shawls', the industrialist Ternaux suggested Napoleon order twelve new designs from the renowned Isabey. Executed in exactly the same *kani* technique as their counterparts from Kashmir, the woven shawls were delivered in 1812 to the Emperor who, in turn, offered them to his wife Marie-Louise. Fortunately, one of these shawls has survived and demonstrates clearly how it is possible to go from a drawing of natural flowers to its woven replicate without losing nuance. A contemporary critique of one of the new designs observed: 'The palms (cones) are replaced by bouquets

Plate 126. French shawl (detail), *pashmina*, design attributed to Isabey, woven by Ternaux, *espouliné* (*kani* technique), 1812.
MUSÉE DES ARTS DÉCORATIFS, PARIS

Opposite, detail pages 186-187:
WM32. Kashmir long shawl (detail)
The phantom shapes of these out of kilter botehs add a mystic touch to what is already an enigmatic pattern. Scalloped arches, reaching across a mysterious mountain of tall cypress trees that is pierced by a large spear-like element, heighten the mystery of the artist's inspiration. The transversal *hashias* exhibit a very Deco flavour. Sikh period, c.1835.
PRIVATE COLLECTION

and garlands imitating the most beautiful European flowers, whose clear colours and fine nuances have something of the appearance of painting' (Plate 126).[234]

It appears that, as the freely spaced flowering plant continued its development on into the eighteenth century, it began to harden somewhat within an outline of a curvilinear shape in what is now known as the cone or boteh. Many shawl patterns with freely spaced bouquets managed to escape curvilinearity but their flowers often became highly geometric in style. While the cone shape is, at times, filled with distinct flowers atypical of the earlier part of the century in which the Mughal floral idiom lingered on, as the decades unfolded the naturalistic look of the woven flowers – including those Mughal flower blossoms exhibiting large areas of solid colour – often degenerated into unidentifiable and, at times, confused patches of colourful mosaic. When the shawl cone finally came into its own, probably towards the first half of the eighteenth century, it was quickly adopted as an identifiable symbol that became synonymous with the shawl. However, it should be understood that, except on the *doublures* of the occasional Kashmiri manuscript, it was, to all intents and purposes, very rarely employed as a design feature before the second quarter of the nineteenth century. Given the dearth of early buta lacquer covers and flyleaves, it is highly unlikely that the lacquer industry of Kashmir had much effect on shawl development. In fact, the reverse is more likely the truth.[235]

Moorcroft had employed manuscript copyists for his own production of books, yet surprisingly, despite his presence in the midst of a thriving industry, the details he provides are but few. Alongside Islamic and secular books, there was also a flourishing industry in Sikh religious manuscripts, most likely in Lahore, whose demand fuelled the industry. In his recently published essay on Sikh manuscripts illustrated with bifolios of illuminated pages, Jeevan Singh Deol introduces them as cultural objects of artistic

merit rather than as an unfolding religious phenomenon of recensions to be studied philosophically, ethically or linguistically. His work sheds light on an art form which is truly Sikh. They offer us a direct insight into Sikh themes whereby the artists were able to embellish their renderings of the Great Gurus with indigenous Kashmiri-style ornaments.

In our search for style and its characteristics, we have already detailed a few of the salient traits associated with the Guler style of painting, such as the umbrella, chair and shield. The

illustrations and illuminations of the *Janam Sakhis* and the *Adi Granth* represent two of the only other known Sikh sources for our study.[236] Of the former, none can be dated prior to the eighteenth century, a fact which tells us something about the growing patronage of the Sikhs under Ranjit Singh. Of the latter, pictorial illustrations, as a general rule, are not to be found, and the rare few that are were invariably executed in the workshops of Kashmir; it is the graphics of the Islamicate *nisans* and *sarlauhs* of the *Adi Granth* that tend to stir our curiosity.

WM33. Kashmir square shawl *(rumal)* Peacocks and 'temples' against a black background with lots of free spacing combine to form a dramatic centre on this *rumal*. The *kani* temple might be a *gurdwara*, a place of Sikh worship. Sikh period, c.1835.
COLLECTION FONDAZIONE ANTONIO RATTI, COMO

The production of illuminated and illustrated Sikh manuscripts was apparently a more serious religious undertaking requiring skills beyond the capability of the average copyists. The ten Holy Gurus, whose portraits were by then rendered into standard recognizable images, became the story themes of the folios, often with intriguing pictographics. In the discussion to follow, we shall explore the possibility of shawl patterns which may have been influenced by these manuscripts.

The mélange of Hindu, Islamic and architectonic motifs found on the shawls of this period reflects, in many ways, the rich blend of spiritual ideas upon which the Sikh religion, which evolved from the devotional traditions of Islam and Hinduism, was formed. In fact, being Sikh then was not altogether a different experience from being a Hindu since the majority of the Sikhs were originally Punjabi Brahmins (or drawn from the Jat community) and shared many similar beliefs; of course the main difference was the breaking of caste.[237] Whether Hindu or Muslim, Ranjit Singh was non-discriminatory when it came to celebrating the festival of each community.

Thus, given the pervasiveness and ancient tradition of the Hindu religion within the Pahari and Jammu regions, one is not at all surprised to find among the illustrated folios

Indic deities. These manuscripts often contain illuminated and/or illustrated opening folios with colourful patterns and motifs which, as expected from earlier periods, depict both typical Islamic and Indic patterns. Although most sacred Sikh manuscripts remain undated, their style clearly falls within the time period of mid-eighteenth to early nineteenth century. This is consistent with the findings of Srivastava who states emphatically that texts of the Sikh gurus or of the *Janam Sakhis* had not been illustrated prior to the late eighteenth century.[238] The vine or 'cloudband' strapwork, swirling interlaced split-leaf arabesques, scenes from Hindu mythology containing, for example, Shiva, Vishnu, Brahma, Devi, Lakshmi, etc., and large petal lotuses, are a few of the motifs that can be discerned, the last of which form a major theme of the illuminated pages.

Left:
Plate 127. *Akal Takhat Sahib*, constructed late 17th century, Amritsar.

Below:
Detail of the *hashias* in WM34 (pages 194-195), c.1835. Small temples (*mandirs* or *gurdwaras*) and unrecognizable building structures are often a part of Sikh period shawls. The identical repeat motif is also found in the long silk-warped *hashias* of the same shawl.

Opposite:
Plate 128. Kashmir *rumal* with temple-like motif, Sikh period, c.1835.
Collection Fondazione Antonio Ratti, Como

Beyond the *Adi Granth* and *Janam Sakhis,* the spiritual paintings of the Sikh Gurus provide few themes we may find reflected in the Kashmir shawl. The sixth Guru, Hargobind, by taking up arms, became the self-ordained ruler of all Sikhs. He carried two swords, one known as *miri*, the other as *piri*, and thus assumed sovereignty over the temporal and spiritual worlds combined. The shawl with two daggers (discussed above) may be a reflection of this idea (WM17). With his assumption of guruship in 1606, Guru Hargobind supposedly undertook the building of a new temple – although there is no direct evidence as to its exact date of construction – to face the Sri Harmandir Sahib (well known as the Golden Temple), at Amritsar. It was called the Akal Takhat (in Persian, 'timeless') and instantaneously it became the key seat of Sikh religious authority and the central altar for Sikh political assembly. It is an impressive four storey building topped by a large golden dome and long finial spire. Eight golden roof-top minarets further adorn the structure (Plate 127). The observation of many small temples found among the Sikh period *kani* weaves has already been mentioned; however, there is one shawl in the Ratti collection which deserves particular mention. Its beautiful black centre is filled with four of the largest peacocks that have ever been *kani* woven and which alternate equally with four massive temple-like structures which one could conceivably equate (with a slight stretch of the imagination) with the Akal Takhat. (Plate 128) Although of the early Dogra

Plate 129. Kashmir long shawl (detail of WM33, page 189), *kani gurdwara* motif (*Baba Atal Sahib?*).
COLLECTION FONDAZIONE ANTONIO RATTI, COMO

period, again in the Ratti collection (Plate 129) we find an unusual long shawl. Its green centre contains corners decorated with temple-like structures that may recall yet another structure from Amritsar, the Baba Atal Memorial Tower (Plate 130). Built in the late eighteenth century, as a memorial to the extraordinary life of Atal Rai who died in 1628 at the early age of nine, the octagon shaped tower is comprised of nine storeys, each representing the life of Atal.[239]

One of the most prevalent architectural structures found on many shawls during this period is the small temple or *gurdwara* (literally the doorway to God), which appears to be used in a myriad number of ways, either as decorating a type of boat or found within the boteh patterns.[240] The Golden Temple, or at that time the Harmandir, was also completed, but it was not gold plated until Ranjit Singh ordered the work done in 1830. Although the various images of these temple-like structures found in *kani* weaves could therefore be abstract inspirations from either of these buildings, one thing is certain, that building activity, both secular and religious, was flourishing at this time. In the later half of the eighteenth century the Harmandir had been completely destroyed no less than five times by Muslim invading forces. Between 1802 and 1839, under the generous patronage of Ranjit Singh, it had been rebuilt and newly decorated, and finally gilded in 1830. There must have been hundreds of architects and designers *(naqqashs)* from far and wide engaged in this building boom.

Plate 130. Golden Temple with view of the *Baba Atal* Temple to the left, Felice Beato, Amritsar, c.1858-60, albumen print, 9⅛ x 11in. (23.2 x 27.9cm).
VICTORIA AND ALBERT MUSEUM, 80093

Left above:
Plate 131. Illuminated Islamic manuscript page.
New York Public Library, Spencer, Indo-Pers. Ms. 19

Left below
Plate 132. Illuminated *Adi Granth* folio with *nisan* (*Mul Mantra*) of Guru Gobind Singh, 17th-18th century, after *Illustration and Illumination in Sikh Scriptural Manuscripts* by Jeevan Singh Deol, Marg, p. 30.
Collection Takht Sri Harimandir Sahib, Patna

Sikh manuscripts, which include, above all, the *Guru Granth Sahib* or, as sometimes called, the *Adi Granth* (Sikh scripture), and the *Janam Sakhis* (the life of Guru Nanak), were crafted by artists who were imbued with the long tradition of their Arabic and Persian senior craftsmen. This is especially apparent in the folios containing *nisans* (handwriting of a guru) or *sarlauhs* – a *sarlauh* (Plate 131) frames the *nisan* or seal – which exhibit Kashmiri geometric and floral infills not unlike what one finds in lacquerware. Illustrated *Adi Granths*, it is important to note, had adopted fully by the early nineteenth century the Kashmiri style. This most likely evolved through the frenzy of artistic activity and patronage in Lahore and the new sphere of Sikh influence over Kashmir, which, after a long period of Afghan rule, sparked a return to Indic roots.[241] This shift was not unlike the incipient patterns of the Sikh Kashmir shawl.

One example in which such a shift can be viewed is an atypical illuminated folio illustrated by Deol which utilizes a particular bold, floral infill decoration, 'drawn from Indian-Mughal motifs', bearing the inimitable style of Kashmiri artistry (Plate 132). The dome section above the *nisan* is composed of a lobed spandrel edged with small pointed leaves, rising to a pinnacle and topped by a finial. Within the *sarlauh's* spandrel, a riot of freely-spaced swirling vines, primroses and spear-shaped leaves with serrated edges decorate the gold background.

Overleaf:
WM34 (detail) A classic Sikh shawl that highlights many of the basic elements of the period discussed in this book: geometric shapes, architecture, quoits, fool's cap, etc. The feature element, however, is to be found in the transverse and long *hashia* patterns, illustrated with a repeat of two buildings (see detail of WM34 on page 190). The larger of the two depicts an upper level with three domed structures. The outer or flanking two might be a kind of *chatri* (a domed shape pavilion) while the centre or taller one contains a more rounded dome. All the niches depict different forms of nondescript vegetation. However the overall feeling of the entire building is one of a grand palace. The second building of the repeat pattern, much smaller, is even less identifiable and the best one can say about it is that its roof appears to display a dome on supporting columns (perhaps also a *chatri*). Sikh period, c.1835.
Collection Karun Thakar

WM35. Kashmir long shawl (detail)
In this fiery mélange of Islamic and Hindu design motifs, such as the strapwork mihrab and zoomorphic or split-leaf hanging vine, an ingenious balance between colour and form is achieved. Sikh period, c.1845. 143 x 56in. (363 x 142cm).
MUSEUM OF ART, RHODE ISLAND SCHOOL CF DESIGN. MUSEUM COLLECTION, ACC. NO. S1986.014. PHOTOGRAPH BY ERIK GOULD

Such flowery work had hitherto not been employed in Islamic *sarlauhs* and seems to have evolved specifically for Sikh manuscripts of the late seventeenth to early eighteenth century. Although there is little relationship of the floral style to that found in the Kashmir shawl, it is the architectural structure which resonates best with the subject at hand. The *nisan* of Guru Gobind Singh is placed within a large lobed medallion which harmonizes well with the lobed sections above and below, and these arching lobed spandrels and *nisan*-like medallions are often seen in Sikh period shawls (see for example WM3). The lobed spandrel – an idea borrowed from Islamic patterns – is again seen on the exterior decoration of the Golden Temple where the *Mul Mantra* is written in Gurmukhi or Punjabi script. (Plate 133).

Since Guru Gobind Singh declared that the next Guru after him would be the *Adi Granth,* the exposure of this holy manuscript to the public had become enormous. Its illuminated and decorated pages could not have failed to inspire the *naqqash* community of the Sikh.

Beyond the Kashmir shawl, painted floral work in other media can at times be difficult to judge against that of the shawl style. This is due not only to constraints of the boteh, whereby asymmetric floral compositions rise from a central axis stem to spread upwards, but also because the *talim* guru, in translating the *naqqash's* design into a coded system of numbers and symbols of warp and weft, distorts the original shape of the flowers to conform to the twill weave of the fabric. Since shading or graduating the colours for shading was rarely done, flower blossoms often appeared flattened and lacking in the contours of plasticity. However, Moorcroft's eight drawings at the Metropolitan Museum of Art, just a few of many he had brought back to England in 1823, provide strong evidence of the contemporaneous artistry prevalent in Srinagar. The designs compare well with those found on book covers and lacquerware.

Many of the holy manuscripts were commissioned by the Sodhis of Haranpur (in particular, Bhan Singh) who were descendants of the fourth Sikh Guru, Guru Ram Das. One of the most important *Adi Granth* manuscripts

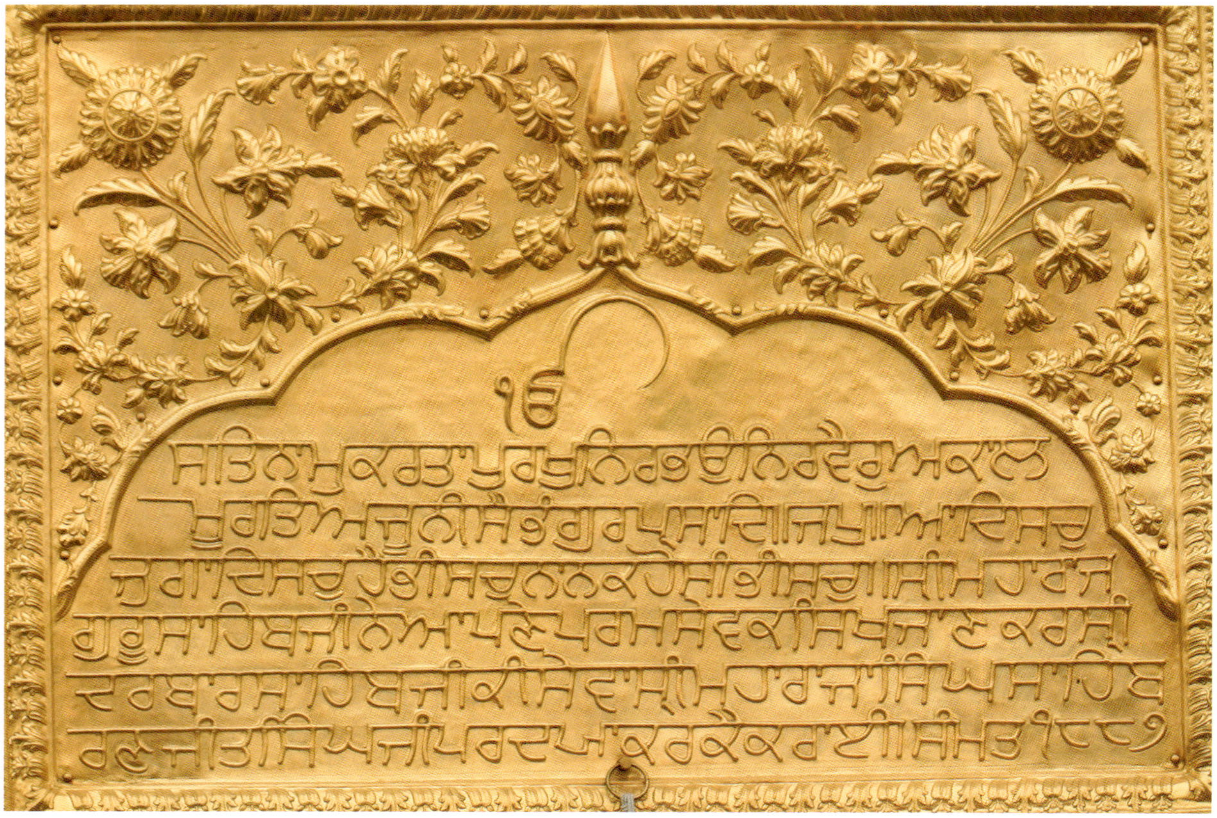

Plate 133. *Mul Mantra* decoration, Golden Temple, gilded metallic exterior, Amritsar.
PHOTOGRAPH BY GURUMUSTUK SINGH

Plate 134. Lotus medallion of Ten Gurus, Kashmir, c.1840, after the *Arts of the Sikh Kingdoms,* gouache and gold on paper, 17½ x 17¾in. (44.5 x 44cm).
National Museum, New Delhi, (59.155/2)

in public collections, and richly illustrated, is attributed to the Kashmir artist, Miha Singh and the Kashmir scribe, Misar Prakas. This is, perhaps, the first mention by name of an artist who is both a Kashmiri and a Sikh. It was made for Sodhi Bhan Singh of Haranpur, district Jhelum. One familiar with the design repertoire of Kashmir lacquerwork would immediately recognize the background pattern of Miha Singh's illuminated folio. The dark blue ground is speckled with tiny flower buds and overlaid with a freely spaced split-leaf, arching cloudband, providing a cosmic setting for the huge lotus-leaf pattern that depicts the constellation of Sikh gurus (Plates 134 and 135).

Plate 135. Painting from the *Guru Granth Sahib,* dated 1839, reclining Vishnu with Avatars, after B.N. Goswamy…, fig. 176, p. 163. 19¼ x 17in. (49 x 43cm).
NATIONAL MUSEUM OF INDIA, 59.155/3.

Although such patterns are not inconsistent with some of the patterns that can be found in shawls, they probably derive from the long tradition of lacquer painting. The colophon within the text provides an enlightening inscription whereby the manuscript's writer avows how much effort has been expended, just as Hanuman knows how difficult it was to cross the ocean. This invocation of a Hindu god by a Sikh scribe is a good example of the strong melding of two neighbouring religions and the often blurring of sacred distinctions.

The importance of this manuscript, and others similar to it, although perhaps less lavishly illuminated, is to be found in the large lotus petals (garland) that form an important part of the illustrations. Their similarity to motifs found in contemporary shawls has heretofore gone unnoticed. The illustrations themselves, however, could have hardly gone unnoticed at the time they were made. The more important books, given their size and lavish work, imply that they were intended for public display. Deol writes: 'Such ceremonial use would be in consonance with long established *Mina* tradition of publicly exhibiting scriptural volumes'.[242] Thus, one thing is clear: the *Adi Granth* was not a book that collected dust on the shelf of a house of worship. On the contrary, not only was it an invaluable item carried into war in battles against the Afghans and Mughals, but it was also admired as an object of aesthetic value among the Sardars and chieftains.[243]

It should be pointed out that the tenth Guru and the last, Gobind Singh, a true warrior, ended Guru lineage. He insisted that 'it was the Granth that should be worshipped, and through it the ten Gurus would receive symbolic representation'.[244] This surely caused a dramatic increase in the publication of the *Granth,* and most certainly of the illustrated *Janam Sakhis* and other Holy Sikh literature, which many households were required to own. Archer asserts that 'Sikh beliefs had become clarified through the spread of copies of the Granth; religion was a morning and evening exercise practiced either in public, under the direction of a prominent disciple, or privately in the house. The community, in fact, could be compared to a network of cells spread across the Punjab'.[245]

The *Adi Granth* is composed of 5894 hymns, written in part by each of the ten Gurus and by Kabir. It is divided into sections which are classified according to the musical modes (*ragas*) of traditional North Indian music. The *ragas* are further classified by a musical key in which each hymn is sung and the closing section of the *Adi Granth* contains a *ragamala* (Garland of *ragas*). With this scriptural *ragamala* in mind and considering the wreath designs that may have filtered down from the medals of honour, we can begin to speculate about the origins of these highly visible garlands, featured in the design of many shawls. The powerfully drawn shawl pattern in WM37, page 203, in a way, expresses the idea of the *mala* (garland, or prayer beads) within the three bold circular medallions (see detail of WM37, below). This unique design, with its 'spinning' medallions – borne aloft by a rising sea of 'angry' waves, evoking the fantastic imagination of the Japanese woodblock printmaker, Hokusai – explodes with kinetic energy. Who would have thought a subtle synesthesia was embedded within these floating Paisley 'ghosts'?

In reading the hymns of the *Adi Granth,* we find that the tree is often cited directly as symbolizing the Lord Himself. For example: 'The Dear Lord is the fruit-Bearing tree;

Detail of WM37 (see page 203), illustrating the 'mala' concept or even the influence of the wreath associated with the Legion of Honor medals.

WM36. Kashmir long shawl (detail)
The shawl artist has eschewed the traditional boteh and instead opted to create a series of flowering stalks against varying ground colours of intensely dyed pashmina. This intensity, acting as a halo, seems to bathe the 'Divine' trees (or stalks) in a warm glow, perhaps symbolizing the connection with their revered status in the *Adi Granth*. Sikh period, c.1840.
COURTESY, NATIONAL MUSEUM, NEW DELHI, NO. 51.2816

drinking in the Ambrosial Nectar, thirst is quenched' (Guru Amar Das, p. 108, line 6); or, 'This Elysian Tree of miraculous powers is the name of the Lord' (Guru Arjan Dev, p. 265, line 5). The tree is thus either directly referred to as the Lord, or mentioned in the context of, for example, 'wish fulfilling', 'celestial', 'miraculous', 'ambrosial', 'Elysian', 'contentment', 'golden', etc. It is not surprising, therefore, to find the tree, often a kind of cypress, as a feature element in many of the high Sikh period weavings (WM32, page 185).

The idea that a Sikh artist from Kashmir has the ability to learn and illustrate complex Hindu iconography, demonstrating his creative abilities, is an excellent example of reaching out and accepting the challenge of articulating new themes. Sikh art was not only promulgated by Ranjit Singh and his entourage of foreign mercenaries, but also, as recent research in this area has come to illuminate, by the noble families of his court. Local and migrant artists and draughtsmen must have been impressed by such public displays of an art form whose impact on the religious community was so great.

Although it is widely accepted that Ranjit Singh's magnetic charisma brought peace and stability along with patronage of the arts, less is known about the interaction of royalty and craftsmen within the Sikh community prior to his phenomenal rise to power as Maharaja. As for Archer's view that Sikh patronage of the arts only began within the first few decades of the nineteenth century, Hari Harinder Singh, Srivastava, B.N. Goswamy, et al., have presented formidable arguments to the contrary. Besides the Sandhanwalias and the Majithias, it is now known that there were, during the second half of the eighteenth century, more than a few Sikh *sardars* who patronized Pahari painters. Jai Singh of the Kanhaiyal *misl,* and his sons Gurbaksh Singh and Jassa Singh Ramgarhia, all dealt with Pahari painters.[246] It therefore comes as a welcome surprise to learn of the names of at least two Sikh craftsmen from Kashmir who worked on the *Adi Granth* as illuminators and the names of the patrons for whom they worked. Artists who worked on the *Janam Sakhis* in the Baba Atal Sahib (a shrine) in Amritsar are identified by Srivastava as Amar Singh, Jaimal Singh and Buta Singh.

While a large corpus of Sikh manuscript literature from the sixteenth to nineteenth centuries can be found spread out geographically throughout Indian and Western museums, university libraries, and private collections, making access difficult, scholars have yet to make it a focus of a major study, especially from an iconographic view. However, one can easily observe the commingling of three distinct styles from the Pahari, Punjabi and Kashmiri regions, although Kashmir had been responsible for producing some of the finest specimens of illustrated Sikh MSS.

Opposite:
WM37. Kashmir long shawl (detail)
The rich emerald green centre casts backlighting, illuminating the bright colours of the very unusual double circle centre, creating a kaleidoscopic effect. The laurel wreath idea was most likely borrowed from design motifs found on the medal of honours which Maharaja Ranjit awarded to his *Fauj-i-Khas* (elite) troops. Sikh period, c.1830. An identical shawl is in the Collection Fondazione Antonio Ratti.
Private Collection

ASKER KAN
mbassadeur de Perse

Chapter 6

Persia and Kashmir:

A Cross-Fertilization of Two Cultures

Multan and Lahore fell sway to Muslim influences via completely different routes and periods. Approximately two hundred miles apart, Multan was the first, in the eighth century, to come under the Arab sphere of Muslim hegemony and then, a hundred years later, to become an Arab state. This portion of India, according to Percy Brown, was more Persian, maintaining relations with Southern Iran. Lahore received its Islamic influence at a later date, through Afghanistan, since it was not until the tenth century that Mahmud of Ghazni wrested the Punjab capital from Hindu rule. The twelfth century saw the construction of Ghaznavid palaces (since gone). As a melting pot of Persian and Central Asian influences, a strong foothold for Islam subsequently developed on the subcontinent. Repeatedly attacked by the Mongols and captured by Babur's troops, Lahore became an Imperial seat of the Mughal Empire under Akbar and later an outpost to Nadir Shah's warring campaigns, until it finally came under the rule of Maharaja Ranjit Singh in 1799.

Ranjit Singh soon extended his kingdom to include all of the Punjab, an area that took in several of the Mughal empires' former *subas* (provinces), which extended from the Khyber Pass to Philaur (near the Sutlej), from the Himalayas to the Sindh frontiers. It was the fertile Land of the Five Rivers, a stretch of *doabs* (the land between two rivers) irrigated by the Sutlej, Ravi, Indus, Chenab and Jhelum, all of which drain down from the Himalayas. The Jhelum River forms at the north-eastern slopes of the Pir Panjal Range, sweeps north cutting across the expansive Kashmir Valley, through the city of Srinagar and Wuler Lake, hooks around Muzafarabad and drops south through the Punjab Plains draining into the Arabian Sea. While in Lahore, the seventeenth century doctor to Aurangzeb, François Bernier, remarked that the quality of the Kashmir shawls woven in Lahore and washed in the Ravi was less than those coming from Kashmir.[247] This defect he attributed to the poor qualities of the Ravi which, passing through Lahore, draws its waters from the northern edge of the Siwali Range, a much higher mountain range (about 23,000 ft. – 7,000m) than that of the Jhelum's source, bordering Chamba and Basohli.

Kashmir sits above the Pir Panjal mountain range and is a large valley running north by north-west and south by south-east. Kashmir's strategic geographic position, lying between China and Central Asia, is such that it enjoyed being an integral part of the Silk Road. Its Indo-Persian culture became well established during the Sultanate period, a period in which waves of immigrants, often known as Sayyids, from Persia and Central Asia alike, came and settled

Opposite:
Plate 136. Portrait of Mirza Ashgar Khan, Ambassador of Persia, Zand period (1750-1779), after Christie's catalogue, 4 May 1995, lot 37.

Plate 137. Shah Hamadan Mosque, Srinagar.

in the Valley. With them came their determination and passion to proselytize and disseminate the embrace of Islam. It was not until a Tibetan prince, Rinchin (1320-1323), took control of the Valley and converted to Islam, that Kashmir witnessed its first state religion and first Muslim king.

Accredited as the most influential of the pious Sufis to have arrived in Kashmir, the peripatetic Sayyid 'Ali Hamadan (1314-1385), endowed with a scholarly genius and saintly charisma, was responsible for thousands of converts to Islam. Persian soon became the language of the court. This was the beginning of successive waves of Sayyids (a highly respected clan of Muslims), Sufi saints and scholars whose Persian language and culture had by then become a subject of righteous learning and education within the major institutions of the Valley. Scholars, poets, mystics, statesmen, writers and Hindu pundits all flourished in what must have been, indeed, a rarefied glorious atmosphere, the likes of which, the world may never see again.

Zain-ul-Abidin (r.1420-1470), often credited with the founding of the shawl industry, descended from a continuous line of the Sultans of Kashmir. His reign is associated with one of the most peaceful, artistic and intellectually stimulating periods in the history of Kashmir. Architecture, music and dance, religious toleration, art and crafts and the pursuit of higher learning became the hallmarks of a long rule, whose reputation had spread throughout Central Asia, the Middle East, Egypt and Mecca. Mention of the word 'shawls' is noted among the many gifts he dispatched as part of his diplomatic relations with Samarqand, a fact which, if it wasn't for the rarity of the wool, may sound ironic, since Samarqand's artisans' excellence in all crafts was probably one of the highest in the world.[248]

Since the fourteenth century, or the arrival of Shah Hamadan and the construction of the mosque (still standing but rebuilt in the mid-nineteenth century – Plates 137 and 138) named after him which has since become a point of pilgrimage, Persians have continued to travel to Kashmir.[249] Under the peaceful and patronizing rule of the Mughals, whose language was also Persian, Kashmiri scholarship continued its intellectual growth in the humanities and sciences. With the decline of the Mughal empire, the Afghans, under the Durranis, moved in and took control of Kashmir (1753-1819). One of the Afghan governors of Kashmir was Amir Khan, a Persian of the Qizilbash persuasion, who began his post in 1771.[250] Unfortunately, records in trade and commerce for Kashmir's Afghan period are severely lacking.

Trade was heavily curtailed with the arrival of the Afghans, causing the disappearance of almost eighty Hindu firms. Kashmiri traders continued their Central Asia interests through business houses in Yarkand, Kashgar and Tibet. Therefore, in assessing design influence from points west of Kashmir, and especially from Persia where patronage, pomp and splendour permeated the changing diplomatic climate of the Safavid, Zand and later Qajar dynasties, trade, however meagre its available evidence, needs to be taken into account. Ann Lambton's in-depth monograph on trade at the beginning of the nineteenth century, under the early Qajars, makes it clear that the absence of trade statistics forms a major hindrance to the advance of mercantile activities among Persia's trading partners. We do know that Persia's foreign politics at this time were somewhat indecisive due to their sporadic conflicts and wars with Russia. Despite these conflicts, where Russia was trying to force its hand over the control of Persian trade, mercantile activity

Plate 138. Ceiling décor of Shah Hamadan Mosque. The mosque was renovated around the mid-19th century and shows a Sikh pattern which was very popular on embroidered *rumals*.
PHOTOGRAPH BY STEVEN COHEN

continued between India and Persia. This activity came via the East India Trading Company who never formally secured a trade agreement with Persia; the Company was more interested in seeing that the Russian sphere of influence remained in abeyance and remote from India.[251]

While Kashmir was under the Sikh rule, Shia traders from Iran, numbering between two and three hundred, formed the largest foreign colony. They fled Kashmir after the Sunni-Shia riot in 1831.[252] This must have had an adverse effect on trade between Persia and Kashmir; from travellers' accounts to Kashmir we know that the shawl industry was in the hands of only a few rich Persian merchants, who also controlled commerce between Kashmir and Tibet.[253]

Since the collapse of Imperial Mughal rule following Nadir Shah's devastation, north-west India and the Punjab were not the safest places for Indians, let alone traders and foreigners. War was everywhere. From the south came the Marathas, to take over the Punjab (1758); from the northwest the Afghans (Durranis made nine invasions between 1748 and 1767); from the north and east the Rohillas and the forces of the Nawab of Oudh, for a face-off against the Marathas who ultimately were decimated. The Afghans under Ahmad Shah Abdali (Durrani), who already ruled Kashmir (1753), finally took control of the Punjab (1759). These were tough, cruel and exacting people who picked clean the pockets of every Kashmiri, ruining the entire economy of the valley. Eighty Hindustani merchants, obviously some of whom were shawl merchants, fled their homes and businesses and returned to their homeland.

Thus, merchants who once travelled under the firm hand of Mughal rule unimpeded along protected routes, suddenly found themselves either locked out or having to establish difficult and circuitous routes of access. Although Forster's recorded comments of merchants enjoying 'full protection … and … commercial privileges' may seem to conflict with the actual state of affairs, I believe he must have been referring to the region confined to the Kashmir Valley, and to points eastward from the Himalayas. He also may not have been aware until after the great famine of 1783-4 hit (Forster entered Kashmir in 1782), that it would not only devastate much of northern India but also affect Kashmir itself. In fact, the rise and prevalence of banditry towards the end of the eighteenth century was directly related to the famine, a famine that purportedly was more destructive than all the wars put together.[254] Twining was constantly warned about the 'mounted banditti', and he observed that to cross the Doab without escort was considered impracticable.[255] According to one historian, the famine, known as the *chalisa,* also affected, besides the Punjab, the north-west provinces, Oudh, and Kashmir, and extended as far away as Bengal, Madras, Bombay and parts of Rajputana.[256] The effect of the famine and the chaotic state of the Punjab was to effectively shut down all creative, mercantile, and industrial activity.

In 1809 Maharaja Ranjit Singh struck a deal with the British to fix the Punjab frontier at the Sutlej, thereby establishing a dividing line between British India and Ranjit's Land of the Five Rivers. The British maintained outposts along or near the Sutlej such as at Ludhiana, where surveillance activities took place. Political tensions were heightened when the British discovered that the French were negotiating with Russia, creating a palpable fear of the two muscling in on British territory.[257] The amount of trade between Persia and the Lahore court should be weighed against scars yet unhealed by Persian invasions, which obviously engendered a deep distrust and vigilant surveillance of that country's intentions. Since the caravan routes would have been unsafe, most merchandise travelling between Persia and Kashmir would have taken place by sea traffic via Bombay or, if by land, via Kashgar and Yarkand. By the time Moorcroft arrived in 1819 Kashmir was once again open to traders from around the world, including many from Persia.

Given the various pictorial references and the extraordinary commercial ties between Mughal and Safavid dynasties, the distinct visual differences between those shawls attributed to Persia and those of Indian origin present a persistent challenge of a much earlier history for the Persian shawl. Written sixty years ago, Phyllis Ackerman's seemingly exhaustive monograph (at that time) on Persian textiles covered important ground. Her study of textiles, in general, revealed not only the various towns and cities but also the artists responsible for the development of intricate and sophisticated weaving patterns for the nobility and the general market. However, given the lacunae of references available to her at the time, her abortive glimpse of the shawl industry hardly did justice to the active role Persia had enjoyed, and certainly prevented her from assigning, prior to the nineteenth century, any shawl history of substance.[258]

It was not until two decades ago that the first firm references emerged to push the shawl industry back to at least the eighteenth century.[259] It was through the likes of two French emissaries, Guillaume Antoine Olivier and Adrian Duprès, travelling there between 1794 and 1807, and also due to the Englishman, Sir John Malcolm in 1801, that we have confirmation of important *kani*-shawl weaving centres, especially Kerman. Recent research has shown that it was in 1640, as discovered through the inventory probate records in Istanbul, that Yazd and Kashan emerge providing multicoloured silks from the former and shawls from the latter, in the form of Kashmir substitutes, though it was pointed out that their quality was not to be compared to the Indian versions.[260] Of course, the type of weave is not mentioned. This important reference also makes note of imitations being produced in Istanbul. Willem Floor cites the poet, Vahshi Bafqi, who, in a poem for the governor (1587-1598) of Kerman, refers to the shawl.[261] From another seventeenth century source we learn about Indian traders who bring into Persia beautiful 'silk' sashes known as *schal,* which are used as turbans because the Indian ones are longer lasting.[262]

Hanway, writing in 1753, noted that sashes and turbans were made of costly Kermani wool and one can be quite confident that their designs were in the Kashmir/*kani* style.[263] It is curious that Hanway, when writing about the sashes and turbans worn by the Persians, cites the quality of the 'costly Kermani wool' which most other writers so often repudiated because of its inferior quality when compared with that of Kashmir's wool. This discrepancy may have had more to do with, among other things, the way the wool was spun, the water used to wash the wool, and even the quality of the dyes. Once a person is exposed to the incredible fineness, texture and warmth of the real Himalayan *pashmina,* it easily becomes the standard against which all others are measured. While in exile in Persia the Mughal Emperor Humayun was hosted by Shah Tahmasp, who saw to his Imperial needs by lavishing upon him, among other things, *shal-e termeh* and *shal-e Kashmir,* which, of course, doesn't tell us where the *termeh* was woven. Thus, however 'substitute' these Kashmir products were, we have here documented proof early on of an industry that was, at the very least, four centuries old.

Uncovering useful data on the commercial movement of shawl, textile and other goods of Kashmiri origin will eventually have to depend on a careful scrutiny of early Armenian, Russian and Middle Eastern mercantile trade and, as already noted, perhaps Turkish probate records. Unfortunately, all the imperial records of the Safavid court were destroyed during the Afghan invasion in 1722. Although many detailed studies of Indian merchants working in Persia, Russia and Uzbek Turan have been published in the last decade or so, statistics on the actual flow of merchandise from Kashmir are lacking.[264] About Russia, Burnes remarked that 'The passion for shawls among the Russian nobles is great, and will account for the exorbitant prices given for them…'.[265] This is borne out by the number of fine shawls bearing Russian customs duty stamps (WM31, page 180). In studying the Indian diaspora of the seventeenth to eighteenth century, and while drawing extensively from Russian archival material, Stephen Dale, in his fact-filled monograph, establishes the great importance the huge number of expatriate Indians placed on commerce between India, Iran, Uzbek Turan and Russia. According to at least one estimate, taken in 1630, as many as ten thousand expatriate Indians lived in Persia.[266] In all the key trading cities such as Multan, Kandahar, Bukhara and Astrakhan, hundreds of India traders were settled. In the latter city resided a large colony of Punjabi traders.[267] From the late sixteenth to the early seventeenth century only was trading more stable and it proved safe to travel in caravans, since both Safavid and Mughal rulers recognized the great importance of guaranteeing a safe passage to the very people who saw to the prosperity of their respective countries.

The Armenians were in competition with the strength of the Indian traders across the Orient. They represented an equal if not more powerful colony of merchants. They were highly trained and educated within their own special schools for mathematics, accounting and the mastery of languages. By the time Shah Abbas I awarded them a monopoly over the silk industry (1606), their network (firmly ensconced in the Middle East) extended from Holland, France, Italy and the Far East to Surat, Agra, Cambay, Diu and Goa. These unsung heroes, bonded by esoteric and religious ties, were considered the best intermediaries for the shipment of rare goods, and the high value of the Kashmir shawl was such that, in all likelihood, it formed a lucrative part of their trade. For example, merchandise destined for Persia travelled through Kandahar. The link Kashmir-Lahore-Kandahar was heavily populated by Indian and Armenian merchants and moneylenders whose established trade colonies were supported by a solid financial and administrative infrastructure. If war or turmoil broke out, goods were immediately diverted through safer regions and points of embarkation. When Kandahar fell to the Persians in 1622, goods were directed instead to Surat for shipment to points west, such as Baghdad, an important entrepôt. The irony of the situation is such that, even if records of shawl merchandise were found, due to the shawl's costliness they probably would not be listed, except perhaps in some secret code. One would find it credible that these precious weavings were treated like rare gems and that their transportation had to be done discreetly.

Floor publishes a long quote from a very informative nineteenth century German source, wherein the author describes in detail just to what extent the Persians had adopted the shawl as an object of high value. Shawls and even shawl fragments were used as cash or as bribes, and it was considered a 'sign of good education' to know how to estimate the price of a shawl. In another reference Floor cites that 'pieces of real shawls are weighed with gold and are considered to be as small pieces of money'.[268] Property was often measured, among other valuables, in shawls, both in the Orient as well in England. Custom House officials in London were savvy about the value placed on the shawls and were not indiscreet when it came to searching travellers.[269] Indeed, one of the most ubiquitous items found in the antique textile market is a small fragment of *kani* woven material, either from Kashmir or Persia. It would have been carefully preserved by a Russian floral-printed cotton backing, while the reverse side perimeter edges were lined with a wide ribbon of silk which had been meticulously sewn down with a type of quilting stitch. If silk was not used, then one might find a ribbon of Yazd type *khatraaz kani* fabric.

Following the death of Nadir Shah (1747), a new ruler rose to power, Karim Khan Zand (r.1750-1779). Karim moved the capital to Shiraz, a city close to the Persian Gulf providing easy access for international maritime trade, especially from Bombay and Surat and points further east. Shipping routes from India to the Gulf were direct as boats passed through the Ormuz Strait and docked at Bandar Abbas or continued up the Persian Gulf coastline to Bushire, at Shiraz's port city. By 1804 the amount of Kashmir shawls arriving in the Gulf region was enormous, estimated

Opposite:
WM38. Kashmir long shawl (detail)
A finely woven shawl with sunburst white centre and corner lyre motifs and a novel *palla* of directional botehs filled with leafy stalks. Notice the Russian customs stamp on the yellow fringe tab. Sikh period, c.1840.
Collection Joan Hart

Above:
Plate 139. *Karim Khan Zand and his Kinsmen,* attributed to Muhammad Sadiq, after 1779, Shiraz, after *Royal Persian Paintings,* L. Diba, 1999.

Left:
Plate 140. *A Girl playing a Mandolin* by Muhammad Sadiq, dated 1769-70, Zand period, oil on canvas.
PRIVATE COLLECTION

upwards of 6,000 pieces.[270] Of course not all of these remained in Shiraz; many went to feed the luxury demands of the markets further west, in Baghdad and Turkey, not to mention the many pilgrims arriving in Mecca.

With the likes of ruthless leaders such as Nadir Shah (1698-1747) and Ahmad Shah Abdali, who followed him, wars in the region were very much part and parcel of eighteenth century life. The seizure of Persia by the Afghans (1722) and the subsequent warring chaos of Nadir Shah culminating in his assassination could not have been much of an atmosphere for the creation of new art forms. India, too, was being plundered for what little booty remained. Yet, somehow, despite the echoing world of clashing swords, dark skies disappeared for a while as a period of peace and prosperity settled in on Shiraz, nurturing it under Karim's rule into a thriving city with cultural aspirations; painting and architecture witnessed a renewed efflorescence.

Plate 141. *An Amorous Couple,* signed by Muhammad Sadiq, dated 1787, Zand period, after Sotheby's NY, 12 Oct. 2005, lot 43.

Zand Painting

A look at the large painting of *Karim Khan Zand and His Kinsmen* provides a strong statement of dress code and etiquette at the ruling court of Kashmir's close neighbour. The turbans are mostly red and white and each one is wound with a slightly different twist, while others appear not twisted at all (Plate 139) In addition, the twisting is quite clear from the white and blue ground *hashias*, which form the features of the long edges of the shawl fabric. As far as design information goes, the only thing we have to go by is multiple flower repeats of the *hashias* and the diapered floral repeats of the men's coats, which contain only small buti or tiny flower sprigs. The butis' leaves, branches and blossoms are highly detailed and are typical of the buti found in the shawl weavings up until, say, the beginning of the Sikh period (1819). What is remarkable in this painting is that one of the dignitaries is wearing almost exactly the same patterned coat as Karim Khan, while two others also sport a similar pattern on their coats. I doubt very much if the colour of the turban was an important sign of hierarchy in this painting, or even at Karim Khan's court in general, since besides Karim's white turban, two others sport white ones as well. What is difficult to determine is whether the material used for the turbans was a complete *dochalla* or narrowed down to serve as the turban, since there are no botehs or even glimpses of botehs as is sometimes customary. A nobleman painted by Mohammad Zaman III in 1795 is shown with a tall white turban and at the very top one can clearly see a piece of the large flower that usually crowns the top of the tall bulbous botehs of that period (Plate 136).

In recent years, four life-size Zand paintings have surfaced, shedding important light on the surprising early development of the curvilinear boteh. Three are from the hand of Muhammad Sadiq (fl.1740-1790), of which two are signed and dated. The first, *A Girl Playing a Mandolin* (Plate 140), is inscribed 1769-1770;[271] the second, *An Amorous Couple* (Plate 141), is

Left:
Plate 142. *Embracing Lovers,* attributed to Muhammad Sadiq, Shiraz, c.1770, Zand period, after *Royal Persian Painting* by Layla Diba, p. 157.

Opposite:
Plate 143. *A Portrait of a Dancing Girl,* oil on canvas by Muhammad Baqir, dated 1778-1779, Zand period, after *Hali,* 139, p. 71.

dated 1787.[272] The third, *Embracing Lovers* (Plate 142), can be firmly attributed to the artist, with the approximate date of 1770-1780. Another recently discovered Zand painting, perhaps the most important for our study of shawl iconography, titled *A Portrait of a Dancing Girl* (Plate 143), is also signed and dated, Muhammad Baqir, 1778-1779.[273] Its sudden appearance at a Sotheby's auction a few years ago created quite a stir among textile historians for two reasons: first, signed and dated eighteenth century paintings, either from Persia or India, with clearly delineated features of the Kashmir shawl, are extremely rare; secondly, the surprise of viewing an otherwise early nineteenth century shawl pattern in a decidedly eighteenth century painting translates into a definite need to reassess the way shawls had been hitherto dated. Put another way, one could almost safely say that, had the painting not been dated, textile and painting experts might have rigorously disagreed over such an early date for this portrait. What all four eighteenth century paintings have in common is the painter's use of the Kashmir shawl to adorn his subjects with clearly identifiable boteh patterns. One may now wonder just how old is this elusive curvilinear boteh, and what about its origins? Does this also mean that shawl boteh patterns which are semi-curvilinear but yet contain a lively bouquet of flowers have to be reassigned to a generation earlier? There is reason to speculate that *A Girl Playing a Mandolin,* given the sharp definition of boteh pattern on her trousers, may easily have been a style created at the beginning of the eighteenth century. There are no parallel Persian art forms, even in woven carpets. Because shawls are so well identified and defined by the shape and style of the boteh pattern, collectors, curators and aficionados have become greatly influenced in dating them according to the ubiquitous patterns of repeat design. While there may be further surprises down the road as other concealed or as yet undiscovered paintings emerge over time, this small group of Zand paintings begins to fill a gap with much needed pictorial evidence.

Over twenty years ago I had seen the painting *A Girl Playing a Mandolin* and felt quite perplexed over the validity of its inscribed date of 1769-1770 (Plate 140). When my research on the Kashmir shawl was about to be published (1986) it was an easy choice not to alter my chronology on the basis of meagre evidence in one painting, locked away in a private collection in Tehran. It was not until 1998, when Layla Diba's magnificent book *Royal Persian Painting* appeared, that my earlier doubts began to resurface.[274] Both paintings were displayed on consecutive pages, facing each other, a fact that further stimulated my curiosity to learn more about Zand painting. Having consulted Diba about the Falk painting, she assured me that both signature and date were clearly inscribed on *A Girl Playing a Mandolin*.[275] With the arrival of the painting at Sotheby's auction house, we now had three eighteenth century Zand paintings with *kani* material of sharply defined, strikingly 'precocious' botehs.

Although life-size Persian painting began in the seventeenth century, its popularity seemingly emerged only at the beginning of the eighteenth, reaching its peak with Fath Ali Shah (r.1798-1834) in the nineteenth century. Karim Khan encouraged the arts and the large scale of many of the paintings proved that they were made for high visibility. Because they were often placed within niches, the canvases were arched at the top and the dimensions often reached from 40in. (102cm) in width to 60in. (152cm) in height. In this way, paintings played a significant role in promoting the latest fashion within the Persian Empire. Since the paintings were often presented to foreign emissaries, exposure to Persian fashion must have made an impact abroad as well.

With the arrival of Karim Khan Zand, a new political stability arose and with it a renewed

interest in painting, as seen in the previously mentioned group of paintings. Similar to the Napoleonic painters who exalted their subjects with the diaphanous folds and exotic patterns of the shawl, these three paintings, through their courtly luxury and refinement, may have been equally emblematic in proclaiming a bold style and fashion for an imported rich fabric.

In *Embracing Lovers* the male's tall red cap is brightly patterned with a buti repeat and his coat is a dazzling red and white striped *(khatraaz)* material with tiny buti, most likely from Yazd or Kerman (Plate 142). His female consort sports a 'Kashmir' coat with buti (small botehs) on a dark blue ground (typical of Persian taste) while behind her is draped a long saffron coloured shawl with an overall pattern of larger buti, bordered by a *hashia,* obviously of Kashmir origin. The girl's billowy trousers, most likely of silk, are patterned with bold curvilinear botehs on a blue ground, while the cone is filled with a hazy, vermicular scribble, something very unrelated to the types of cone-fills one would typically find in Kashmir. In the admixture of textiles and romance, it is worth noting Diba's approach to the painting's higher symbolism:

> *An idealized image of the luxury and refinement of court lifestyle is conveyed by the rich fabrics, lavish gilt patterning, and impasto of the jewelry…in a broader sense however, the image exemplifies the romanticism of Persian poetry. The modeling of the faces and bodies is counterbalanced by the rich interplay between the striped and floral textile designs and the figure's limbs, which combine to form an abstract pattern.*[276]

One cannot help but feel that Henri Matisse, whose own lavish Oriental fabric collection served him as a working library, would have felt right at home among the Zand and Qajar artists.

Scrutiny of *Mandolin* shows that the trousers' pattern clearly reveals sharply pointed botehs containing a vase and dish flanked by leafy fronds and a large flattened flower placed at the top and in the centre, all typical features of the Kashmir pattern. In addition, a long shawl is obscurely draped behind the girl, but, due to the lack of a proper colour photograph, little can be decoded.

Although *kani* material can at times be extremely finely woven and rendered into quite thin material, it could also be argued that the women's trousers in both paintings were made of silk, since *kani* material might have been considered too warm or heavy for comfort. Postulating that these trousers were of silk suggests that the time capsule for the boteh pattern in Persian silks equally requires re-evaluation. Silk, it appears, was the only fabric used as waistband material, as indicated from Persian painting up until the time of the Zand. With the evidence of these paintings, both silk and *kani* boteh patterns appear to be in fashion. A distinct likelihood that the silk industry of Persia was first responsible for the creation and dissemination of these curvilinear boteh patterns should not be overlooked. Thus, Persia's mercantile influence, its centuries old renowned silk industry, *kani* products, noble thirst for fashion and possible introduction of the Zand cone into the repertoire of its shawl industry have yet to be fully investigated.

Baqir's *A Portrait of a Dancing Girl* depicts a woman with a wonderfully detailed long Kashmir shawl that has been wrapped around her waist and tied in front around her belt buckle (Plate 143) As she pinches one end up with her castanets, the other falls down in a smooth telescopic twist with the pattern clearly visible. At the beginning of the nineteenth century, the *dochalla's* (long shawl) *hashias* (borders) were extremely narrow and comprised a finely laid out floral meander of usually four or five flowers, flanked by an insignificant guard border whose width was no more than a few millimetres. A decade later, it appears that the *hashias* widened with more evolved guard borders.[277] Baqir's *hashia* meander, however, fits in well with other known eighteenth century ones in so far as it shows only a two-flower repeat. In general, eighteenth century *dochallas* were woven with a four or less flower repeat in the *hashia;*

earlier ones often displayed only one or two.[278] This idea of blossom repetition normally applies to the long vertical *hashias*. On fine shawls, both the vertical and horizontal *hashias* would actually mirror each other's patterns.

Baqir's botehs are sharply curvilinear and filled with flowers that are not simply mosaic in style, but exhibit clearly identifiable features from the known repertoire of Kashmir designs. Baqir's enthusiasm for the shawl, though not as meticulous in his details as, say Ingres, is nevertheless such that he leaves us little doubt as to the shawl pattern's floral content. Although close in format, but not in detail, the boteh does resemble those found in the Moorcroft patterns dispatched to England in 1822.[279] However, in *Dancing Girl*, Baqir's boteh is clearly from an earlier generation. There is a large blossom at the top, while at the bottom we find, flanked by leafy sprays, a vase spewing forth the familiar flower buds and blossoms. More surprising yet, for this early date, where one would have expected to see at least some remnants of natural flowers still in fashion, is the representation of a boteh tightly enveloped by a dense thicket of flowers, which mimics the boteh's interior and which covers most of the red ground.

These three key paintings by Sadiq and Baqir represent an important milestone in shawl history in so far as they not only symbolized a form of noble decadence, but may also have heralded the beginnings of a new (court?) fashion, not unlike the success of shawl fashion under Napoleon. The Zand period ushered in patterned *kani* dress accessories with tiny patterns; a transfer of the decorative motif of the shawl. According to the visual evidence the figural paintings afford, the curvilinear boteh appears on women's trousers and jackets and in men's turbans and waistbands. Because the Persian fashion dictated that turbans and waistbands be wound and twisted, tiny patterns or butis were usually preferred. Twisting a full-blown Kashmir boteh or other large pattern into a waistband would have broken up the design, rendering the total effect less appealing. Wrapping a classic Zand high turban was different; *dochallas* were often used, making good use of the long *hashias* as decorative swirls while the *pallas* were mostly hidden except, on occasion, one could glimpse part of a tall boteh (Plate 136).[280]

The exciting revelatory boteh graphics in these three paintings seem to instantly overthrow all our previous ideas of chronology for the shawl by at least thirty years, establishing a new time-line paradigm. The implications are huge and suggest the possibility that the curvilinear boteh first developed in Iran. They provide us with surprising new iconographic reference points. The fact that they come from Persia, and that they represent the earliest of dated pictorial sources for the Kashmir shawl, underscores two things: first, a lack of knowledge of Persia's textile and decorative arts of the period prior to the nineteenth century and secondly, and equally lack of knowledge of mercantile trade between Kashmir and Persia.

A perusal of paintings executed during the Safavid and Afsharid (1736-1747) periods that preceded the Zand illustrate characters who are lavishly dressed in rich floral-patterned silks. However, their costumes show a marked absence of anything resembling Kashmir or the boteh pattern. Similarly, there is a void with regard to the wide *hashia* Indian *patka* in all three periods. Indeed, Safavid *kani* shawls, where one might expect to see, at least, designs with the bird-and-tree-stump cliché, appear to be nonexistent. Equally, in the pre-Zand period we find little among the works of the master Ali Ashraf (fl.1740-56), who worked with lacquer and oils and specialized in flower designs, medallions and birds. What is important to note from all this is that, despite Iran's rich weaving industry, where once great designers such as Shafi Abbasi (c.1740s to 1770s) and Muhammad Zaman (1649-1704) were active, transitional elements that might link typical Safavid designs to those found in the *kani* shawl – either in Kashmir or Persian shawls – appear to be patently missing.

Chapter 7
Some Further Musings on the Boteh

Although the development of the boteh has been previously discussed, the ability to develop better chronology has often been hampered, surprisingly, by lack of pictorial evidence from India.[281] Until recently the earliest Indian paintings found in which one can say for sure that the shawl has been well replicated, with its distinctively identifiable features, have been from the first quarter of the nineteenth century. While eighteenth century Indian paintings certainly contain many instances of the Kashmir shawl, the detailing is so sparse and indecipherable that the pictorial barely resembles the extant evidence.[282] From the former time frame, two paintings of exceptional detail stand out. One is of eight successful horse traders of hill tribe or Afghan origin, three of them wearing red *dochallas* (Plate 144). Red and other dark colours were popular in that region. The second painting depicts a group of wealthy jewellery merchants seated on a rich carpet in front of a Mughal style home with servants (Plate 145). What stands out here are the beautiful moon shawls: two red ones, perhaps an identical pair; and an elaborate white one. The dates – somewhere around the second decade of the nineteenth century – given by Archer to these rare sartorial paintings would appear to be spot on, given the moon shawl patterns.[283] Imam Bakhsh

Above:
Plate 144. A group of Afghan horse traders, painting by William Fraser, 1816-1820, after *India Revealed,* by Archer and Falk, fig. 99, p. 111.

Opposite:
Plate 145. Lalita Parshad seated with four companions, c.1820, painting by James Fraser, after *India Revealed* by Archer and Falk, fig. 84, p. 105.

Left:
Plate 146. Geometric motif, painting by Imam Bakhsh Lahori, 1837-1839, from *Jean de la Fontaine*.
COURTESY MUSÉE JEAN DE LA FONTAINE, CHÂTEAU THIERRY

Opposite:
Plate 147. Geometric motif, painting by Imam Bakhsh Lahori, 1837-1839, from *Jean de la Fontaine*.
COURTESY MUSÉE JEAN DE LA FONTAINE, CHÂTEAU THIERRY

Below:
WM39. Moon shawl (detail)
An ingenious use of hooked vines, sharply hooked botehs and a repeat of *gurdwaras*, or temples, combine to form a bold pattern on a red *pashmina* ground. Sikh period, c.1845.
COLLECTION FONDAZIONE ANTONIO RATTI, COMO

Lahori's celestial quincunx patterns which he used to illustrate Jean de la Fontaine's book of fables offer tantalizing suggestions (Plates 146 and 147), which will be taken up in a future study devoted to the moon shawl, an area that needs to be seriously addressed.

In the Western world one had to rely on the Empire (1804-1814) painters such as Ingres, Baron Gros, Godefroy and David who meticulously featured the Kashmir shawl in their paintings. For the textile historian, unfortunately, they only depicted two types of shawl patterns that were then in vogue: the *buti* or tiny flower repeat and the boteh or

Plate 148. Madame Bansai by Ingres, 1795.
MUSÉE DU LOUVRE, PARIS

cone. Other more floral types were certainly available. Ingres, in a delicate sepia sketch, depicts Madame Bansai draped in a shawl with an end decoration of bouquet repeats (Plate 148) which are drawn with just enough detail to discern the non-curvilinearity of the bouquet.[284] Certainly had this sketch made its way into oils, Ingres would have left us with a very compelling and colourful shawl pattern. At present, there are no other French paintings of significance prior to the last decade of the eighteenth century featuring Kashmir shawl patterns. French textile printers wasted no time in seizing a design opportunity, as can be seen in the album of the Oberkampf estate, bearing the inscription: 'Most were copied from the first shawls and scarves which were introduced in France at the beginning of this century (c.1800) by the officers of the Egyptian army'.[285]

In the Near East, the early Qajar period (reign of Fath Ali Shah, 1797-1834) of painting, more than any other contemporary period, is replete in shawl illustration. Qajar nobles revelled in Kashmiri cloths. The types of patterns they enjoyed most appear to be narrowly focused on either tiny buti repeats or on diminutive curvilinear botehs. Thus, Qajar painting appears to act more as a confirmation of Persian fashion rather than as a source of new stylistic information. Looking at extant shawls themselves, held by institutions and collectors, there are basically no dated shawls, either from this period or earlier. Therefore, before c.1800, until the discovery of the Zand paintings, there was basically nothing available, either from Western or Oriental pictorial sources. Evidence of the curvilinear boteh developing well into the eighteenth century, as attested by Baqir's *A Portrait of a Dancing Girl,* serves, therefore, to confirm the pictorial legitimacy sought by textile historians.[286]

A broad overview of this noble period is acquired through the languor and opulence of the court paintings, where colourful textiles and shawl stuffs often dominate. We observe that the freely spaced, natural flower so prevalent in Mughal times is no longer in fashion. Maybe it was then that the style of the curvilinear boteh, vying with the floral boteh, developed and began to impose itself on Kashmir. The big European markets for the shawl hadn't yet opened up; until then the market was mainly Turkey, Persia, Central Asia, Russia and, of course, India. The other possibility is that the cone emerged directly, and perhaps to a large degree independently, from within the enormous silk weaving industry in Persia and, thereafter, merged with the design repertoire of the Kashmir shawl.

Another theory is that the style remained localized. One might speculate that it was a new fashion; these curvilinear botehs captured the fancy of the ruling classes of Zand nobles and dignitaries. What makes all this so intriguing is that the cone is absent in carpets, lacquerware, architecture and all the other decorative art forms until the end of the eighteenth century. Curiously, I have never heard any of the Kashmiris speak about Shirazi or Tehrani styles, but they do indeed speak of Hyderabadi and Jaipuri styles. Some of the old-timers will mention Pathani style, which is in reference to the hill tribe and Afghani people.

In Moorcroft's trade/commerce notes (1822) Persia tops the list as recipient of the highest percentage of different shawl items exported from Kashmir. Given the nature of his mission, we find 'An Account of Shawl-Goods…' skimps on the exact nature of the various markets at which the shawl was aimed. However, of the eighty-four items listed under 'Trade Name', Persia is named as a destination thirty-eight times, while Turkey (where flowers in the Ottoman period were worshipped) is named twenty-two times and Afghanistan twenty-six. Whether the goods were reshipped once they reached their destination is unknown. Moorcroft, writing in 1822 from Srinagar, pointed out in his voluminous notes that the quality and pattern of the various shawl goods were produced in 'conformity to the taste of the markets for which they are intended in a degree probably not suspected in Europe'.[287] Nevertheless, in his account under 'Remarks' he leaves us with very succinct descriptions. Only one item, labelled 'Kuddhar', comes close to a description, about which he says 'With large groups of flowers somewhat in the form of the cone of a pine with the ends or points straight or curved downwards'. Although here we learn something about the pointed shape of the boteh, of the precise terminology as applied to the shawl, Wilson's transcription of Moorcroft's notes provides the following:

> Buta *is the generic term for flower, but is specifically applied, when used alone, to the large cone-like ornament which forms the most prominent feature of the* pala. *Sometimes there is only one line of these ornaments, extending from the lower* Zanjir *to the upper one. When there is a double row, one above the other, the* butha *is called* Dolkad*; up to five,* Sehkad*, after which it takes the name of* Tukaddar. *Each* butha *consists of three parts; viz., the* Pai*, or foot or pediment of leaves generally; the* Shikam*, or belly, and the* Sir*, or head. The head is either erect, or straight, or curved, or inclined. If the butha slope[s] generally, it is named* Butha kaj. *The* Thal*, or net, is the work which separates the different* Buthas*, but sometimes the interstice is without ornament.*[288]

For a historic description of the boteh, this is about as good as it gets from our man Moorcroft. Nowhere among all the other eighty-three items published in Irwin does he mention the word 'cone' and, in fact, out of this number forty-three have no descriptions at all, while what remains are paltry descriptive words such as 'sprigs', 'flowers' or 'ornaments'. Although slight in detail, other early travellers and writers have given their observations on shawl decoration. Legoux de Flaix, who supposedly visited Kashmir in 1782, submits: 'The price of the shawl is dependent on the size of its flowered ends (*pallas*). The ends must be 16 to 18 inches [41 to 46 centimetres] in height in order for the shawl to bring the highest price'.[289] A retired French military engineer, Flaix offered up some outlandish ideas about the shawl industry, but his observations about the pricing of the shawls appear to be accurate.[290] His height dimensions corroborate well with the prevailing evidence and, although they may seem unusually large for the period in question, based on the newly dated Zand paintings appearing on the market (and the Napoleonic paintings as well) the validity of Flaix's notes now appear sustainable. They also serve to rectify a key misconception that has hitherto been propagated for many years: that it wasn't until Napoleon's return to Europe from his military campaigns in Egypt that a sudden growth in the size of the ornamentation evolved. It can be said that it was at least two decades earlier that such a phenomenon came about, perhaps due to unusual market activities of the Middle East or of the subcontinent itself. Delhi, not to mention Awadh, for example, during the early eighteenth century enjoyed probably one of the most cosmopolitan scenes in all of India, for the rich and famous, noblemen and aristocrats and the royal court. 'They spent huge sums of money on entertainment, festivities, musical soirées, sumptuous banquets and spectacular shows; they were all for ostenstation, formalism, and elaboration in their daily routine of life'.[291]

In our study of ornamentation, perhaps there is no early nineteenth century Indian painting more important than that of the court of Begum Samru for style, taste and the donning of the shawl itself.[292] Begum Samru began in youth as a *nautch* dancing girl, rose as head of a mercenary army, leading her troops into battle, turned Catholic and died immensely wealthy. In this Company style painting (Plate 149), with no less than eighty Indian and European characters illustrated, we find approximately thirty-two are donning the Kashmir shawl at her court. What is interesting in this great frieze is that none of the shawls, despite their great numbers, is either of the Mughal period or of the just beginning Sikh style; all of them appear to be of the conservative *dochalla* type that falls somewhere between that found in Muhammad Baqir's painting of 1778-1779 – the Afghan period – and the style seen in Moorcroft's drawings of 1823, with mosaic infill around the botehs. The only thing Mughal about the painting is the way each of the characters has chosen to drape his shawl. It is either wrapped around both shoulders or around only the left shoulder with the material passing under the right arm, while the decorated *palla* in both cases hangs vertically down the left shoulder, a typical seventeenth century fashion. Clearly this painting illustrates a definite regional taste for a specific shawl style. In our discussion of Flaix's measurements above, one should bear in mind that we cannot eliminate the traditional taste for the less expensive, smaller graceful flowers or cone shapes, which surely continued to vie concurrently with the more expensive ornamentation of larger *kani* woven botehs.

One curious fact about this impressive painting is that it was supposedly executed by '…a freelancer only temporarily hired by the Begum…a virtual unknown', who signed his name Muhammad A'zam. Viewed from a

Plate 149. Begum Samru and her household by Muhammad A'zam, painted c.1820-25.
THE TRUSTEES OF THE CHESTER BEATTY LIBRARY, DUBLIN. ACC. # IN74.7

costume perspective, it is obvious that the painting is a virtual fashion show for Kashmir shawls. All of them exhibit similar patterns, leading one to speculate as to whether the Begum had insisted that all members of her family wear the same style, including the servants. Being expensive items, the servants probably received them as gifts, although given the 'caught in the headlights' look on their faces, one is tempted to say that most of the shawls belonged to the Begum's wardrobe and may have been loaned specifically for this portrait. Since it is usually the case that several artists would work on a tableau of this magnitude, one should not discount the possibility that the costumes and shawls were executed by another artist. The Begum normally commissioned her paintings from the Delhi artist, Jiwan Ram, an artist trained in European techniques who had worked for Akbar Shah II and Ranjit Singh as well.[293] Whoever the artist responsible for the fine detailing of the Kashmir shawls may be, this tableau could not have failed to have a resounding impact on the fashion and style of the period.

Equally well known as an important document of royal courtly life in the early nineteenth century, but perhaps not quite as sartorially dazzling, is the darbar scene of Akbar II (r.1806-1837). Of particular note in this painting on ivory (Plate 150) is the marked difference in style of donning the Kashmir shawl. On the left are two characters, each wearing two shawls (of which one appears to be a moon shawl), both of which are draped over their heads, a reminder that the early morning in the Delhi winter months, when this scene takes place, can be quite cold. Concerning the fashion for patterns, we find little difference between the tastes of Delhi and those of Begum Samru's region, Sardhana.

While Moorcroft was still in Kashmir (1822), the French shawl manufacturer cum writer, Jean Rey, was busy publishing the first book on the Kashmir shawl. He contended that floral decoration 'prior to this period was never more than 9 inches [22.9 centimetres] in height'. Given the *palla* height of contemporaneous shawls, obviously this was incorrect. One wonders where he was when David and Ingres were exhibiting at the Salons.[294] Rey makes known his obvious disappointment in the likes of Forster and Flaix and their 'general silence' about divulging the secrets of shawl weaving. One or the other must have witnessed the actual weaving; the secret is carefully hidden with them, he bemoans.[295] Napoleon's return from Egypt was the main cause for the shawl's explosive popularity in France and Europe. Legoux de Flaix notes clearly that he had returned to France from India in 1788 and had brought some shawls with him which he offered as gifts. He lamented: 'no woman was flattered by them'. This precludes any notions that France played a role, say before the advent of the Jacquard loom in shawl weaving around c.1815, of influencing the *palla* height of the shawl.[296]

Since one would certainly assume that the princesses, baronesses and other noblewomen of Europe would not have worn old shawls, one could safely say that these shawls represented newly minted fabrics of the latest Oriental fashion. Comparing a Baqir to an Empire style shawl now becomes a challenge, for the former style would appear to be much later. Although the shawls of Kashmir were in fashion in England perhaps as much as a generation or so before they caught on in Europe, the shawl's surge in interest among the nobility didn't come about until Napoleon's Egyptian campaigns and the pictorial power of the Empire painters. There is little evidence in painting, either French or English, that could show other shawl styles or the transition of one style to another; European paintings with freely spaced and natural flowers are virtually non-existent.[297] Without doubt we learn from dated paintings the periods in which certain patterns were in vogue. We do not know for just how long the shawls were popular before they made it to representation in the paintings. In the case of the Empire painters it would appear that they took a boteh style that had been long in fashion in the Orient, perhaps in Persia to be precise, and adapted it to French taste, while other trends of whimsical or even conservative taste came and went. Just as Irwin stated, there were novelty patterns alongside those that expressed the market tastes of the conservatives and ultra-conservatives, while concomitantly there were the exotic patterns created for foreign markets that gained local

Opposite:
Plate 150. Delhi Darbar of Akbar II, c.1820.
British Library, London, Add. Or. 3079

popularity by dint of innovation and originality.

Does this mean that many of the shawls with this type of design previously dated to 1815-1820 now have to be reconsidered? The immediate answer to that question is 'yes'; the long-term answer will take, well, a little longer. Why? There are several factors. We need to look at the dyes used, as well as the botanical rendering of the boteh, and we need a thorough knowledge of the *hashia* pattern repertoire of the Afghan-Sikh period. In addition, much as a painter's brushstroke can identify the artist, the outline contours must be carefully weighed against the floral naturalism of the content. The effect of all this is to narrow the playing field, placing a heavier demand on the researcher to be more precise in shawl pattern recognition.

Despite the long history of Persia competing with Kashmir to produce a fine shawl, there is no convincing *kani* evidence for Persian products of the eighteenth century. Almost all the beautiful long shawls, *jamawars* (long gown shawls) and moon shawls we know of attributed to this period are from Kashmir. Eighteenth century shawls possess a distinct colour palette of rich and exotic hues and unique botanical details and, so far, none attributed to Persia has been found enriched with these characteristics.

The approach of the Qajar period in Persia, which was concurrent with the high Sikh Period in India, seemed to bring about a radical change in fashion, as evidenced by the widespread use of the sharp boteh pattern on many other costume elements. This is especially apparent in the figural painting of nobles sporting long fur-lined robes, while in India a similar transference occurred except that the draping of the shawl still remained the custom.

As more eighteenth century Persian paintings begin to surface (as well as objects in lacquer), the origins and development of the boteh motif will most likely experience further dramatic changes in understanding, forcing us to re-evaluate old theories and critical notions of Oriental decorative arts. Because the cone design is also a major motif found in Oriental rugs and carpets, the benefits of research in this area can be extremely helpful in dating floor coverings (Plates 151 and 152). The paintings instruct us, above all, to regard fashionable patterns in the Kashmir shawl which remained in vogue for a conservative Persian taste while, parallel to that trend, other fanciful motifs came and went, fulfilling a niche for the exotic and whimsical. The Persian silk and *kani* industry and its patronage should be carefully reviewed to develop a better understanding of the propagation of motifs within the historical nexus of the international shawl industry. Whether the court painters had more influence than the textile and lacquer artists on the popularization of a particular motif is difficult to tell; that their activities were very much tied together is a known fact.

It is well known that in Persia the various crafts were organized into trade guilds – including the *naqqashs* – which offered opportunities to the young who perhaps had not inherited their talents from their parents. On the other hand, in India skilled professionals, such as the *musawirs* and *naqqashs,* developed their trades as handed down from father to son within the tightly knit family circles that defined the organization of craftsmen in the Punjab and the Hill States, and most likely in Kashmir. In Persia, however, at the beginning of the nineteenth century the guilds offered many artists the chance, through government subsidies, to travel to Europe where it was believed the best experience for a painter could be achieved. While we know little about if or how many Persian art students may have gone to Europe during the eighteenth century, we have firm evidence

Opposite:
Plate 151. Palace carpet with vermicular field pattern and bold 'strapwork' meander. Its Kashmir-inspired design exhibits split-leaf end botehs standing tall and 'snarling' face à face within the arches created by the thick meander. Knotted sheep wool, Sikh period (Lahore?), approx. 14 x 21ft. (4.25 x 6.5m).
COLLECTION BEAUVAIS CARPETS, NEW YORK

Plate 152. South Persian carpet with boteh motif. 18th century or earlier.
COLLECTION JIM BURNS

that, as early as 1811, many were sent to Paris, Rome and Great Britain to 'master the art of European painting'.[298]

From the seventeenth century on, beginning with the likes of such great artists as 'Ali Quli Bayg Jabbadar and Muhammad Zaman, whose inspired paintings were directly linked with European techniques and subtleties, the Perso-European art form had become standard practice among artists, often copying directly from or mimicking engravings, prints and oils as they entered the country. A large number of European sketches, drawings and prints surely found their way back to Persia via art students who had gone to immerse themselves in Western world art. Such cross-cultural links with Europe may have first begun under Shah Abbas I (r.1687-1729); a treaty with France was signed in 1708. However, Persia's conflicts with the Ottomans made any serious European connections extremely difficult.

It wasn't really until the arrival of the diplomatic missions headed up by Guillaume Antoine Olivier, Amédée Jaubert and General Gardane at the beginning of the nineteenth century that serious trade agreements were undertaken. Thus this period was probably the most propitious time for students travelling abroad to France. Although the best of the shawl artists often worked on a commission basis for the nobility or royal workshops, the main source of income and survival for the artists came from the commercial market, which may have been the dynamic impetus for Persian art students to travel to Europe. Such events should not be ignored in evaluating the overall design influences of a shawl industry that was, for the large part, controlled by Persian traders, who most certainly arrived in Srinagar armed with fashion trends popular in Tehran, Isfahan, or Meshad, etc. Although open to speculation as to how certain designs may have infiltrated the shawl 'canvas', many woven during the turn of the nineteenth century exhibit design elements borrowed from Napoleonic era ideas. To mention a few of the First Empire design devices found in contemporary shawl patterns, we have the Greek palmette, laurel crown, garland, rectilinear leaf branch, cornucopia, split-leaf rosette, vase and urn. Many of these motifs were incorporated into the *hashia* patterns.

Whether these motifs made their way to the shawl through the mercantile impact of the Persian traders residing in Kashmir is certainly an unresolved point; that Persian art students returning from abroad had been exposed to and copied such great artists as Ingres, Jean Godefroy, David, Baron Gros, Gérard, Mosnier and Prud'hon would be difficult to refute. All this expands on possible sources of an ever widening international market that, by the turn of the nineteenth century, and given the heavy burden on Kashmir's looms to meet world demands, became increasingly sensitive to world fashion. While there were many artists of talent working in the various large cities of Persia such as Isfahan, Kashan and Tehran, there seems to be little known about their works in general and even less about their biographies. Nevertheless, one artist, Mirza Baba of the Imami family from Isfahan, cited by Floor, from the period 1785-1810 produced oil paintings, manuscript illuminations, miniatures and lacquer covers. His wide ranging talents included the creation of flower paintings as well and he was esteemed as one of the most renowned artists of his day; his talents became legendary and were considered almost divine.[299] This period of Mirza Baba is, of course, of particular importance when weighed against the change in shawl patterns developing in Kashmir, as it falls well before the direct influence of the Europeans who found employment with Ranjit Singh.

In mulling over the market forces acting on fashion, somehow the words of John Irwin keep ringing in the air: '...great importance on novelty and fashion... independent evidence of a documentary nature... place them within the framework of when they were first known to have appeared...'. Maybe we can frame them to a degree, but then the imagination takes over and we find ourselves musing over the maturity of the boteh and claiming that it needed several decades to achieve its look.

WM40. Square shawl *(rumal)*
There is something about the design of this *kani* piece reminiscent of the pattern found on the ceiling of the Shah Hamadan mosque in Srinagar (see Plate 138). The bull's-eye centre of concentric circles is unusual. Late Sikh period, c.1850.
COURTESY INDIANA MUSEUM OF ART, INDIANAPOLIS

Epilogue

Nothing can replace years of experience in the handling of *kani* shawls. Like Oriental rugs, one can talk and read about them ad infinitum, but to understand them fully one has to expose sensitive fingers to their tactile qualities and eyes to their inimitable colours. One has to roll up one's sleeves and, by opening and unfolding these large tapestry weavings, feel their weight and softness. Granted, the study of the Kashmir shawl differs from Oriental rugs in the sense that the type of weave usually remains the same: twill tapestry and double-interlocked. On the other hand, rugs come in hundreds of sizes and shapes, often woven with cotton and wool combined, containing wefting and various types of knotting and distinctive warp depression and a myriad other details that set them apart as a truly ethnographic artefact: tribal, village, urban, court, etc. Since all *kani* shawls are woven in the same technique they can, for the most part, be divided up into long and square, making them much easier to sort out; but, for the novice, determining the difference between a Persian and a true Indian, regardless of how many books read, would not be an easy task. One needs to get hands on with them. Few are the number of museum curators trained with the skills of determining the provenance of the *kani* shawl, not to mention the differences between European and Indian ones. The older Persian rug dealers, of course, would be more likely to have this knowledge and especially the shawl wallahs of India whose families, for centuries, have been trading in and repairing them.

Museums and institutions overlooked a golden opportunity during the Persian diaspora when the Shah of Iran fell.[300] Thousands of rug dealers fled to other countries taking with them family treasures and rich collections of Safavid textiles, including caches of Kashmir shawls. New York was a good place to be at that time and if one was in the rug and textile business there was no need to travel abroad to various cities such as Kerman, Yazd, Isfahan or Shiraz. It was all there, safely tucked away in the shops and homes of the newly established businesses of the expatriate Persian community of the Big Apple. It was a tremendous learning experience to see these various groups of textiles that had been collected over the years. The Persian shawls stood out clear as day from those woven in India. True, the *kani* shawl was woven in many Persian cities as well as in many of North India, but, by and large, there were significant differences in the dyes used, the patterns employed, the piecing and, of course, the quality of the wool that separated them from their Indian counterparts.

To comprehend fully the material, historical or picture book knowledge is not empowering enough. The Persian art scholar, Phyllis Ackerman, in her ground-breaking work on Persia, *A Survey of Persian Art*, inaccurately attributes a magnificently patterned, very late nineteenth century Kashmir shawl to the seventeenth century, exclaiming it's '…so definitely Persian in floral character and so unlike anything from Kashmir that its Persian origin can be assumed…'.[301] With this unabashed postulation, she continued to push

Opposite:
Detail of WM20 (see page 121).

further into the quagmire of misattribution with a description, albeit absorbing, of its pattern matched only by a theory of which town, Kerman or Characin, might be ascribed to its origin. Of course sixty years ago errors such as this were easy to make. Had Ackerman set foot only once in a Delhi bazaar she would have quickly learned that these types of shawls represented Kashmir's last floral gasp at supplying their indigenous markets. A similar error occurred with our doyen of shawl history, John Irwin, when he chose to illustrate his 1955 and 1973 monographs with a nineteenth century fragment of the same ilk, though he doesn't refer to it in his text. Perhaps it was not surprising, therefore, to find in Ackerman's monograph on Persian textiles only one thin paragraph on Persian shawls. In their research, Western scholars of the early twentieth century depended mainly on western sources, Latin languages or translations thereof. Today's cyber world has made available a deluge of information. In this rapidly shrinking world the emergence of this new technology and e-material is stimulating and, for an enlightened bevy of polyglot scholars, knowledgeable collectors and historians, this can't help but bode well for the future of art history.

The most serious attention given to the Persian textile industry since Pope and Ackerman has been from Willem Floor, whose dense monograph is jam-packed with refreshingly early and important references, many culled from a great variety of multilingual sources. This assiduous work, with a ground-breaking chapter on the Persian shawl industry, brings a new and invigorating focus to an area that has for a long time remained unexplored. For the student of the nineteenth century shawl there is much to be found. Tracing the etymology of the word *shal* to at least the tenth century, Floor's relentless blitz of critical references to the industry straight through to the nineteenth century ends with a thorough description of the industry in Kerman. However, in the wake of this thorough but unillustrated exposé of facts, little can be gleaned aesthetically from any of the patterns discussed. Unlike Ackerman and Irwin and others before him who stated that it was merely difficult to know the difference between the Persian and the Kashmir shawl, Floor openly declares that he is completely flummoxed when it comes to that point. There is a palpable sense of plaintive frustration as he hammers away at each of his numerous references in an attempt to squeeze out a final answer of enlightenment, only to end with the wry phrase 'I leave this pleasant task to art historians and textile experts…'.[302] None the less, Floor's exasperation is perfectly justifiable considering the paucity of literature on this subject, both by textile dealers and academia.[303]

As discussed above, the Iranians placed a great value on the shawl and even the smallest fragments were coveted. Evidence of this can be seen in the many fragments which have been carefully backed, the edges carefully wrapped with strips of *kani* material, often exhibiting a *khatraaz* pattern and silver or gold type of lacing, or fringe, attached. This was an inimitable technique of care and preservation unique to Persian culture. *Royal Persian and Kashmir Brocades*, published in 1975, has been little discussed or its impact assessed during the course of recent publications on the *kani* shawl. Nevertheless, the one hundred or so full-page colour-illustrated *kani* swatches which it features were collected over a period of fifty years by a prominent Iranian antique dealer from Tehran, who willy-nilly had developed an eye for 'home-grown' textiles from his native soil. Of the 104 colour plates, approximately forty-two, it would appear, have been rightly attributed to either Kerman, Khurasan, or Yazd, with the remaining assigned to Kashmir. As one would expect of the former cities, almost all contain small repeat patterns and none appears to be older than early nineteenth century, while of the latter there are motifs which are obviously dating from the eighteenth century. As attested by the substantial chapter on mordants and dyes, the authors had extensive knowledge in dye techniques and bring therefore a trained eye to discerning the various nuances between the Persian and Indian *kani* products. I believe that a short apprenticeship of a hands-on experience in handling both types of regional textiles would enable textile enthusiasts to detect and make apparent their differences. Since there are no other books either by dealers or scholars devoted to Persian *kani* shawls, the value of this book should be acknowledged, if only for the rare ethnographic light it sheds on the geographical provenance for the Iranian shawl.

In sum, the particular Sikh patterns, with strange shapes and geometric patterns that have so far been discussed are best understood through the perspective of cross-cultural forces that have defined the Punjab. We have seen how Persia's Zand painting can define a fashion; Pahari painting inflect an aesthetic sensitivity; and how Punjabi artists ply their trades. There is no doubt that these cross-cultural forces derive from the French mercenary officers in command of a Punjabi army trained in the Napoleonic style, or from the might of a Sikh Khalsa movement in full expansion under the powerful Maharaja Ranjit Singh. If the Sikhs broke caste through their Khalsa Brotherhood, they also broke from the past with their new shawls, creating an inimitable style whose impact is still in fashion today.

WM33. Detail of WM12 (see page 100).

Notes

1. The first *Exposition des produits de l'industrie française* took place in 1798 and subsequently in 1801, 1802, 1806, 1819 (London and France), 1823, 1827, 1834, and so on....
2. Stella Kramrisch, *Exploring India's Sacred Art* (selected writings), Barbara Stoller Miller (ed.), University of Pennsylvania, 1983, p.16.
3. Lafont, *Maharaja Ranjit Singh*, p.129.
4. Ames, 'A Kashmir Paradigm Shift', *Hali*, 2005, issue 139, pp.70-75.
5. Manucci, II, p.341.
6. *Tarikh-i-Rashidi*, p.425.
7. *Memoirs of Jahangir*, pp.143-144.
8. Modave, p.360.
9. Flaix, p.298.
10. Archer, *Painting of the Sikhs*, 1966.
11. *Tarikh-i-Rashidi*, p.434.
12. Chandra, p.9.
13. Some interesting observations on the antiquity of Kashmir's celebrated wool can be found in *Commerce between the Roman Empire and India,* where the author discusses the trousseau connected with the marriage of the Sassanian King, Homisdas, to the daughter of the King of Kabul (E.H. Warmington, Octagon Books, 1974, p.161).
14. Bernier (about 'embroidery made on the loom...').
15. Flaix, p.294.
16. Blochmann, vol. 1, pp.91-92.
17. Ibid, p.91.
18. Foster, p.169.
19. *Tuzuk-i-Jahangiri*, pp.147-148.
20. Indeed, Akbar had established a veritable battery of chroniclers to record every detail of his reign, with Abul Fazl at the head. Thus there is every reason to believe that some parts of the chronicle could be missing. See Pal, *Court Paintings of India,* 1983, p.36.
21. Ethnic Afghans from the North-West Frontiers.
22. Beach, *The Imperial Image*, p.58.
23. Flaix and Fraser were there but obviously they were not interested in detailing information on the industry, especially since it had not yet achieved its great success in the West.
24. Moorcroft and Trebeck, *Travels in the Himalayan Provinces....*
25. In the words of F.S. Aijazuddin: 'Lahore was the fulcrum of the Punjab'.
26. It should be pointed out that, although the stylistic nature of these four important periods has been underlined, there would be very little technical variations in the weave since all the significant weavings are from Kashmir; a serious study has yet to be conducted on shawls attributed to areas outside Kashmir.
27. Scott, 192. One should also mention *Recueil de Décorations Intérieures.*
28. For an comprehensive and fascinating discussion of the French military and their advanced technology in India, see *Indika,* chapter 6.
29. Fahr-Becker, p.108.
30. Bamzai, p.610.
31. The area of European design that engendered the creation of the style Art Nouveau has yet to be fully studied vis-à-vis the impact of the Indo-French Kashmir shawl industry.
32. Use of the term 'Kashmir shawl' or *kani* shawl, unless otherwise noted, denotes a *pashmina* wool shawl woven on the loom in the double-interlocked, twill tapestry technique. Although a few museum examples do exist, *kani* shawls of *shah tus* from the 19th century are extremely rare. Besides being difficult to dye, *tus* is so delicate, soft and breakable on the loom that it requires very special treatment. Weaving ornamentation into a *tus* twill weave using the *kani* technique is virtually impossible without somehow strengthening the foundation, often with the addition of heavier wefting as in the normal *kani* shawls.

33. Irwin, *Shawls* ,1955.
34. Ames, 2003, pp.85-97.
35. Irwin, 1955, pp.11-13.
36. Fazl alludes to this; see *Ain* (vol. 1, 1873, pp.91-92).
37. Personal communication, 7 Aug. 1979.
38. Forster notes that a '...long and very narrow, with a large mixture of black colour in it, is worn as a girdle by the Northern Asiatics (*A Journey from Bengal...* Vol. 2, p.19).
39. Irwin, *A Decorative Motif...*, pp.37-45.
40. *The Kashmir Shawl* , Marg, 1952, Vol. 6, No. 1.
41. See, for example, 'The Court of Kay Qubad', an illustration from the epic *Shahnameh*, 1540-50 National Museum, Delhi, acc. No. 48.8/30, 'Mughal and Deccani Paintings', Dr. Daljeet, 1999, p21; or, *Painting for the Mughal Emperor,* Susan Stronge, pl.42 [1590-1595], p.63.
42. 'More Persian poetry was produced in India than in Persia proper' (Annemarie Schimmel, *A History of Indian Literature,* Otto Harrassowitz [ed], Islamic literatures of India, Wiesbaden 1973: vol. VIII, Fasc. I, p.32
43. Forster, vol. II, p.19.
44. Ismailova, p.15.
45. *Tuzuk,* op. cit., Vol. II, pp.144-145. Jahangir seems to have been fixated on the term 'Sweet scented' mentioning it four times in just a few pages.
46. See Pl.88, p.261, of Ames, *The Kashmir Shawl....*
47. This can be better understood through V. Rich's article 'Mughal Floral Painting...' (1987) in which it can be seen how the Mughal artist interpreted these engravings.
48. Desmond, p.259.
49. *Tuzuk,* p.144.
50. Barrett and Gray, p.87.
51. Schimmel, *Pain and Grace,* p.2.
52. Forster, Vol. 2, pp.115-116.
53. Ames, 2003, pp.84-85.
54. One of the earliest appearances of this elusive flower, perhaps a few decades even before the completion of the Taj Mahal, can be found on the door surround of the Ibrahim Rauza in Bidjapur, a mausoleum built for Ibrahim II's queen, Taj Sultana, completed in 1626. Although now mostly faded or worn away, one can still see the clear outline of freely-spaced flowers or shrubs that had once colourfully embellished the profusely calligraphic doors that lead into the tomb. (These shrubs are in the typical pre-Mughal idiom, Persian model.)
55. Skelton, pp.147-152
56. 'Sweet scented' is mentioned six times in one paragraph of his *Tuzuk* (p.145).
57. Much like Mansur, but differing in significant ways, was his contemporary in Iran, Shafi Abbasi, an artist at the court of Shah Abbas who, according to Phyllis Ackerman, also 'elevated flowers to a primary place and [he] takes rank as the first outstanding painter to make them his principal concern'. Ackerman (& Pope), *A Survey...* pp.2129-2131. Celebrated as a gifted painter of birds and flowers, Shafi's design inspirations descended via Iran's historic connections with the Far East.
58. Dürer, vol. 2, for example p.710, 'The great piece of turf'.
59. Rich, Doctoral Thesis.
60. Ibid, p.38.
61. Atasoy, p.48.
62. Habib pp.128-131.
63. Koch, p.8.
64. Ibid, p.44.
65. Brown, p.167.
66. Prakash, pp.25-27.
67. MacLagan, p.48. An excellent account of the ecclesiastical debates and frustrating dilemmas of the Jesuit Fathers at the Imperial courts.
68. Pierre Vallet, *Le Jardin du Roy Très Chréstian, Loys XIII, Roy de France et de Navarre 1608.*
69. Greene, vol. 1, p.368.
70. Prior to the Mughals, the Muslims, under the Lodi dynasties (Delhi Sultanate), had their own illustrated herbals which were still based on the Greeks, such as the works of Dioscorides *(Materia Medica,* Pliny and even Theophrastus, fifteen hundreds years earlier.
71. Greene, vol. 1, p.384.
72. Greene, vol. 2, p.858.

73. Until now no insects have been found woven into the early *kani* weaving, though Rich has found that the adoption of this embellishment derived mainly from two European herbalists, Vallet and Passe, but with their own markings and colour.
74. Arber, p.215.
75. Welch, *India!*, p.177.
76. Skelton, p.150.
77. Illustrated in *King of the World* (Beach and Koch), pl. 5.
78. Skelton described them as 'bird's-eye view'. He further suggests that because of the butterflies and the flowers being grouped in rows, a common trait found in European engravings, influence from this source is possible (personal communication, 9 Dec. 05).
79. *King of the World*, pls. 10-11.
80. Ibid., pls. 5 and 11.
81. Cohen, *An Ideal Reality....* Although Cohen concludes that for textiles and rugs the Windsor *Padshahnama* is unreliable, this should not distract from the essential point of this section.
82. Anand, p.7.
83. *The Arts of the Sikh Kingdoms* 1999-2000, Victoria and Albert Museum, The Royal Ontario Museum and the Asian Art Museum in San Francisco. More recently, *I See No Stranger* at the Rubin Museum of Art in 2006, along with their accompanying rich catalogues, have added significantly to our understanding of Sikh Heritage.
84. Stronge, *The Arts of the Sikh Kingdoms*, p.63.
85. Schmitz, *After the Great Mughals*, p.75.
86. Moorcroft, MS Eur 266, f.21. Sharma, p.210.
87. Srivastava, 1991, p.91.
88. Dalrymple**,** *The Last Mughal.* p.32.
89. Forster, vol. 1, p.293.
90. Ibid, vol. 2, p.20.
91. Sharma, D.C, 1983, p.26.
92. Lafont asserts that a 'serious economic history of the Punjab cannot be written because there are not enough contemporary documents' (Indika, p.344).
93. Certainly during the high Mughal period of 17th century Lahore there existed a Kashmir-Lahore centric nexus (see Ames, *Woven Legends).*
94. Burnes, vol. 2, p.399.
95. *Kashmir Shawls: woven art & cultural document,* exhibition catalogue by T. Falk and V. Murphy.
96. Forster, 1798, vol. II, p.20.
97. Sharma, D.C., p.174.
98. Ibid, p.273, p.213.
99. Archer, *Paintings of the Sikhs,* p.22.
100. Sharma, D.C., p.48.
101. For a full treatment of this, see Datta, pp.77-105. It appears that so much shawl wool was being diverted from Tibet to Jammu that in one pleading letter to Ranjit Singh an officer in Kashmir complained that '...Kashmire had become absolutely deserted and its affairs had gone from bad to worse'. (Suri, p.213). Archer states that 'part of Runjit Singh's enigma was his attachment to the Dogra brothers' (*Paintings of the Sikhs,* p.34).
102. Archer, op.cit., p.38.
103. Ibid, p.22.
104. Ibid, pp.20-21.
105. Jacquemont, *Voyage...*, vol.3, p.289.
106. Moorcroft, British Library, Mss. Eur. 260, p.1.
107. For further discussion of this see Willem Floor's informative essay, 'Art (Naqqashi) and Artists (Naqqashan) in Qajar Persia', *Muqarnas* 16 (1999), pp.129-58.
108. B.N. Goswamy, 'A Painter's letter to his Raja Patron: An Old Ta_kr_i Document', *Journal of American Oriental Society*, 1966, vol. 86, pp.209-210.
109. For a discussion of the principal artists and their families see Srivastava, *Punjab Painting...*, pp.47-53. Bishan and Kishan Singh are both mentioned in Archer's discussion of Baden-Powell's review of the arts and crafts fair held in Lahore in 1864, p.61.
110. Stronge, pp.98-99.
111. Ibid. p.101.
112. Goswamy, *Painters at the Sikh Court...*, p.11.
113. See, for example, Pratapaditya Pal's *A Buddhist Paradise: the miracles of Alchi Western Himalayas*, published by Ravi Kumar, Hong Kong, 1982.
114. Khandalavala, p.31.
115. Pal, p.99.

116. Illus. 44, p.136.
117. This may be the only painting in Indian art illustrating a Chinese textile.
118. *Painters at the Sikh Court*, p.2.
119. See, for example, fig. 4, p.52 or fig. 6, p.55, *Painters of the Pahari Schools*, Sept. 1998, vol. 50, no. 1. See also 'Blindman's Buff' by Manaku of Guler, 1750-55, p.100 in *Indian Court Painting* by Steven Kossak, Metropolitan Museum. of Art, 1997.
120. Welch, *Gods, Kings & Tigers*, fig. 64, p.204.
121. Paintings by Indian artists for the British or by the British themselves.
122. See, for example, *A Tiger Hunt* by Hanraj Joshi, p.272, plate 272, c.1777, in *In the Realm of Gods and Kings* (Topsfield).
123. See floral design for an embroidery in *Kings, Gods & Tigers*, p.170, pl. 47.
124. Jacquemont, *Letters...*, pp.280-281.
125. The Universal Expositions of 1834 and 1839 represented important turning points in the dimensions of Jacquard loom engineering (see Ames, pp.145-155).
126. See Chapter Two in Ames, 2003 p.53.
127. Ibid, pp.41-44, letter from the union of shawl manufacturers....
128. Actually, Allard's and Ventura's very first entry into Lahore mostly likely saw them disguised as Oriental merchants; Ranjit Singh thought them spies until checks proved otherwise. See Indika, p.206
129. Lafont, *Maharaja Ranjit Singh*, pp.55-57.
130. Garrett, p.94.
131. Ibid, p.34.
132. This was probably before changes in the design of the medal, which came about with the first *Restauration*, whereby the head of Napoleon was replaced by King Louis XVIII and the other sides introduced the fleur-de-lis.
133. Garrett, p.106.
134. Personal communication with J-M Lafont, 4 Sept. 2004. 'The medals were certainly given to the rank and file of the Fauj-i-Khas. The one kept today in the Patiala Palace Museum must come from an Indian officer of the Fauj'.
135. Personal communication, Lafont, 29 Aug. 2004.
136. Jacquemont, vol. 1, p.359.
137. Archer, *Paintings of the Sikhs*, p.87.
138. F. Bernier, writing in 1670 about his impressions of the great beauty of the Kashmir Valley (*Voyage dans les Etats du Grand Mogol*, pp.301-302).
139. Bamzai, p.519.
140. Zutshi, p.203, 285.
141. Farooque, pp.117-118.
142. Hugel, p.108.
143. Archer, *Paintings of the Sikhs*, p.28.
144. Latif, pp.493-495.
145. The boat in funerary rituals harks back to Greek mythology where Charon the oarsman steers the departed souls across the river Acheron towards Hades.
146. Goswamy, *Nainsukh of Guler.*
147. Garrett, p.90.
148. Burnes, vol. 1, p.9.
149. Garrett, p.102.
150. Zain-ul-Abidin wrote two books in Persian: one on pyrotechnics, *Islamic Culture* (an English quarterly), Vol. LI, No. 1 Jan, 1977, 'Persian Influences in Kashmir in the Sultanate Period (1320-1586)' by Dr. Mohammad Ishaq Khan.
151. Garrett, p.99.
152. Burnes, vol. 1, p.13.
153. Archer, *Paintings of the Sikhs*, pp.79-92.
154. Jacquemont, *État politique...* (1830), p.379.
155. Burnes, vol. 1, p.29.
156. Hugel, pp.283-284.
157. Lafont and Schmitz, *The Painter Imam Bakhsh of Lahore*, After the Great Mughals, B. Schmitz (Ed.), Marg Publications, Mumbai, 2002, pp.76-77.
158. Court also married a Muslim Kashmiri; Allard married in 1830 into a royal family, Ventura a Christian Indian woman, around 1830, who came from the circle of people of Begum Sombre, and married with a big celebration in Lahore, under the eyes of Ranjit Singh. From Jean de La Fontaine, *Le Songe d'un Habitant du Mogol, and autres fables*, illustrées par Imam Bakhsh Lahori, Réunion des Musées Nationaux. 1989. Miniatures conserved at the Jean de La Fontaine de Château-Thierry, Paris, c.1995, p.177 (includes an essay by J-M. Lafont).
159. *After the Great Mughals*. p.78.

160. Charles Percier, *Recueil des décorations intérieurs comprenant tout ce qui à rapport à l'ameumblement comme vases, trépieds, candélabres* ...etc. Paris, 1812.
161. Burnes, vol. 2, p.404.
162. Personal communication, Lafont, 15 Oct. 2004. 'Leurs contacts étaient par Calcutta, ou démeuraient ou voyageaient leurs chargés d'affaires, amis ou parents français (Meifredy, Mazar, Falcon). Mais par Wade (à Ludhiana) et par John Palmer à Calcutta ils faisaient certains achats en Europe.'
163. *The French and Lahore*, p.103.
164. Ames, *Hali* (op.cit), issue 139.
165. For a detailed discussion of these motifs see Ames, 2003, pp.104-108.
166. Ibid, pp.105-107.
167. Karpinski, pp.116-124.
168. Moorcroft, Mss. Eur. 260, p.1.
169. Quoted by Archer in *Indian Painting from the Punjab Hills*. Archer explains that 'he is the only Pahari ruler to be actually portrayed seated with courtiers holding "picture sessions" scrutinizing miniatures and passing them around from hand to hand. (p.70).
170. Moorcroft, Ms. Eur. 260, p.1.
171. Moorcroft, Ms. Eur D 265, pp85-100. It is possible that Joo was the same one responsible for the collection of coloured illustrations of Kashmiris hard at work at the various prevalent trades. (eighty-six drawings at the British Library, Add. Or. 1660). Mildred Archer has found these paintings to be of mid-19th century origin. Given the late pattern of the shawl over which the *naqqash* is bent, applying his colours (see Irwin, 1973, p44), they are probably from c.1870.
172. Irwin, 1973, p.24.
173. Moorcroft, MS Eur 264, p.258.
174. Moorcroft's notes, besides being very difficult to read, are filled with duplications and deletions. Wilson H. Wilson, who prepared his notes for publication in 1841, admits that 'Mr. Moorcroft's writings were so voluminous, so unmethodical and so discursive....', thus making his manuscript exceedingly difficult to analyze. Assuring that inferences drawn from his manuscript are entirely free of inaccuracies would be a daunting task for the most obsessive investigator of primary source material. Because Moorcroft's notes are so indispensable to the history of that era and it is now more than a century and a half since their only publication, perhaps the time has come for a fresh transcription.
175. Alder, p.295.
176. Sharma notes that after the great famine of 1833, these numbers were reduced to about 100 (Sharma, D.C., p.211).
177. Garrett, p.69, obviously referring to the Afghan period.
178. Personal communication 9 Jul. 2004.
179. Garrett. p.27.
180. K. Goswamy has studied Kashmiri manuscripts and found them to be extremely hard to date. Books from both Kashmir and Shiraz resemble each other in colour schemes and standardization of composition. (*Kashmiri Painting*, p.28.)
181. One wonders if the *tarah* and *talim* gurus were actually required in the weaving of the especially large Sikh patterns, the finer ones often seamlessly woven.
182. Moorcroft, MS Eur 264, p65; MS Eur 266, f.21.
183. Bates, p.56.
184. D.C. Sharma, pp.172-173.
185. With all the new workshops opening in Punjab and hill regions, experienced artists must have been in great demand. Many of course, due to famine, had to leave the Valley anyway.
186. Aijazuddin, p.29.
187. Ibid, p.29.
188. Lafont, *Indika*, p.267.
189. Both Allard and Ventura collected Indian miniatures; Allard, two years before his departure for France, had dispatched 'a case of paintings weighing 98.5 kg' (Indika, pp.271 and 257).
190. Lafont and Schmitz, p.92; a copy exists at the Ranjit Singh Museum, Amritsar. Between 1750 and 1793 more than 1,000 French officers served in India.
191. Lafont, *Maharaja Ranjit Singh...*, p.53.
192. Allard's first born, Marie-Charlotte (born Nov. 1826), was supposedly painted by Bakhsh.
193. Lafont and Schmitz, p.90.

194. Vigne, p.124.
195. Losty, pp.286-289.
196. Jean de La Fontaine, op.cit. For Plaideurs and Renard, see pp.104 and 48.
197. The Brooklyn Museum's collection has an amazing unique French Jacquard shawl (unpublished) with chinoiserie motifs, frigates and a host of other fantasy design elements.
198. Two other *quissas* exist, one at the Bibliothèque Nationale (89 illus.) and one in Chandigarh. It should be mentioned that *Tales of A Thousand and One Nights* was already known among Indian artists.
199. Burnes, vol. 1, p.23.
200. New York Public Library, Spencer, Indo-Pers. Ms. 19.
201. Barrow, p.71.
202. The world's largest collection of indigenous South Asian maps is in the Maharaja Sawai Man Singh II Museum, City Palace Museum, Jaipur (Gole, *Indian Maps and Plans*).
203. Barrow, p.84.
204. See, for example, illus. 4 and 5 (pp.79-80) of Lafont and Schmitz; also p.101 of *The French and Lahore*.
205. *Piety and Splendour*, p.191.
206. Mughal artists had been invited to Chamba by Raja Umed Singh (1748-17) (Hall).
207. *Album du Cachemirien.*
208. Couder, normally a great trendsetter in the designs of shawls, has left us few examples of his sketches from this early period. One, a 'harlequin pattern', with compartmentalized botehs, exhibited at the Museum of Industrial Arts, Paris, is important for its date of 1823. However, in this sketch there is little that might foreshadow the coming of the Sikh designs. One can speculate as to whether he drew his inspiration from an Indian pattern or whether the pattern was developed out of his own fertile imagination. Whatever the case, the harlequin shawl represents the earliest dated full design of a European shawl.
209. Ames, 2003, pp.40-41.
210. Vigne, vol. 2, p.85. Schimmel cites a long standing feud in Kashmir between Sunni and Shia beginning from the 16th century (Schimmel, p.6).
211. Rey, pp.142-143.
212. Adamova and Greck, p.59.
213. This is very similar to Mughal carpets and textiles, whereas the 18th century appears to be pretty much a black hole.
214. Losty, *The Art of the Book*, p.119.
215. See also Ames, *A Kashmir Paradigm Shift*, pp.70-75.
216. Beach, p1. 67.
217. K. Goswamy, *Kashmiri Painting*, p.28. Goswamy laments the poor quality as 'bazaar work'.
218. A. Adamova & T. Greck, p.56.
219. Adahl, pp.3-18. One of the late governors of Kashmir, under Afghan rule, was a Qizilbash, Amir Khan, of Persian origin. The Qizilbash are traditionally considered to be the descendants of Persian Shia mercenaries and administrators left behind by the Afshar Emperor Nadir Shah Afshar (1736-47) to govern the Afghan provinces. (Vigne, p.14).
220. Adamova and Greck, p.57.
221. Mikosch, p.14.
222. Ames, 2003, pp.166-168.
223. Garrett, p.27 (section on Jacquemont).
224. Raby, See, for example, p.105, a work signed by Muhammad Zaman, invoking the injunction to the Twelfth Imam, 'Ya Shahib al-Zaman'.
225. Personal communication, S. Digby, 2005. Two hundred years later, Vigne describes the riots between the two sects, vol. 2, p.85). Jacquemont commented 'All the commerce of Kashmir with Tibet is in the hands of the Mussalmans, Shiah of Persian extraction, who live in Ladakh and business is very prosperous' (Garrett, p.72).
226. What was once a colourful and beautifully drawn rare map shawl in the Sri Pratap Singh Museum of Srinagar is now sadly, due to broken windows and neglect to the museum's building, a faded piece of cloth.
227. Ames, 2003, see Colour Plates 145 and 146, p.283. There is also a *naramala* shawl at the National Museum, Delhi, with *kani* scenes of Krishna and Radha at either end. The Tapi Collection has a *rumal* containing a narrow meandering procession of figures.

228. Ames, *Woven Legends*, pp.192-209. Contains a detailed discussion of Lahore and Kashmir as a nexus of craft production.
229. Schmitz, *Islamic and Indian Manuscripts...*, 'A unique feature of the Lahore painting style is that it seems to have originated with the work of a single artist, the gifted Imam Bakhsh Lahori', p.185.
230. Titley, p.211. The British Library's Divan of Hafiz (BM 1879) may also contain some early 18th century specimens of fine Kashmiri work. See Losty, p.143. Although all these characteristics of painting are obviously important for the understanding of the Kashmiri manuscript style and how it may have been applied to or found in the artistry of the *kani* and embroidered shawl, this brief investigation cannot hope to cover all the critical aspects of a complex subject which extends beyond the scope of this book, but opens the ground for future exploration.
231. It should be mentioned that Hermann Goetz, the first to point to a separate Kashmiri school of art, defined the style as 'Mughal-Afghanistani', Goetz, p.14.
232. N. Titley and K. Adahl.
233. See the Rajaur manuscript dated 1719 [18804(97a)], Plate 43: Alexander the Great pursuing Darius across the Euphrates. *Shahnameh* of Firdausi. ('Typical for the Lund Nava'i, as for all Kashmiri illustrated manuscripts, is a tree with concentrically arranged leaves', Karin Adahl, p.9).
234. Ames, 2003, p.168.
235. Seminal works dealing with Kashmiri manuscripts can be found among the following authors: Adamova, Greck, Losty, Titley and Schmitz (see bibliography).
236. Textiles in general of this period have up to this point not been found with any known Sikh designs.
237. Ranjit Singh's funeral was presided over by Brahmin priests and Gurus (Archer, p.29). 'The entire vocabulary and philosophic terminology of the Sikh faith stems from Hindu sources' (Talib, vol. 1, p.495).
238. Srivastava, *Punjab Painting*, p.53.
239. Marg Publications, p.39.
240. A *gurdwara* (Punjabi) is a Sikh place of worship, the temple, where the Guru Granth Sahib dwells and where a triangular orange coloured flag is flown. The prevalence of the Khanda weaponry symbol is a phenomenon of the late 19th century and thus bears little importance to the discussion at hand (personal communication, 19 Oct. 2006, J.S. Deol).
241. Deol, p.33.
242. Ibid, p.41.
243. Singh, Dr. Kirpal, pp.viii-ix.
244. Archer, p.3.
245. Ibid, p.2.
246. Goswamy, *Painters at the Sikh Court.*
247. Bernier, *Travels...*, pp.402-403.
248. Zutshi, p.58. Tamerlane, throughout all his conquests, always spared artisans, bringing them to Samarqand.
249. Although the mosque was rebuilt in 1732, it is obvious that its ceilings were redecorated some time during the late Sikh period, using popular shawl motifs taken directly from the industry. The author is grateful to Dr. Pal for having brought to his attention the ceiling pattern of the Hamadan Mosque (personal communication of 1 Apr. 2007).
250. Vigne, Vol. 2, p.14.
251. Lambton, pp.215-244.
252. Sharma, D.C., p.28.
253. Garrett, p.72. See also Jacquemont, *Voyage...*, vol. 3, p.289.
254. Sharma, S. (see chapter 2).
255. Twining, p.210.
256. Srivastava, *The history of Indian Famines...*, p.21.
257. Treaty of Tilsit in 1807 between Napoleon and the Tsar Alexander I.
258. Pope and Ackerman, vol 3, p.2199.
259. Ames, *The Kashmir Shawl*, pp.119-124.
260. Veinstein, see Chapter 5. p.102.
261. Floor, *The Persian Textile Industry...*, p.300-301.
262. Ibid, p.301.
263. Hanway, vol 1, p.331.
264. See, for example, Floor, Dale, Chaudhury and Morineau.
265. Burnes, vol. 2, p.435.
266. Maloni, p.28.
267. Rishi, p.135. Rishi points out that this huge Indian presence is reflected by the enormous number of Indian manuscripts and

books (about 600 in thirty languages) found at the Institute of Oriental Studies of the Academy of Sciences, Leningrad.

268. Floor, *The Persian Textile,* p.318.

269. Dalrymple, *White Mughals,* p.470.

270. Olivier, vol. 2, p.55.

271. Falk, *Qajar Painting,* fig. 9, p.28.

272. Sotheby's catalogue, 12 Oct. 2005, lot 43.

273. Sotheby's catalogue, *Arts of the Islamic World,* London, 13 Oct. 2004, lot 23, p.44.

274. Diba, *Royal Persian Paintings,* As the one in Toby Falk's book, Diba had revealed another chronologically 'unsettling' painting *(Embracing Lovers)* of a similar date and artist.

275. Diba explains: 'The Forouhgi *(A Girl with a Mandolin)* painting location is unknown but it is likely to be somewhere in Tehran, if it has survived the revolution. As to the dating, although it cannot be read more clearly, it is unlikely to be incorrect since the painting is clearly signed as the work of the painter Muhammad Sadiq a painter active, according to his dated works, from the 1740s to 1790s'. (Personal communication, 13 Nov. 2002.)

276. Diba, 1999, p.157.

277. See Ames, 2003; compare Plates 139 and 144 with Plate 125.

278. One should be careful not to confuse *patkas* with *dochallas* in that the former almost always have larger *hashias.*

279. For detailed description of Moorcroft's drawings see Ames, 2003, pp.103-107.

280. See also Diba, ill. 44, p.190.

281. Ames, 2003, pp.81-118.

282. Archer and William, see, e.g., vol. 2, p.150; see Goswamy, *Nainsukh of Guler.*

283. Archer and Falk, see ill. 84, p.104, and ill. 99, p.111. See also, Goswamy, B.N., Nainsukh... Nainsukh included in his works many textiles in great detail but seems to have never been taken in by the Kashmir shawl. To be clear, since this discussion is solely centred around the curvilinear boteh, we are not talking about the well-known Deccani miniatures (see Ames, 2003, pp.84-85) with easily identifiable (Mughal) Kashmir shawls.

284. Ingres' grisaille painting of Madame Bansai, c.1797, Paris, Musée du Louvre, Cabinet des Dessins, no. R.F. 11684.

285. Ames, 2003, pp.163-164.

286. Two small shawl fragments in Tipu Sultan's (1799) jacket lining were found by the Victoria and Albert Museum. They exhibit no curvilinearity. See Irwin 1973, pls. 4 and 12

287. There is no reason to dispute the same work ethics being carried out among the merchants waiting for their goods in Yazd, Kerman or Meshad.

288. Moorcroft, *Travels...,* Vol. 2, p.190.

289. Forster, pp.317-318. Forster also equates the rising price of shawls to the introduction of flower work.

290. As much as Flaix voices some erroneous remarks about the origins of the wool, his details of the washing and processing of the wool provide valuable information.

291. Malik, p.361. See also *White Mughals,* p.237: Hyderabad's big 'urs festival at Koh e-Sharif, attracting hundreds of thousands of people, late 18th century, was also a bazaar where, among many other items, 'fine woollen *pashmina* shawls' were sold.

292. See Leach, p.789.

293. Ibid., p.791.

294. Irwin, in his first monograph of 1955 (p.33), restated Rey's assertion, rightly contradicted it due to the obvious extant evidence, though for some reason, in his later revised edition of 1973 (p1. 5), he again quotes Rey but without the caveat.

295. Rey, p.146.

296. Flaix, p.291

297. The only known exception to this rule would be Ingres' grisaille painting (op.cit.).

298. Floor, *Art (Naqqashi) and Artists (Naqqashan)...,* p.131.

299. Ibid, p.140.

300. Ackerman astutely pointed out this lack of Persian fabrics in museum collections, p.2154.

301. Pope, vol. 5, p.2154.

302. Floor, *The Persian Textile Industry,* p.353.

303. Ibid. Richly dense in refreshingly new references, Floor has plumbed the depths of both Oriental and Western literature to arrive at a valuable account of the ebb and flow of Kermani, Yezdi, and Kashmiri shawls, rare wools, carpets and textiles.

Glossary

Akali – tribe of religious fanatics from the Punjab
Baradari – audience hall
bract – a small stem leaf usually located just below the flower
buta – Indian term for the Paisley design
calyx – a group of petals (sepals) that lie just below the flower
chakla – district
cis-Sutlej – beyond or south of the Sutlej, controlled by the British
darbar – court
dhurrie – a flat woven floor covering
diwan – high official
doab – the land between two rivers
dochalla – literally two shawls; one of a pair.
doublure – the reverse sides of a manuscript's end covers
emir – a chief, prince, or governor
Fauj-i-khas – Ranjit Singh's elite troops
gompa – Ladakh Buddhist temple
ghazal – A poetic form in the Indo-Perso-Arabic literature, expressing love, pain of separation or longing
gul-bulbul – rose and nightingale motif in Persian art
gurdwara – Sikh temple
Gurmukhi – Punjabi script, used in the Sri Guru Adi Granth
hashia or *hashya* – the border of a shawl
jagir – land granted by a ruler
jharoka – throne seating area of a ruler
kalamkar – hand painted Indian textile
kani – twill tapestry, double-interlocked woven
karkhandar – shawl weaving workshop
Khalsa – literally 'pure'; the Sikh Brotherhood
khatraaz – striped shawl pattern
kunj botehs – Paisleys that decorate each corner of the shawl's field *(matan)*
maharao – variation of maharaja
mansabdar – a military rank or grading
mihrab – an arching niche associated with the direction of Mecca
misls – a Sikh brigade and its territory
musawir – trade organization of artists; an artist
naqqash – Indian or Persian artist
naqsha – Farsi for drawing
nisan – seal of the Guru; handwriting of the Guru
nizam –a ruler of Hyderabad
palla or *pallu* – the end section of a shawl with decoration
pashmina – wool woven from goats of the Himalayan Chang Tang region
patka – waistband
prasad – blessed food that has been offered in prayer to a Hindu deity
quissa –Persian fairy tale
quoit – curved, flat, sharply pointed throwing weapon used by the Akalis
rafugar – tailor, or the one in charge of piecing a shawl together
raga – Indian mode of music
rumal – square shawl
Samadhi – A state of transcendent union; an Indian funeral; burial monument
sardar – military chieftain
sarlauh – a frame for the *nisan* or invocation of the Guru
shah tus – extremely fine and rare wool from the high-altitude Himalayan antelope, chiru (endangered species)
talim –the card that records, in esoteric Kashmiri language, the weft colour and warp number of the shawl pattern
talim guru – the one who records the pattern information
tarah guru – the one who records the shawl colours
termeh –Persian name for *kani* woven cloth
toji – wooden needles used to insert the shawl wefting
toshakana – royal wardrobe
unvan – an illuminated frontispiece found in Islamic manuscripts
zamindar – a landholder who pays taxes

Select Bibliography

Marg Publications, 'Homage to Amritsar', nd (c.1985?)

Exhibition catalogue: *Kashmir Shawls: woven art & cultural document*, Veronica Murphy, Toby Falk, and Mildred Archer, for Kyburg Limited, London, 7-24 June 1988

Album du Cachemirien: Reproduction exacte de tous les beaux châles des Indes et de la Perse fabriqués à Lahore, Ispahan, Téheran, Caboul, Kashmir, et Candahar qui arrivent en Europe calqués fidèlement et dessinés aux traits simples dans leur grandeurs naturelles. Ouvrage précieux pour server de matériaux aux dessinateurs de manufactures, Paris and Kashmir, 1837. Bibliothèque Nationale, Dept. des estampes, Paris

Adahl, Karin, *A Copy of the Divan of Mir Ali Shir Navai,* Persian Painting: from the Mongols to the Qajars: studies in honour of Basil W. Robinson, Robert Hillenbrand (ed), London, 2000, pp.3-18

Adamova, A. & Greck, T., *Miniatures from Kashmirian Manuscripts*, 'Iskusstvo' Leningrad Branch, 1976

Aijazuddin, F.S., *Sikh Portraits by European Artists*, New York/London, 1979

Ain-i-Akbari, H. Blochmann (trans.), Calcutta, 1873

Alder, Gary, *Beyond Bokhara: the life of William Moorcroft, Asian explorer and pioneer veterinary surgeon, 1767-1825.* Century Publications, London, 1985

Ames, F., 'A Kashmir Paradigm Shift: Qajar and Zand Paintings as Evidence for Shawl Dating', *Hali,* 2005, issue 139, pp.70-75

Ames, F., *Woven Legends: Carpets and Shawls of Kashmir 1585-1870*, The Arts of Kashmir, p.Pal (ed), Asia Society, NY, 2007, pp.192-209

Ames, F., *The Kashmir Shawl and its Indo-French Influence*, UK, 2003

Ames, F. 'A Unique Mughal Kashmir Shawl at the Musée Guimet', *Orientations,* Oct. 2007, pp.69-72

Ames, F. 'Lost Horizons: The Stylistic Development of the Kashmir shawl', *Hali* 6, no. 4, 1984

Anand, Mulk Raj, *Painting Under the Sikhs*, Marg, Vol. VII, N. 2 (1954)

Anand, Mulk Raj, *Maharaja Ranjit Singh as Patron of the Arts*, Marg Publications, Bombay, 1981

Anavian, Rahmi & Anavian, George, *Royal Persian and Kashmir Brocades*, Senshoku To Seikatsusha Publishing Co. Kyoto, 1975

Arber, A.R., *Herbals: Their Origin and Evolution 1470-1670*, Cambridge University Press, 1938

Marg, Vol. VII, n.2, 1954

Archer, W.C., *Indian Painting in the Punjab Hills*, London, 1952

Archer, W.C., & Falk, S.J., *India Revealed: The Art and Adventures of James and William Fraser 1801-1835*, London, 1989

Archer, W.G. and William, G, *Indian Painting from the Punjab Hills: A Survey of History of Pahari Miniature Painting*, London, 2 vols, 1973

Atasoy, Nurhan, *A Garden for the Sultan*, Aykaz, 2002

Bamzai, P.N.K, *A History of Kashmir*, New Delhi, 1973

Barnes, R., Cohen, S., Crill, R., *Trade, Temple and Court,* Mumbai, 2002

Barrett, D. and Gray, B., *Indian Painting*, Rizzoli, New York, 1978

Barrow, J., *Making History, Drawing Territory: British mapping in India, c. 1756-1905* New Delhi, 2003

Bates, Charles Ellison, *A Gazetteer of Kashmir* , Calcutta, 1875

Beach, M.C., *The Imperial Image: Paintings for the Mughal Court*, Washington D.C., Freer Gallery of Art, Smithsonian Institution, 1981

Beach, M.C. and Koch, E., *King of the World* : *Padshanama*, Sackler Gallery, 1997

Bernier, François, *Voyage dans les états du Grand Mogol*, Fayard, Paris, 1981

Blochmann, H., *Ain-i-Akbari*, Calcutta, 1873

Brown, Percy, *Paintings under the Mughals*, Oxford, 1924

Burnes, Alexander, *Travels into Bokhara…1831-33.* Karachi (reprint), 1973

Chandra, Moti, 'Kashmir Shawls', *Bulletin of the Prince of Wales Museum,* vol. 3, 1954

Chaudhury and Morineau, *Armenian Merchants of the Seventeenth and Early Eighteenth Centuries: English East India Company Sources,* Vahé Baladouni and Margaret Makepeace (eds.), American Philosophical Society, Philadelphia 1998

Cohen, Steven, 'An Ideal Reality: Carpet Images in the Windsor Padshahnama', *Hali,* 1997, issue 95

Dale, S.F., *Indian Merchants and Eurasian Trade, 1600-1750,* Cambridge, 1994

Daljeet, Dr., *Mughal and Deccani Paintings,* New Delhi, 1999

Dalrymple, W., *White Mughals*, Viking, New Delhi, 2002

Datta, C.L., *Ladakh and Western Himalayan Politics 1819-1848,* Munshiram Manoharlal Publications, Delhi, 1973

Deol, Jeevan Singh, *Illustration and Illumination in Sikh Scriptural Manuscripts,* Marg, Mumbai, Vol. 54, No. 4, June 2003

Desmond, R., *The European Discovery of the Indian Flora*, Royal Botanical Gardens, Oxford, 1992

Diba, Layla, *Royal Persian Paintings*, Brooklyn Museum exhibition, London, 1999

Dürer, Albrecht, *The Complete Drawings*, New York, 1974

Fahr-Becker, Gabriele, *Art Nouveau,* Koneman, Cologne, 1997

Falk, S.J., *Qajar Painting*, London, 1972,

Farooque, A.K.M., *Roads and Communications in Mughal India*, Delhi, 1977

Floor, Willem, *The Persian Textile Industry in Historical Perspective, 1500-1925*, Harmattan, Paris,

Floor, Willem, *Art (Naqqashi) and Artists (Naqqashan) in Qajar Persia*, Muqarnas 16 (1999), pp.129-58

Forster, George, *A Journey from Bengal to England: through the Northern Part of India, Kashmire, Afghanistan, and Persia,and into Russia, by the Caspian-Sea*, London, 1798

Foster, William, *Early Travels in India*, 1583-1619, H. Beveridge (ed.), London, 1921

Garrett, H.L.D., *The Punjab a Hundred Years Ago: as described by V. Jacquemont (1831) and A. Soltykoff (1842)*, Punjab, 1971

Goetz, H., 'Die Moghul-Malerei Nordwest Indiens unter Persischer und Afghanischer Herrschaft', *Zeitschrift der Deutschen MorgenLandischen Gesellschaft, Wiesbaden*, 1969, S. 912

Gole, Susan, *Indian Maps and Plans,* Manohar Publications, New Delhi, c1989

Goswamy, B.N., *Of Patronage and Pahari Painting, Aspects of Indian Art,* Pratapaditya Pal (ed.), Leiden, Brill Publications, 1972, pp.130-138

Goswamy, B.N, *I See No Stranger : Early Sikh Art and Devotion*, Antique Collectors' Club (distrib.), 2006

Goswamy, B.N., *Journal of American Oriental Society,* 1966, vol. 86

Goswamy, B.N., *Nainsukh of Guler*, Zurich, 1997

Goswamy, B.N., *Painters at the Sikh Court, a study based on 20 documents, Wiesbaden,* University of Heidelberg, New Delhi, 1975

Goswamy, K., *Kashmiri Painting*, Shimla, Institute of Advanced Study, Aryan Books International, New Delhi, 1998

Greene, E.L., *Landmarks of Botanical History,* Stanford University Press, 1983

Habib, Irfan, *Mughal Gardens*, Westcoat & Wolshke-Bulmahn (eds.), Washington D.C., 1996

Hall, M., 'The Victoria and Albert Museum's Mahabharata Hanging', *South Asian Studies*, 12, London, 1996, pp.83-96

Hanway, J., *An Historical Account of the British Trade Over the Caspian Sea*, London, 1753

Honigberger, J.M. *Thirty Five Years in the East*, London, 1852

Hugel, Karl Alexander, *Travels in Kashmir and the Punjab…*, Punjab, 1970, p.108

Irwin, John, *Shawls: a study in Indo-European influences*, Victoria & Albert Museum, London, 1955

Irwin, John, *The Kashmir Shawl* , Marg, India, 1952, Vol. 6, No. 1

Irwin, John, *The Kashmir Shawl*, Victoria & Albert Museum, London, 1973

Ismailova, A.M., *Oriental miniatures of Abu Raihon Beruni Institute of Orientology of the USSR Academy of Sciences*, Tashkent, 1980

Jacquemont, V., *Correspondence de V. Jacquemont pendant son voyage dans l'Inde, 1828-1832*, 2 vols., Paris, 1841

Jacquemont, V., *Voyage dans l'Inde*, 4 vols., Paris, 1841

Jacquemont, V., *Letters from India, 1829-1832*, London, Macmillan and Co., 1936

Jacquemont, V. *État politique et social de l'Inde du Nord en 1830; extraits de son journal de voyage, avec une intro. de Alfred Martineau*, Paris, Ernest Leroux; Masson, 1933

Jahangir, Tuzuk-i-jahangiri (memoires), Henry Beveridge (ed.), Alexander Rogers (trans.), 2 vols., 1974

Karpinski, Caroline, 'Kashmir to Paisley', *Metropolitan Museum Bulletin*, Nov. 1963

Khan, Mohammad Ishaq, 'Persian Influences in Kashmir in the Sultanate Period (1320-1586)', *Islamic Culture* (an English quarterly), vol. LI, No. 1, Jan. 1977

Khandalavala, Karl, *Pahari Miniature Paintings in the N. C. Mehta Collection*, Gujarat Museum Society, Government Museum and Art Gallery, Chandigarh, c.1982

Koch, Ebba, *Mughal Art and Imperial Ideology*, Collected Essays, Oxford University Press, New Delhi, 2001

Kossak, Steven, *Indian Court Painting*, Metropolitan Museum of Art, 1997

Kramrisch, Stella, *Exploring India's Sacred Art* (selected writings), Barbara Stoller Miller (ed.), University of Pennsylvania, 1983

Lafont, Jean-Marie *La presence française dans le royaume Sikh du Penjab: 1822-1849*, Ecole Française d'Extrême-Orient, Paris, 1992

Lafont, J.M. & Schmitz, B, *The Painter Imam Bakhsh of Lahore*, After the Great Mughals, B. Schmitz (ed), Marg Publications, Mumbai, 2002

Lafont, Jean-Marie, *Maharaja Ranjit Singh: Lord of the Five Rivers*, Oxford, Univ. Press, New Delhi, 2002

Lafont, Jean-Marie, Indika: Essays in Indo-French Relations, 1630-1976, Manohar Publications, New Delhi, 2000

Lafont, Jean-Marie, *The French and Lahore*, Lahore, 2007

Lafont, Jean-Marie, 'Observations sur le commerce du Penjab et du Cachemire, d'après un rapport de C.-M. Wade, 1832', *Bulletin de l'Ecole Française d'Extrême-Orient*, LXXIV, Paris, 1985, pp.58-78, 3 maps

La Fontaine, Jean de, *Le Songe d'un Habitant du Mogol, and autres fables, illustrées par Imam Bakhsh Lahori*, Réunion des Musées Nationaux, Paris, 1989

Lambton, Ann K.S., *Persian Trade Under the Early Qajars*, Islam and the Trade of Asia, (ed.) D.S. Richards, University of Pennsylvania, 1970, pp.215-244

Latif, S.M., *History of the Punjab*, New Delhi, 1964

Leach, L.Y., *Mughal and other Indian Paintings from the Chester Beatty Library*, London, 1995

Legoux de Flaix, *Essaie historique géographique et politique sur Indoustan*, Paris, 1807

Lévi-Strauss, Monique, *The Cashmere Shawl*, London, 1986

Lévi-Strauss, Monique, *Il Cachemire*, vol. IV, Ratti, 1995

Losty, J.P., *The Delhi Palace in 1846, Arts of Mughal India,* R. Crill, S. Stronge and A. Topsfield (eds), Victoria and Albert Museum, London, 2004

Losty, J.P., *The Art of the Book*, British Library, London, 1982

MacLagan, Edward, *The Jesuits and the Great Mogul*, London, 1932,

McClenaghan, Tony, *Indian Princely Medals,* New Delhi, c.1996

Malik, Zahir Uddin, *The Reign of Muhammad Shah 1719-1748,* Asia Publishing House, Bombay, 1977

Maloni, *European Merchant Capital and the Indian Economy*, Manohar Publications, New Delhi,1992

Manucci, Niccolao, *Storia do Mogul India, 1653-1708*, William Irvine (trans.), 4 vols., London, 1906.

Mikosch, E, 'The Scent of Flowers: Kashmir Shawls in the Textile Museum, *Textile Museum Journal,* vol. 24, Washington D.C.,' 1985

Milstein, Rachael, *Islamic Painting in the Israel Museum*, Jerusalem, 1984

Modave, Comte de, *Voyage en Inde du Comte de Modave, 1773-1776*, Paris, 1971

Moorcroft, W., MS Eur 264, p65 ; MS Eur 266, f.21, Ms. Eur D 265, British Library, London

Moorcroft, William,*Travels in the Himalayan Provinces of Hindustan and Panjab; in Ladakh and Kashmir; in Peshawar, Kabul, Kunduz, and Bukhara,* by Mr. George Trebeck and William Moorcroft from 1819 to1825, London, 1841, 2 vols.

Olivier, G.A., *Voyage dans l'Empire Ottoman, l'Egypte et la Perse etc.*, Paris, 1804

Pal, Pratapaditya, *Court Paintings of India,* Navin Kumar Publications, New Delhi, 1983

Percier, Charles, *Recueil des décorations intérieurs comprenant tout ce qui à rapport à l'ameublement comme vases, trépieds, candélabres*, p.Didiot l'Ainé, Paris, 1812

Pope, A.U. (ed) and Ackerman, P., *A Survey of Persian Art,* London, 1958

Prakash, Gujarat Sahitay, *Jesuit Presence in Indian History*, Anand Amaladas (ed), India, 1988

Raby, J. (ed), *Lacquer of the Islamic lands, The Nasser D. Khalili Collection of Islamic Art,* The Nour Foundation, Vol. XXII, Part One, London, 1996

Randhawa, M.S., *Basohli Painting*, New Delhi, 1981

Rey , Jean, *Etudes pour servir à l'histoire des châles*, Paris, 1823

Rich, V., 'Mughal Floral Painting and its European Sources', *Oriental Art,* Summer, 1987, pp.183-189

Rich, Vivian Anne, 'The origins of Mughal floral paintings and its development with particular reference to the 17th and 18th centuries', thesis (Ph.D.), University of London, School of Oriental and African Studies, 1981

Rishi, W.R., *India and Russia*, Roma Publications, Chandigarh, 1982

Schimmel, Annemarie, *Islamic India and Pakistan*, Brill, Leiden,1982,

Schimmel, A, *Pain and Grace,* Brill, Leiden, 1976

Schimmel, Annemarie, *A History of Indian Literature*, Otto Harrassowitz (ed), Islamic literatures of India, Wiesbaden 1973, vol VIII, Fasc. I

Schmitz, Barbara (ed.), *After the great Mughals : painting in Delhi and the regional courts in the 18th and 19th centuries,* Marg Publications, Mumbai, 2002

Schmitz, Barbara, *Islamic and Indian Manuscripts and Paintings in the Pierpont Morgan Library*, New York, 1996

Schmitz, Barbara, *Islamic Manuscripts in the New York Public Library*, New York, 1992

Scott, P, *The Book of Silk*, London, 1993

Sharma, D.C., *Kashmir Under the Sikhs*, India, 1983

Sharma, Sanjay, *Famine, Philanthropy, the Colonial State: North India in the early 19th century*, New Delhi, 2001

Singh, Kirpal (ed.), *Descriptive catalogue of Manuscript section (Gurmukhi)*, Government-Museum and Art Gallery, Chandigarh, 2005

Singh, Khushwant, *History of the Sikhs*, Princeton University Press, 1984

Singh, Khushwant, *The Illustrated History of the Sikhs*, New Delhi, 2006

Skelton, R., *A Decorative Motif in Mughal Art, Aspects of Indian Art*, Brill, 1972

Soltykoff, Prince Alexis (1806-1859), *Habitants de l'Inde: dessinée d'après nature. Lithographiés a deux teintes par J. Frayer*, Paris (1859)

Soltykoff, Prince Alexis, *Indian scenes and characters : from drawings made on the spot* by Prince Alexis Soltykoff, Edward Eastwick (ed.), London, 1859

Srivastava, H.S., *The History of Indian Famines and Development of Famine Policy, 1858-1918*, Agra, 1968

Srivastava, R.P., *Punjab Painting: study in art and culture*, Abinav Publications, New Delhi, 1983

Srivastava, S.P., *Art and Culture: Heritage of Patiala*, Sundeep Prakashan, Delhi, 1991

Stronge, Susan (ed.), *The Arts of the Sikh Kingdoms*, Victoria and Albert Museum, London, 1999

Stronge, Susan, *Painting for the Mughal Emperor*, Abrams, London, 2002

Suri, Lala Sohan Lal, *Umdat-ut-Tawarikh Daftar 111, parts (1-V), Chronicle of the Reign of Maharaja Ranjit Singh, 1831-1839 A. D.*, Chan & Co., Delhi, 1961

Talib, Gurbachan Singh, *Sources of Indian Tradition*, Ainslie T. Embree (ed.), Columbia University Press, 1988

Tarikh-i-Rashidi by Mirza Haidar Dughlat, c.1500, see English translation of W.M. Thackston, Harvard Univ., c.1996

Titley, Nora, *Persian Miniature Painting and its influence on the Art of Turkey and India.* The British Library Collections, University of Texas Press, 1984

Topsfield, Andrew (ed), *In the Realm of Gods and Kings*, London, 2004

Twining, T., *Travels in India one hundred years ago...*, London, 1893

Vallet, Pierre, *Le Jardin du Roy Très Chréstian, Loys XIII, Roy de France et de Navarre 1608*, Paris

Veinstein, G., *Commercial Relations between India and the Ottoman Empire Late 15th to Late 18th century, Merchants, Companies, and Trade : Europe and Asia in the Early Modern Era*, Sushil Chaudhury and Michel Morineau (eds.), Cambridge University Press, 1999

Vigne, G.T., *Travels in Kashmir*, (1844), Sagar Publications, New Delhi, 1981 (reprint)

Welch, S.C., *India!*, Metropolitan Museum of Art, New York, 1985

Welch, S.C., *Gods, Kings & Tigers*, Harvard University Art Museums, 1997

William, D., *The Last Mughal*, 1857, London, 2006

Zutshi, N.K., *Sultan Zain-ul-Abidin of Kashmir: An Age of Enlightenment* , Jammu, 1976

Index

Page numbers in bold type refer to illustrations and captions

FORTRESS OF TH